Beginner's Guide to Enneagram

Waking Up to Journey into Self-Discovery, Spiritual Growth; Creating Happy, Healthy Relationships (Understanding the Enneagram and Personality Types)

By:
Glinda Porter

Table of Contents

Introduction

In life, we feel like there is some kind of unbalance. We feel like we are living a life that lacks spirituality, balance, and overall health. Oftentimes, as we move through each day we just deal with stress as if it were the norm.

And yet we do nothing about it because it seems like we don't have any control over it. Another thing we often ask ourselves is why do we act the way we do? Why are we perfectionists when it comes to doing something we are passionate about?

What is it about us that makes us loving and caring for others? Or what makes someone who wants to be recognized for their achievements? There are so many similar answers, but the answers can be found in something that is known as the Enneagram.

What is the Enneagram? You will find out in more detail shortly. This book will show you how it can be helpful in transforming your life into something healthier.

You see, the Enneagram is based on personality types. And it is believed that we behave a certain way based on a certain unique personality type that we possess. There are nine 'types' of the Enneagram.

And each and every one of us has a type. The question is, which type are you? Are you a Type One or a Type Eight?

Are you a Type Seven or a Type Three? If you don't understand this, don't worry. You will once you get deeper into this book.

What we can tell you is that the Enneagram is something that wields quite a bit of power. When you know about its power, you will understand why so many people (religious or non-religious) rely on it so much. And when they want to know about their personality types, they take a test to unveil which one fits them best.

The Enneagram and How It Can Help You

The Enneagram can be helpful in improving your life, your relationships, and other areas. And it all depends on your personality type. Keep in mind that no personality type is superior to the other.

And there is no personality type that is considered to be a friend or an enemy. The Enneagram defines your personality type right down to your core beliefs, your traits, and how you handle certain situations in life such as stress, happiness, professional settings, and romantic relationships.

It can help you in many ways. It can help you achieve personal growth based on your type. It can also help you achieve calm when things get tough. And it will help you understand people based on their own personality types as well.

Not everyone will act and behave the same way as you. There will be people who will have the same personality type as you. Likewise, there will be others with a different type.

So, it is important to understand your type while being able to understand the others. Especially when you want to communicate with other people. Even couples in relationships may have different Enneagram types with each other and still manage to get along just fine.

What This Book Will Cover

This book will be separated into two major sections, each separated into two parts. In the first section, we will talk about understanding the Enneagram as a whole. You will learn about what the Enneagram is in detail and how it works.

Next, you will learn about discovering yourself and being able to develop yourself using it. You will learn about its power and how you can properly utilize it. You will also learn about how it can contribute to your growth and change as a whole.

The Enneagram has a complicated history as no one knows the true origin. But we will talk about theories on where it came from and tie it into modern insights. You will also learn about terms such as the centers, the Nine Enneagram types (or 'Faces of the Soul'), and finally, you will take a test to learn about your true Enneagram type.

Once you find out what your Enneagram type is, you will take this opportunity to find out more about yourself. You will learn about things you may know about yourself (as well as things that may surprise you about your personality). But nevertheless, you will prepare yourself for a journey that will lead you towards growing into a better version of yourself.

In the second part, you will learn in more detail about your Enneagram type. This includes the personality traits that you possess, how you behave in a healthy and unhealthy manner, and what makes you the way you are based on your 'wings'. You will learn about your needs while learning about what you need to do in order to become your best self.

In the second section, you will learn about how you can repent for your past mistakes while reorienting yourself towards a better life. You may also come face-to-face with what is known as your idealized self-image. You will learn that this fabrication of yourself is not who you are, and you will learn how to get rid of it accordingly.

You will also find out about the elements of the universal growth process and the general principles of the Enneagram. Then, you will learn about how you can practice the Enneagram in both the personal and professional areas of your life.

Finally, you will finish up the book with certain practices that you must follow with the Enneagram. This includes a personal growth plan, breathing exercises, how you should communicate or work with your Enneagram type and others based on theirs, and how you can improve your relationships.

What's Next?

Now, it's time to make a choice. Are you willing to go on what might be a personal and spiritual journey towards personal growth? Are you ready to make the improvements in your life that will provide you with what's missing?

Are you eager and willing to learn about your true personality based on the Enneagram? If you answered 'yes' to these questions, then you are about to embark on a journey that will change you for the better. After reading through this and applying what you have learned, you will be able to feel changes in both your physical, spiritual, and mental health.

And it's all part of making the improvements with the Enneagram as your guide. When you're ready, let's start with the first chapter and explain what the Enneagram actually is.

Chapter 1: What Is The Enneagram and How It Works

In this first section, you're going to learn what enneagram is and how you will be able to understand it. You will also learn your personality type based on the system itself. If you don't know what enneagram is, don't worry.

We will explain what it is in the beginning of this section. If you are curious what your personality type is, this book will give you a deeper understanding of it. You may find yourself thinking 'this is very true about myself'.

We will discuss the process of self-discovery and self-development using the enneagram system. You'll also learn how to utilize its power. We will also talk about its history dating back to ancient times (along with modern insights regarding enneagram today).

You'll learn how to cultivate awareness, the three centers including your gut, heart, and your head. And you'll learn about the nine faces of the soul. After this, you can then take the enneagram test (complete with instructions on how to do it).

After the test, you'll learn which type you are and understand it deeply. From there, you'll learn how to proceed with life using your newfound discovery. This book is jam-packed with lots of information about every personality type.

We're going to go really in-depth on these personality types. The deeper you know about your own personality type, the better you will understand yourself. Let's now jump right in and explain what enneagram is and how it works:

What Is Enneagram

The Enneagram is a personality system that is used to describe patterns in how people understand and interpret the world around them. At the same time, this system also describes how people handle their emotions as well.

The Enneagram consists of nine different personality types. These personality types are put together on a map-style diagram that will illustrate these personality types (and how each one relates to each other).

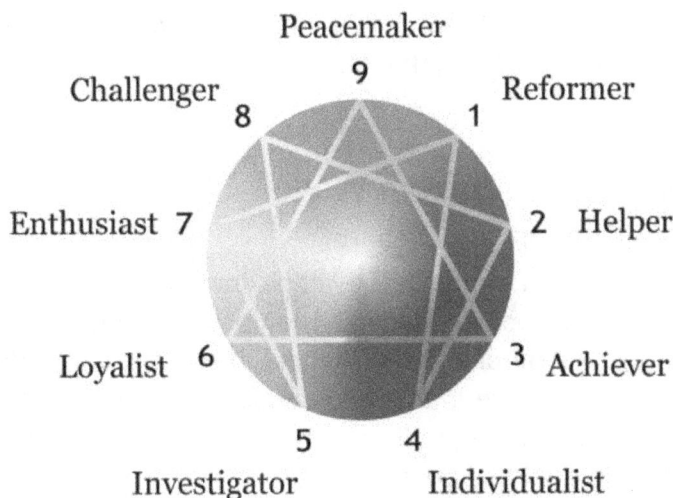

This is what the map looks like so you get a good idea of how it all connects with some of the other personality types (if you are listening to this book in audio format - be sure to download your PDF version of the book so you can see the diagram). As you can see above, these are the nine personality types of the Enneagram:

1. **Reformer**
2. **Helper**
3. **Achiever**
4. **Individualist**
5. **Investigator**
6. **Loyalist**
7. **Enthusiast**
8. **Challenger**
9. **Peacemaker**

Now that you know the personality types, you might already have a good idea of which type you might be on the diagram. Your assumption may be right. However, you might be surprised that it may not be the case once you have taken the Enneagram test.

How The Enneagram Works

The Enneagram system has symbols that represent the 'big picture' of someone's identity. They are based on the gut and triad centers of a person's mind, body, and soul. What you need to realize is that you shouldn't take shortcuts in order to understand the Enneagram (and that's why we're going as in-depth as possible).

It's important to understand yourself at a deeper level. And we'll be glad to help you with that. We want you to focus on the Enneagram as more than just a single number.

You want to focus more on the qualities in the nine numbers that are associated with the diagram. From there, the complexity of the Enneagram will become much clearer. At the end of the day, the system is all about the nature and values of each personality type (and not so much the type of behaviors that you exhibit.

Let's say you take the test, and you end up with the 'Enthusiast' personality type. Most people will translate enthusiasm as their way of saying that they value the experience of the things they enjoy most. But the real question is: is there anything else that they value?

Each personality type has its own definition. We will start with the definition based on three things: what you value, seek, and what motivates you. So, you might be enthusiastic about something, but you may go into a deeper understanding about what you look for and what will motivate you to find what you value most.

It's hard to understand the Enneagram. By the time you finish reading this, you will have a much deeper understanding of it. Even if you've read books before this, this might be the most in-depth you've read up to this point.

You may even have your personality type pegged down and have already taken the test. If that's the case, then you may want to skip to the section based on your personality type on the Enneagram. Keep in mind, we dig pretty deep when it comes to each personality type.

Enneagram Is Not A Personality Quiz

The Enneagram is more of a language that you're learning as you go. So do not consider the test or the like to be some kind of personality quiz that you constantly take online. This is very different.

If you are new to learning the Enneagram, you will approach this as if you are learning a foreign language. If you were in school and took a language course, you probably remember how it began. You started with the basics, learned the alphabet (if different from the regular one), phrases and sayings, and so much more.

You will notice that with every language you learn, it seems to have its own structure. Whether you are learning Spanish and the Enneagram at the same time, you'll notice that it's not so different in terms of structure or how it's even used. Before you even seek the idea of being understood by the Enneagram, you want to understand it yourself.

What makes the Enneagram different from the others

There are various behavioral systems and personality models that exist. However, they focus on two major things: the how and the what of what you're doing as a person. The Enneagram system is considered to be one of the most accurate of its kind when it comes to describing you as a person.

Using this system, you'll be able to know what actually motivates you. You will have a deeper understanding of why you engage with the world in your own special way. At the end of the day, the Enneagram will help you gain better self-awareness.

When people like you begin to understand the Enneagram, you will learn some things you might not know about yourself. You will understand the mental spaces that you seek refuge in, if you are faced with stressful or traumatic situations. You will also learn a lot more about the coping mechanisms that you use and why you rely on them.

The Enneagram doesn't just focus on that. It also helps people identify their true strengths. And it allows them to seek opportunities in terms of growing. That's because you will learn about your reactive behaviors in terms of stressful situations.

You will also find out about the different patterns and how you can use conscious choices to make sure that you take a certain action that you won't regret later on in life. Specifically, you could be in a stressful situation and say the wrong thing out of anger to someone. If you understand the Enneagram, you may find yourself in a situation where you can stop short of that and make a better, more conscious decision.

You will handle stressful situations better than ever. But that's just part of the personality that you develop. You will notice the patterns and practices that you can perform knowing your true personality.

How Should You Not Approach The Enneagram

If you are someone that is expecting that a number will tell you everything you need to know about yourself, you're approaching the Enneagram the wrong way. If you are using this as a parallel to astrology, then you may have a hard time understanding the system. You'll end up focusing on one single thing and never dig deeper beyond that.

However, many people commonly approach the Enneagram like this. However, they need to look beyond the labels of their reductive behaviors. They need to have a much deeper understanding and integration for the purpose of their overall health.

Also, you don't want to utilize the Enneagram as a weapon to use against yourself. Specifically, a weapon where you shirk your responsibilities of being yourself (especially someone who is healthy mentally, physically, and beyond). Last but not least, the Enneagram should not be used as a weapon for stereotyping other people.

If you use the system as a way to jump to conclusions, hurt people, brag about what you know, point out flaws in someone's argument and beyond, you are basically abusing its power. You're going to learn not to do that. Instead, you want to use the power of the Enneagram as a greater good as opposed to a weapon of mass destruction.

That greater good is used for growth. You will grow to be more compassionate, empathetic, and for your own inquiry.

Focus on that instead of using it as a way to twist arms and burn personal or professional bridges along the way.

Final Thoughts

Now that you know the definition of the Enneagram and a basic, bare-bones understanding of how it works, you can soon use it to your advantage. But you don't want to just yet.

Before you even use it to determine your personality and use it as a tool, you'll want to understand it. Once you do, it will return the favor and understand you. It's a two-way street.

You are aware of the nine personality types that are mapped out in the diagram. And there is usually a connection between one type or another. Keep in mind that you don't want to focus on the numbers.

Instead, you want to focus on the things you value, seek, and the things that motivate you to find it. You could assume right off the jump the kind of personality type that you are. But it may be different after taking the test.

Speaking of the Enneagram test, we do not want you to approach it like one of those personality tests you see online. You want to approach the system as something that has a set of tools. It's tools that will help you grow as a person over the course of your life.

Everyone's timing is completely different. They will develop more compassion and self-awareness quicker than others.

At the same time, you will have a much deeper level of self-awareness than ever before.

The Enneagram is a tool for the greater good. It should not be used as a weapon where you bring people down. The Enneagram system is a powerful thing.

To quote a famous superhero movie, 'with great power comes great responsibility'. When you have a deeper understanding of the Enneagram and how it works, you will understand its true power. And it will be so powerful to the point where abusing it would be the stupidest thing that you ever do.

In the next chapter, we will discuss the process of self-discovery and self-development using this system. This is the next step that will help you get a better understanding of how it all works. The journey towards growth begins by turning the page.

Chapter 2: The Process of Self-Discovery and Self-Development Using Enneagram

The enneagram is designed to help you better understand yourself. From there, you can use the tools to grow beyond your current state. In this chapter, we will discuss the process in its entirety.

You will also learn how to use it so you can grow personally. When you discover yourself and your true personality, you'll be shocked by some of the things you may not know about yourself. The mystery of it all sounds quite exciting enough, does it not?

Using the Enneagram will be like second nature by the time you understand it and use it to your advantage. You may not even recognize your 'new self' once you become part of that personality system. Keep in mind that the Enneagram is a lot different than any other system and is way different than the Myers-Briggs personality test (and the like).

One of the true keys of self-discovery and self-development is mindfulness. Without practicing mindfulness, you will have a very hard time observing your personality and the mechanisms that put it all together. Speaking of mindfulness, we will discuss what that is and how to practice it now and for as long as you live.

What Is Mindfulness?

As mentioned, in order to get the most out of the Enneagram and how to discover and develop yourself, it all starts with mindfulness. Mindfulness is defined as having the basic ability to be fully present. You are aware of what's going on around you, what you're doing, and where you are at the present moment.

Being mindful means that you are not overwhelmed or overactive about what's going on. What you may not understand is that everyone has this quality of being mindful. But there is a catch.

Not every person practices mindfulness right from the jump. Their ability to be mindful is actually dormant and buried underneath the surface. In other words, you need to find a way to access this mindfulness.

How to Access Your Mindfulness?

Now, let's discuss how you can unearth this mindfulness ability. There are a few proven techniques that will allow you to do that. Let's take a look at what you can do:

Meditation: This can be done while you are walking, standing, sitting down, or in motion. You can try this lying down, but you may fall asleep by accident (that's happened to some of us). Meditation can take anywhere from 5 to 10 minutes from the start. Once you have a routine down, you can increase the time by another 5 to 10 minutes.

Short pauses: These can be brief pauses as you go about your everyday life. It can be something where you can set aside 5 to 10 minutes of your time where you can 'hide' somewhere and think about where you are right now, how you feel, and what's going on around you. Think of it as an opportunity to realize the level of mindfulness you are at right now.

Merging meditation with physical activities: Whether it's yoga or playing intramural sports, you can forge mindfulness and meditation with what you're doing while on the move. You'll realize where you are, what you're doing, and be on top of your game at the same time.

The Benefits of Mindfulness

When you practice mindfulness, you will achieve so many benefits. They include but are not limited to the following:

You are less stressed: When you are mindful and aware of what's going on, you feel like you're less stressed. You'll also feel like you are handling the situation like nothing else. Stress becomes an afterthought. You just power through it all and get through the tasks at hand.

Increased overall performance: Whether it's at your job or when you are performing your favorite personal tasks, when you are mindful, you tend to perform a better job. You may make fewer mistakes and you are a lot more concentrated.

You gain better insights: When you are mindful, you will have better or even deeper insights about things. You will look at things from plenty of different angles. This will work to your advantage if you are having a conversation with someone about any topic you can think of. You can provide excellent insights on the Enneagram with someone who knows something about it.

More awareness: You will be aware of what is happening, what's around you, where you are just by observing with your mind. That's simple enough.

Better self-development and self-discovery: Using the Enneagram and combining your mindfulness abilities, you will be able to have a better chance at developing yourself at a rapid pace. And your self-discovery will be a lot deeper compared to on the surface.

Things You Need to Know About Mindfulness

There are some things about mindfulness that you want to be aware of:

Mindfulness is not an obscure thing: Even though we have it, unearthing it is your responsibility. We are familiar with it because we know we have it. So, it's not some new thing that someone introduces to you. Think of it like buried treasure. Someone will tell you that there is buried treasure underneath your feet. All you need to do is dig it up and it's yours. That's what mindfulness is.

You don't need to change yourself: This may sound a bit confusing. You don't need to change your identity or everything that makes you...well, you. Once again, because your mindfulness exists the day you are born. It's accessing it that makes it the task. No need to change your style, your personality, and everything else. You can be you, but a more upgraded version.

Anyone can practice it: People can practice mindfulness if they know how to do it. Just doing one of the three tasks listed above like meditating, you are practicing it.

There's a lot of evidence in favor of it: Mindfulness is not some pseudo-scientific phenomenon. Mindfulness is not something that is considered faith-based. But science can prove that mindfulness can provide you with excellent benefits regarding your overall health, happiness, relationships, and everything in between.

It can spark innovation: If you are looking for ideas or develop some kind of innovation, mindfulness can open up plenty of doors. You may come across something that will allow you to test it out and see how it works. The world is getting a little more complex. To be innovative will keep you slightly ahead of the curve.

Mindfulness is not always in your head: Mindfulness goes beyond what's in your mind. It also goes with the rest of your body. Rather than solely focus on your mind, focus on the rest of your body as you practice mindfulness on a regular basis.

How to Meditate

One of the easiest ways to practice mindfulness is meditation. Lucky for you, we will show you exactly how to do it. If you are new to meditation, it's good to start out small in terms of the timing of your sessions.

Let's begin and show you how it's done:

1. Sit down somewhere

Though we mentioned standing or walking, we are going to take the seated approach. If you are new to meditation, this is how you will start out. With that said, find a stable chair or cushion. Please note that the seat should not allow you to perch or hang back.

2. Observe what your legs are doing

Next, you want to observe what your legs are doing. This will depend on how you are seated. If you choose to sit in a chair, make sure that your feet are planted on the floor. If sitting on a cushion, cross your legs.

3. Maintain a straight, not stiff, upper body posture

Next, you want to make sure that your back is straight. Do not stiffen up as you assume posture. Allow your head and your shoulders to rest comfortably on the top of your spine.

4. Make sure that your upper arms are parallel with your upper body

Now, you want to allow your hands to rest on the top of your legs. Your upper arms must be at their sides to ensure that your hands fall properly. Don't go too far forward as it will allow you to hunch. Also, don't go too far back as it will cause you to stiffen.

5. Allow your chin to rest and your gaze fall slightly

At this point, you can close your eyes a bit (but not completely). Do this almost to the point where you are simply relaxing. If something appears before your eyes (i.e. - a cat walking past you), allow it to appear and don't focus on it too much.

6. Be in the moment

This is the point of mindfulness. You want to be in the moment. So, relax.

Just be there. Your body will feel relaxed. You will let your mind wander through.

7. Repeat

Once you have the correct posture, follow your breath. Breathe in through the nose and out the mouth. Do this again for about five minutes.

Once you get the hang of it, you can increase the time. You can go for 10, 15, 30 minutes or beyond that.

8. You're done

That's basically how you do it. You can do this once per day (or multiple times per day like morning, afternoon, and evening).

Beginner's Tip: If you're a beginner, try meditating for at least five minutes. You can set a timer. Make sure the alarm sound doesn't 'jar' you out of your state. Also, if you want a more guided meditation, we recommend that you check out some of the meditation apps that are available.

Apps like Calm are available on either Android or iOS (iPhone/iPad).

Meditation and Self-Discovery

"Meditation is not about making your mind quiet. It is a way of entering into the quiet that is already there - buried under the 50,000 thoughts the average person thinks every day."
- Deepak Chopra

The words above are a golden nugget by who else, but Deepak Chopra. And he's absolutely right. Mindfulness is that quiet in your mind. And it's buried underneath all the thoughts racing through your head every single day.

So, meditation is the way to dig through all that to find that mindfulness. What you're thinking is essential when you are meditating. You will be able to get a deep understanding of your emotions, reactions, the sensations running through your body, and the behaviors.

When you are finding a way to discover yourself, it's important to meditate as often as possible. Let's say for instance that you feel a negative feeling (i.e. - anxiety). Rather than let it control you, meditate on it and figure out why you are feeling that way.

Instead of asking what you should do about it, ask yourself the following question: 'Which part of me is greatly disturbed by this?' From there, you will be able to locate where that negativity originates from. With a little deep digging via meditation, you may discover some insecurities and experiences that may derive from this feeling.

A lot of people can't figure out why they are feeling those negative feelings. That's because they are buried by the thoughts that continue to stroke the flames. If you just take a moment to focus on the cause of it, you will understand yourself better than anyone else.

Now, what if you're feeling happiness? What if you're on the receiving end of something that feels good like the sun hitting your skin on a warm summer's day? Obviously, you meditate on it.

Focus on the sensory data that is processing in your brain. At the same time, you will experience a new level of mindfulness like no other. Don't be surprised if that good feeling is amplified even more over time.

The key takeaway here is this: no matter how you feel, whether it be negative or positive, meditation will help you dig deep into how you're feeling, why you're feeling, and what's causing it all. The data process that your brain goes through will be easier.

You will easily describe the feelings, what's causing them, and even touch base on the positive or negative emotions of past events. If every person on the planet unearths their mindfulness, they will have a better understanding of themselves to the point where they can change their behaviors and get in tune with their real selves.

Mindfulness in Motion (And in Rest)

Earlier, we discussed the idea of being mindful while you're in motion. We will show you how to be mindful while performing some outdoor activities. Furthermore, we will talk about how you can be mindful as you prepare to go to sleep.

Even those who were mindful in motion ended up winning one of the top prizes in the world. Thanks to a trainer named John Kabat-Zinn, the USA Men's Rowing Team that won two gold medals in 1984. It is further proof that with mindfulness, even athletes can achieve top-quality performance almost every single time.

24

With that said, let's talk about the activities you can do while achieving mindfulness at the same time:

Running

A lot of people are tempted to bring their phones with them to listen to music or podcasts. When you're going for a run, you may want to leave the phone at home. Also, you want to do this running outdoors as opposed to doing it on a treadmill at the gym.

The reason why we suggest this is because you will be able to have a deeper, much stronger connection if you are outdoors with nature surrounding you. Start off with a brisk walk with ten mindful breaths.

This breathing exercise as you walk will allow you to be in tune with your body. At the same time, this will help you build up from walking to running. Take note of how your breathing rate changes over time.

Focus on that breath every time you feel your mind starting to wander away from the present. You'll be able to feel your heartbeat and the rhythm of your feet as they strike the ground. There will be times when you will feel things like areas of your body tensing up or even the warmth of the sun hitting your face.

Be sure to observe whatever thoughts appear as you are running. Resist the urge to judge them. If you feel any sort of pain during your run, feel free to slow down. Don't stop.

If you are a complete newbie to running, start out at a slow brisk pace. Think of it like a jog rather than a regular run. After you finish running, do a mini-meditation session (less than 5 minutes) and observe the effects of your run.

Swimming

Swimming is quite therapeutic. Especially when you throw mindfulness into the mix. As for where you should swim, consider doing that in a pool rather than a natural body of water.

As you approach the pool, start off with some mindful breathing techniques. As you do this, observe the effect the water has on you. As you enter the pool, feel the temperature of the water as it hits your body.

What are the thoughts that surface in your mind as you enter the pool? When you swim, be mindful about the water making contact with your body. As you get into a swimming rhythm, you should be aware of your heart, breath, and the muscles in your body.

It can get to the point where you feel one with the water. After you experience this, you can observe how both your mind and body feels.

Cycling

Before you sit on the bike, do some mindful breathing. As you situate yourself on the bike, you want to feel your body weight, the contact your hands make with the handlebars, and your feet on the pedals.

As you begin to pick up speed, take note of the sound of the wind blowing. As you speed up, you'll want to take note of your leg muscles in motion. Forget about your intended destination and focus on the now.

After you ride your bike, dismount and feel that sensation. Detect any feelings you may have after your session is completed.

Mindfulness before sleep

You need sleep. We all need it. So how can you make it easier to acquire?

Mindfulness will make that happen. You'll end up in a much deeper sleep as a result. You'll wake up feeling a lot more refreshed than normal.

Unlike exercise, mindfulness exercises prior to sleep will be a bit more complex. So, you're going to need to do the following in order to get the best night's sleep. Let's take a look at what you should do:

Plan a regular time to sleep and wake up: Set a time to where you can go to sleep and wake up. And be sure to stick with it. Because if you wake up early one day and get up late the day after that, your body's clock will get thrown off course.

Power down any electronics: Electronics like your phone, television, or computer will cause a lot of overstimulation. For this reason, it would be wise to power down at least 90 to 120 minutes prior to your scheduled bedtime. So if you're planning on going to bed at 9:30 PM each night, power down as early as 7:30 PM but no later than 8PM.

Do yoga or gentle stretching: Stretching or even yoga might be a good way to get your body relaxed and ready to go. The more relaxed your muscles are, the better you'll adjust into a sleeping state.

Do mindful exercises: If there is one thing you can do, it's meditation. You know the deal.

Do some mindful indoor walking: This may sound like a weird thing to do, but it helps. Take at least five to ten minutes and walk around your house. As you do this, be mindful of your surroundings and the sensations running through your body. Do this at a slow pace.

Lay down and feel your in and out breaths: Here's a trick, rather than focusing on the main goal that is falling asleep, focus on your in and out-breaths. Count your out-breaths up to ten. As you breathe out, say the number in your head. If you notice your mind wandering off, start back with one.

If you feel worried, accept it: If there is a certain worry that seems to arise in your mind, it's better to recognize it and leave it be. Don't judge it. The more you fight it or give it attention, the more powerful it becomes. Acknowledge and move forward.

Mindfulness and Your Enneagram Type

When it comes to mindfulness, there are key strategies for every Enneagram Type. Later on, when we discuss each type, we will explain what you will be more focused on. For example, if you are an Enneagram Type 1, you're focused on experiencing the bliss of letting go.

We will also discuss things like the hurdles that every Enneagram type faces whenever they are achieving mindfulness. This is followed by a remedy and ally that each Enneagram type can rely on. There is definitely a lot of information that we will be unpacking as we introduce your Enneagram.

If this doesn't inspire you to dig down one rabbit hole or another, we're not sure what will. But for now, we're going to focus on the basics of mindfulness. You also have yet to discover what your true Enneagram type is.

Final Thoughts

When it comes to understanding the Enneagram, one of the key things you will need going forward is accessing your mindfulness. Once you unearth it from all the many thoughts rushing in your mind on a daily basis, that's when you will be more in tune with yourself.

On top of that, your mindfulness will help you become more aware of yourself. You will be able to discover why you are feeling the way you feel (be it stemmed from a negative or positive experience). Mindfulness can be acquired whenever you are sitting down or in motion.

The best way to unearth your mindfulness is by performing regular exercises such as breathing and even meditation sessions on a daily basis. If you are new to meditation, you can start out small. Even a five-minute meditation session would be perfect.

As you get the hang of it, you can add more time to your meditation sessions. This will give you more time to get in touch with yourself and get to know who you are. You will probably find out a little bit more about yourself and not know it.

How does this all tie into the Enneagram? You will be able to use mindfulness to better understand your Enneagram type. We will break it all down when we dive into each chapter that focuses on your respective type or number.

At this point, you already have a key pillar to rely on when it comes to finding and understanding the type of personality you have according to the Enneagram. Now is the time to consider putting together a plan to access your mindfulness and use it for the better.

Practice as often as possible. Because you're going to use it to your advantage later on.

Chapter 3: The Power of Utilizing The Enneagram

The Enneagram is a powerful thing. In this chapter, you will learn how to utilize it for various purposes. Whether it's at home or work, using it to your advantage will be worthwhile. And that's why you have this book in your hand right now.

Not only will you be using it for your own personal growth and development, but it can also be used for healing. You might have undergone a traumatic or painful event in your life. Using it for the purpose of healing and becoming your best self might be one of the main goals.

You have the mindfulness down-packed. As we've said before, you won't be able to utilize the true power of the Enneagram without it. Now, let's discuss how using the power of the Enneagram is so important and how it can help you out personally.

The Enneagram and Addiction

One of the afflictions that causes a lot of pain in a person is addiction. They have something that they want around the clock. Without it, they go through withdrawals and cannot function properly. Such addictions include but are not limited to cigarettes, drugs, alcohol, food, even sex.

It's no secret that at one point in our lifetime, addiction has affected us. And we don't even have to be addicted to anything. This could be something that involves a friend, family member, even someone we love.

Because of addiction, we have witnessed lives unraveling in front of our eyes. They lose their jobs, their health, self-esteem, and their most important relationships. One could describe it as watching someone die slowly (but without actual death not occurring).

This is perhaps one of the saddest experiences one person can go through. Those who are fighting addiction will be in a constant state of denial. They will angrily dismiss those who tell them that they have a problem and must deal with it.

No matter how hard we try to save those we hold as important, it seems like a tough task. Some of us may feel like giving up and letting nature take its course. The truth is, giving up will hurt us more than it will hurt the person who has the problem.

What does addiction have to do with the Enneagram? It all comes down to getting in touch with your personality. You will be more in touch with your unconscious features of your personality type.

These unconscious features of our personality have been with us since birth. But using the Enneagram will allow us to access it. And the knowledge of who we really are as an individual can help us heal in the process.

You will feel more aligned with yourself than ever before. It will get to the point where you will realize that it has never been a part of who you are. And getting rid of it will be easier than you think.

Recovery from addiction is a long road. And staying on the path will be the goal. People will do their best to stay the course, only to veer back into addiction because of some traumatic or depressing experience. These happen all the time.

For someone fighting addiction and eventually reverting, both you and the person dealing with the addiction may feel a deep sense of shame and failure. But the important part is getting back to the beginning and starting over again (but this time, we are more prepared with what could trigger a relapse). Can the Enneagram work with those recovering from addiction?

The answer is yes. Whether you are fighting addiction or someone else is, you will realize that the power of the Enneagram will help you mature and develop as an individual. Each of the nine personality types has their own unique way of forgetting about what's important to their recovery.

A relapse can and will occur if one forgets how important their recovery is based on their personality type. Picking up their addiction of choice will become second nature at this point. And the process could get even harder from there.

That is why it is important for those fighting addiction to be more in tune with their personality type while finding a way to stay the course based on that. Needless to say, the Enneagram helps us become more aware of our limitations.

Furthermore, it allows us to see the opportunities for growth that those with addiction will need to take. Because of this, it will help them recover and become a better person. Leaving the pain of the past is the name of the game.

As we go through every personality type, we will discuss how each one deals with addiction. If you or someone you know is dealing with addiction or in the process of recovery, this is vital information that you'll want to put to good use. However, don't skip to those chapters just yet (since we have plenty left to discuss in order to help you understand the Enneagram more).

Enneagram and Mental Health

Our mental health is important to us. But when we are dealing with traumatic events and the like, mental illnesses can develop. These mental illnesses could lead to more pain and affliction than we can handle.

Those struggling with mental illness may be susceptible to severe depression and are more likely to commit suicide. The truth is, a lot of people are ashamed of disclosing their struggles with mental illness due to a stigma that continues to exist. However, that stigma is not as prevalent as it once was in the past couple of decades.

More and more every day, people are opening up about their struggles with mental illness. They know that it affects not just themselves, but also their families as well. Rather than feeling a sense of shame, they feel like people are listening to them.

They are aware that there are times that they will feel like they are battling it alone. But the reality is, no one should feel like they are. There are many people who deal with some kind of mental illness (either themselves or via a family member).

When you understand your Enneagram type, it becomes clear that you will better understand it. And it can work towards improving your mental health even more. The Enneagram is a useful coping mechanism for those dealing with mental illness and the like.

At first, the person struggling with mental illness may have trouble identifying themselves using the Enneagram. However, some of them may be immediately drawn to some personality types based on how they feel and what they do. If you gravitate towards a certain personality type, make a note of it (since it may possibly run in line with the test results you will be taking later).

There are many positive practices for your mental health based on your Enneagram type. Once you find out which type you are, you will learn how to put them to good use so you can improve your mental health overall. You will forget about your struggles and do your best to live the life you want to lead.

The Enneagram and Your Personal Life

If there is one thing that you should use the Enneagram for, it's in regard to your personal life. Could you be connected to someone who may or may not have the same personality type as you do? Is this person a friend or a romantic partner?

As we break down every personality type, you will learn about your relationships with people and how to adapt. Which personality types will bring your life better balance? Which types are not worth it?

Your friendships and romances might improve through the Enneagram. You might have some rough patches in your current romantic relationship, and you are looking to find a way to make things right. Improving relationships using the power of the Enneagram is possible for both you and that person of interest.

Let's face it, it may be easy for a lot of us to make friends. Even though we live in the age of social media apps and the like, we find a way to make friends even if there are times when we feel lonely. The real question is: is it possible for you to find a good friend a lot easier if you know their Enneagram type?

The answer is a resounding yes. However, there are three pillars to keep in mind about friendship. They consist of honesty, loyalty, and kindness. Those are what friends need the most from each other.

As we go through each personality type, we will discuss how each one should deal with friendships. And we will do the same in regard to romantic relationships. Sure, there are strengths and weaknesses that you will be able to identify.

But you will also look for ways to double down on those strengths while figuring out how to handle the weaknesses as well. You're probably excited to know which Enneagram types you match better with. But you won't be able to understand it fully with the little information you have on the Enneagram at the moment (so keep reading).

Could you stand being with a partner that may or may not have the same Enneagram type as you do? Is marriage on the horizon? There is definitely a lot for us to uncover as we go along.

Your Professional Life

Shifting gears from your personal to professional life now. How can the Enneagram be used in the workplace? Are you someone who considers themselves a team player or a leader?

How do you handle your co-workers (both the nice ones and the not-so-nice ones)? The Enneagram might work wonders on your relationship with your co-workers. You may also use it to your advantage in terms of how you can advance in your career.

Speaking of careers, are there any careers that are best suited for Enneagram types? Sure enough, there is. You might already be years into a successful career in one field that may have been a great fit all along. But don't be surprised that the field you're in at the moment is opposite to your type. Later on, we might be able to pinpoint why you might have found success in a career that isn't a fit for your personality type. It may not be too late to make a change in terms of careers (especially if the current one you're in may feel like it's not fulfilling enough).

In the professional world, you could be working with teams on various projects. Think about the last time you worked on a group project. Were you someone who was a leader or a follower?

Were you someone that was willing to put in the work or pull as little weight as possible? There are so many questions that we can ask about your ability to work with teams. Some may not even be comfortable working with teams.

It's not because they are anti-social. It's likely because they put in their peak performance when they work by themselves. Could that be part of an Enneagram type?

The Enneagram Can Define Your Life

The Enneagram can be the basis of how your life is defined in both the personal and professional sense. We might know a lot about ourselves. And that may explain why we gravitate towards certain personality types.

Your personality type may be based on how you behave in a friendship, relationship, or in a professional setting. At work, maybe you don't see yourself as a leader, and that may be based on your Enneagram type. You'd rather work behind the scenes and be comfortable with such responsibilities rather than lead others.

You could be a friend that is loyal and caring to others. You feel that your self-interests are not as important in times when a friend needs you most. This could be all defined by this complex system that you are learning about right now.

Simply put, the Enneagram can define your life and you might not even know it. Once you understand it, learn more about your personality type, and every little thing about it, it will all make sense.

Final Thoughts

The Enneagram is powerful indeed. But harnessing its power will be something that you will learn over time. It does play a role in how it defines your life and the personality you have. You may gravitate towards a certain personality type based on the way you behave, who you look for in a partner, and so on.

Once we dive into each personality type and examine them individually, you will likely say to yourself 'yes, that definitely sounds like me' or 'hey, I didn't know that about myself'. Either way, you're probably feeling a mix of excitement and mystery right about now.

The Power of the Enneagram is not just about finding out more about yourself. It's also about finding a way to heal. Whether you are dealing with addiction, mental illness, or even relationship problems, the Enneagram does have the ability to help you manage the pain and even heal in the process.

That healing process can help you improve the relationship or improve yourself, whichever may be considered more of a priority. Sometimes, the Enneagram will suggest that yourself is more important than, say fixing a relationship that has no sense in being repaired. But nevertheless, using this system will help you become a better person.

Chapter 4: Growth and Change

If you are someone who has struggled to find ways to grow and make changes in your life, keep reading. The Enneagram is a great source where you can grow and change in many aspects of your life. How that will impact you will depend on how much work you are willing to put in.

How can you apply the Enneagram to your own personal growth? How will it change you for the better? You will find out in due time.

We are going to discuss how you can chart your path towards growth and change. Obviously, your path will be based on your number or personality type. As you already know by now, each type is unique in its own way.

You can use the Enneagram based on the wing points and the arrow-line points that we have explained earlier on in the book. If you are a Type 9, what does that mean for your wings (Types 1 and 9)? Or what about your arrows (Types 3 and 6)?

For the first time in this book, we will give you a quick peek into how some of the types work with others. We will show you some examples, so you know what to expect. We may bring this up again once we break down every personality type later on in the book.

Now, let's give you a glimpse of how to put the Enneagram to good use with the intent to grow as a person.

Using The Enneagram for Your Self Development

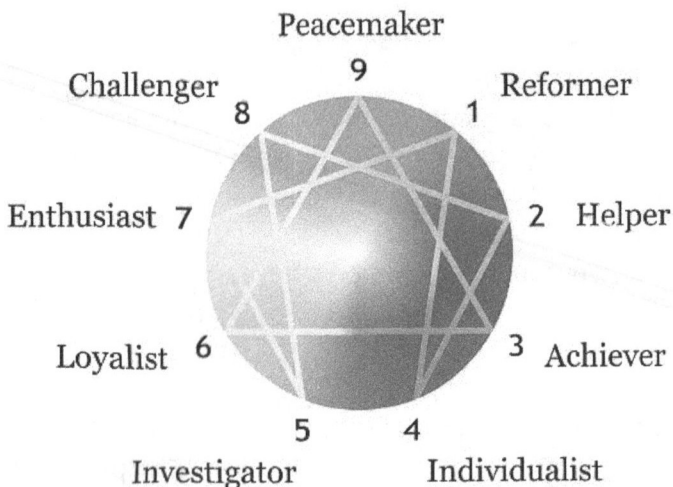

Peacemaker
9
Challenger   Reformer
8   1
Enthusiast 7   2 Helper
Loyalist 6   3 Achiever
5   4
Investigator   Individualist

In the diagram above, let's use Type 9 as an example. Its wing points are Type 8 and Type 1. Whereas its arrow points are Type 6 and 3. As far as growth is concerned, what do they each offer? (If you are listening to this book in audio format - be sure to download your PDF version of the book so you can see the diagram).

How to Grow Using Your Arrows

Your wing points will allow your growth and development to be gentler. Meanwhile, your arrows will focus more on the radical growth and changes. If you are a Type 7 for example, you may make changes based on the Type 5 arrow line.

If you are dealing with emotions such as anxiety, take a moment to meditate and identify the source of that anxiety. At the same time, you will learn how to think through the things you are doing in the moment and learn about them in much greater detail.

But what about the Type 1 arrow line? If you are someone who is a creative person and a Type 7, you will use that arrow line to give you a good idea of what defines 'perfect'. After all, Type 1 personalities are usually perfectionists.

For example, you may learn from Type 1s about how you can follow the rules, put together a well-structured plan that has to be executed to a T, and be sure that you fulfill time commitments. A Type 7 is someone who may have a hard time adjusting to structure, but will come around to embrace it once they realize it gives them more freedom to do whatever they want.

Growth Based on Wings

As mentioned before, growth and development based on wings are not as radical compared to your arrows. For this example, we will stick with the Type 7. The wings for the Type 7 are 6 and 8.

With the help of the 'Six Wing', you will learn the ability to detect negativity from a mile away. You may even detect a subtle hint of it. From there, you will have a responsibility to know how to deal with it before it grows into a much bigger problem.

Meanwhile, you will be able to develop skills on how to solve problems based on bad news, risks being made, and the things that may be considered a threat. As someone who is creative, you will be able to get a good idea of what's working and what's not working. So, you find a creative solution to eradicate any negative problems on the horizon.

In other words, you'll have the ability to put out the fire before it even spreads. And that can be hard to do for most people. This will provide some kind of balance for those who consider themselves natural optimists.

You'll be using this wing as a way to balance the good news and bad news. You will see the positive and the negative of things. The best thing you can do is find a time where you have the opportunity to listen to good and bad news.

The next wing is the 'Eight Wing'. Using this wing in particular, you take more action using as few ideas as possible. Since you are a creative, you tend to double down on your brainstorming abilities. You imagine as many possibilities and solutions as humanly possible.

For this reason, you have so many big ideas that are taking up a good part of your mental space. The solution is obvious: empty that mental space and put those big ideas into practice. Don't let it sit there and collect dust.

You could be someone who might start a business. You have gathered enough intelligence to put together this one big idea. The real question is: will that idea see the light of day?

Most people don't take action because of their fears of failure and rejection. That happens. Some ideas will work, and others will fail because of one reason or another. If one business idea fails, it could be due to factors such as getting it in front of the wrong kind of people (i.e. - your market).

Without relying on this wing in particular, your ideas will collect dust and never come to fruition. Don't let your mental space become that attic or basement filled with items that have collected years, even decades of dust. If you are someone who is an aspiring entrepreneur or leader, Type 7s will be fortunate to have a Type 8 as a wing.

Type 7s can be leaders. They have an idea and will execute it on a dime just to see how it goes. Since they have the ability to handle bad news in accordance with the 'Six Wing', they can process the bad news (i.e. - the idea failed because…), they can move on with the next idea. They are optimistic in knowing that with every idea they have, at least one of them has to stick.

When it comes to growth and change, your wings and arrows will definitely provide you with a lot of ways to become a better person. This was just a preview of how we will break down every personality type and how they benefit based on their arrows and wings.

The Key Takeaway Regarding Wings and Arrows

Every personality type has its own wings and arrows. Your wings will be useful for growth and support. Meanwhile, the arrows will give you growth to the point where you are doing things outside of your usual comfort zone.

Simply put, to successfully grow, it will take getting out of your comfort zone on a regular basis. If we stay in one place where we are comfortable, then growth and change simply cannot happen. The timing of it all will vary from one person to the next.

If you are willing to change yourself for the better, you will need to know your true Enneagram type. From there, you will need to find those who are considered your 'wings' and your 'arrows'. Finding those kinds of people may be difficult, but the time invested in it will be worthwhile.

Stress and Growth Lines Explained

In the Enneagram, there are two types of lines: stress and growth. Let's explain each of these lines in a bit more detail:

Stress lines

The stress lines apply to how each personality type handles all kinds of pressure. When dealing with it, people will find a way to push through it. However, they may do this at the expense of taking on a major weakness of their personality type.

At that point, they could feel the stress brought on by the pressure. They will feel discomfort in taking on a personality trait that isn't naturally developed (or even as part of their Enneagram type). Type Eights may have the knowledge and curiosity as part of their identity, but they may tend to pull themselves away from other people for a long period of time if they find themselves in stressful and often uncomfortable situations.

For this reason, their arrows, the Type 5 personalities, will often pick up the slack and gain strength and experience from the tasks delegated by Type 8s (if any). Type 8s are often the leader types.

And leaders will use their skills to delegate responsibility to other people in order to take the pressure off themselves. That's because they need time to themselves to focus on the other complex tasks that currently exist. That should explain the reason why they distance themselves from others, even if it's for a lengthy period of time.

They require almost 100 percent attention and focus on the task at hand. Thus, it gives fives the opportunity to strengthen any weaknesses they may have while doubling down on their current strengths.

Growth Lines

Growth lines are where you can find ways to grow based on your personality type. Sticking with the Type 8s in this example, they tend to be people who will spend more time with friends and family despite living a busy lifestyle. It's as if they are finding the time without making any excuses of not having to spend time with them.

Type 8s are helpful and caring towards people when they are in a comfortable and less stressed state. That's because when their minds are clearer, they will come up with a solution on the fly to solve a problem. At the same time, they are also people who will relax and take time to explore themselves.

With growth lines, you will use this as an opportunity to grow and gain further insight that will help you become more self-aware and able to heal your inner self.

Growth Practices Based on Your Centers

There are different growth practices that you can focus on based on your personality types and your centers (heart, gut, and head). We will delve more into that when we discuss the chapter on these three centers. Some of these growth practices of using these centers may also be based on some Enneagram types.

For example, for Types 2, 3, and 4 you will focus on growth practices that will focus on the heart center. The head center will focus more on Types 5, 6, and 7. When we discuss this, you will learn about the key themes for reflection.

Handling Change Based on Your Enneagram Type

Once you find out your true Enneagram type, the question you ask yourself is: how do you handle change? Needless to say, when you do change, don't expect it to be stable at all. Because things change over time as it is.

Change can be a daunting thing. And you will go through a lot of emotions and feelings over time. Fight or flight will be ever-present with change.

For some, change can be beneficial. If you know how to respond to change positively, that will allow you to cope using empathy and better understand why these changes happen. You will also understand why your behavior will change once you make some shifts with your everyday routines.

Every Enneagram type has a unique way of handling change. Are you a Type 1 that is stubborn, but willing to push for a better solution over time? Or are you a Type 2 wondering if such change will benefit others compared to yourself?

Final Thoughts

The Enneagram is instrumental to growth and change. Not only will it teach you to grow using your wings and arrows, but it will also help you confirm your personality type even further with the way you behave. As for the way you handle change, your personality type will also define that.

You could be stubborn to change and two things can happen. You either accept it as it is, or you find a better solution that may benefit you the most. Personality types have their own growth and stress lines.

You will learn how to handle stressful and high-pressure situations based on your true Enneagram Type. Sure, you may have a preliminary idea of what your type is. But the question is: does the way you behave and handle certain things change that?
With that said, we will now jump into how the Enneagram applies to obsessions we may have.

Chapter 5: Obsessions

Obsession - 1. *The state of being obsessed with someone or something* **2.** *An idea or thought that continually preoccupies or intrudes on a person's mind.*

Above are the definitions for obsession. The questions regarding obsession are why, what, and how. Why are they obsessed with something or someone?

What is it about that one person or thing that triggers such an obsession? How did it all start? These questions apply to the Enneagram as well.

Somewhere in the Enneagram, we find the answers to these questions. For one type, why are they so obsessed about what the future holds for them? What is it about the future that it gets to the point where they think about it all the time? How will they handle it once their obsession becomes some kind of reality?

You might be thinking that obsessions are unhealthy. Well, yes and no. Some obsessions are bad because it might be something where it can make another person uncomfortable. For example, someone could find another person to be a potential love interest.

It can get to the point where your obsession will surface and leak into how you behave around that one person (or other people for that matter). Those behaviors may even be unhealthy for both people in the mental sense. If you are obsessed with someone, it might just get to an unhealthy level if unchecked.

As for the good obsessions such as the future, it can drive you to work harder and focus more on the task at hand. Let's say for example your future is likely going to be a prosperous one. The obsession with making more money for the purpose of financial security can be the absolute driving force.

Under the surface, what is it about financial security that gives you that obsessive drive? Is it because you want to take better care of your family? Is it because it can provide you with more freedom?

To be obsessed with something that can and will yield beneficial results is something you can focus on without making it look unhealthy. It can help become your fuel to succeed. If you are a Type 8, you may be obsessed with the future because the more you work on something to get an expected result, the more motivated you will become.

Speaking of obsessions, there are people out there who are obsessed with the Enneagram in general. They want to know exactly what type they are, what makes themselves...well, themselves, and are figuring out what to do to become better.

Are There Obsessions Based on Enneagram Types?

One of the questions often asked is what kind of obsessions exist among Enneagram types? For example, Type 4s tend to be obsessed with longing for something or someone. They could be obsessed with finding success in their own right or finding someone that will love them for who they are as a person.

Type 7s are the kind of people who are known to be obsessed with the future. As if there is some kind of goal that they want to achieve. However, they are a long way off from it.

Can they use that obsession to drive them closer to what they want in the future? Yes, so long as they take action. If something in the future is an obsession, that could be enough motivation to work on getting close to that goal or whatever the future holds.

Last but not least, let's take a look at Type 1s. As noted before, they are perfectionists. So, the one thing that they are obsessed with is planning.

They want everything to be executed right down to the littlest of detail. They plan something out, sleep on it, go back and make adjustments whenever something minute pops up in their head. Type 1s are obsessed with planning and make no bones about putting it all together with such militant precision.

Simply put, every Enneagram type has a healthy obsession with something. And they will make sure that they will put that to good use in order to maximize their abilities and live out their personality type. If a Type 2 is a giving person, they are obsessed with doing so with large amounts (and even making many self-sacrifices as a result).

As we explain each of the 9 types in detail, we will touch base on those obsessions. When you do find out about your type, you will start to put all the pieces of the puzzle together. You might find out everything you know or have done all along may be accurate.

You could be the giving type for others. But does that make you a Type 2? You never know.

The Enneagram Can Become an Obsession of Itself

Here's another crazy thing about the Enneagram. The more you understand its power and use of it, you may even use it to read other people. You may find yourself obsessed with it to the point where you can read a TV or movie character and make a basic assumption of their Enneagram type.

But this identification will usually go beyond identifying fictional characters. Sure, actors will have a character that may be one Enneagram type (even one that is different from their own in real life). You can also observe your friends and family and be able to read enough into what their Enneagram type is.

It's all about observing and processing the data in your mind. You can determine what their personality most likely is. Your reading may be accurate or not.

So, don't be surprised when you have a deep understanding of the Enneagram and use it regularly, you start to 'type' people. At the same time, you may 'type' them for some kind of purpose. Could it be for friendship, love, or something else?

You might be obsessed with connecting with people who are different types. There are different types that can blend well with others, so why not be excited or even 'obsessed with it'?

Final Thoughts

On the surface, obsessions may sound like a bad thing. But that depends on what person is obsessed with it. The Enneagram allows us to focus on the 'good obsessions'.

Each type has some kind of 'obsession' that is all part of who they are. Type 1s are obsessed with planning, Type 2s with giving, and so on. You can even become obsessed with the Enneagram itself once you know how to use it fully.

You may end up 'typing' people and make an executive decision on whether you should connect with them or not. We all have obsessions deep inside us. However, not a lot of us know what we are specifically obsessed with until we unearth our true personality type.

Using the Enneagram, we figure out that mystery for ourselves. You might already know what you are obsessed with. If so, write that down somewhere since you'll probably need it later on when we talk about your personality type.

Chapter 6: Ancient Roots, Modern Insights

In this chapter, we are going to dive into the history of the Enneagram. You will learn about the roots that are said to be dated back to ancient times. We will also look into modern insights regarding the system.

While the insights of the Enneagram will probably change or stay the same over time, it is interesting to learn how it all started. At the same time, you will learn about how it became something tied to a person's type of personality. There have been different schools of thought regarding the Enneagram from various scholars from around the world.

Let's dive right in:

The Origins of The Enneagram

The Enneagram is a combination of two Greek terms:

Enneagram = Nine

Gram = Model or Point

The true roots and origins of the Enneagram are still a matter of dispute even as you read this. However, it is said to be connected to various spiritual, philosophical, and mathematical traditions. There have been many assumptions as to where the Enneagram originated from.

Let's take a look at some of these claimed origins:

- Some believe that the Enneagram may have originated from Ancient Greece. It is said that there may be a connection between two different types of mathematics including Pythagorean mathematics.

- There may be a connection between the Enneagram and the Christian faith. Specifically, there are medieval references to the Enneagram and the '7 Deadly Sins' that have been outlined in the Bible.

- Judaism and the Enneagram may have a possible connection. Specifically, the philosopher Philo may have originated the thought that the Enneagram is closely associated with the branches of the Tree of Life in the Kabbalah.

- Athanasius Kircher, a Jesuit mathematician, created a drawing that resembled the Enneagram in the 17th century, furthering the argument that Christianity may have played a role in the development of the personality system.

You may spend time reading and doing research on where the Enneagram may come from. And you may draw your own conclusions as you go. One thing is for certain: you don't need to be religious or be part of any organized religion to truly understand the Enneagram.

Long after its development over the course of centuries, many scholars and experts continue to share their insights on the Enneagram. As the 20th and 21st century passed, more information about the Enneagram has come to light.

The Modern Insights of The Enneagram

The earliest known insights of the Enneagram were believed to be from a Russian scholar named George Gurdjieff. He called the Enneagram a symbol of 'perpetual motion' and used it in his teachings. Because of this, he proclaimed himself as a 'teacher of dancing'.

Gurdjieff claims that his discovery of the Enneagram stemmed from a visit to Afghanistan in the 1920s. He said that it originated in a monastery in the country but did not go further in-depth regarding the true origin itself.

More than 40 years later and half the world away, Oscar Ichazo used the Enneagram in his newly founded school in Bolivia. He had developed theories over time that would be known (and termed by him) as 'protoanalysis'. Ichazo also passed the Enneagram along to a Chilean psychiatrist named Claudio Naranjo.

Naranjo continued using the Enneagram in his teachings, even up until his passing in 2019. Those who were students of Naranjo used the Enneagram in their own unique teachings. One of those students was Robert Ochs. Ochs utilized the Enneagram to many people in the Christian community to names much familiar to the system itself (names like Riso and Hudson, for those who may be familiar as well).

It's a matter of debate as to whether the Enneagram has a religious association or not. But once again, you don't need to subscribe to a specific religion in order to use the Enneagram to your advantage. Some may use it while relying on a higher power to get through things.

What Christianity Says About The Enneagram

While the Enneagram has been introduced to many in the Christian faith, there are those that have shared their thoughts about it. Their response can be stemmed from Deuteronomy 18:9-13:

"When you enter the land the Lord your God is giving you, do not learn to imitate the detestable ways of the nations there. Let no one be found among you who sacrifices their son or daughter in the fire, who practices divination or sorcery, interprets omens, engages in witchcraft, or casts spells, or who is a medium or spirits or who consults with the dead. Anyone who does these things is detestable to the Lord, because these same detestable practices the Lord your God will drive out those nations before you. You must be blameless before the Lord your God."

By the sounds of it, the Bible curries no favor to the Enneagram. They state that it goes everything against the word of God. Be that as it may.

But it's further proof that the Enneagram and the Christian faith have no direct association with each other in terms of its origin. If you are a Christian and considering the idea of using the Enneagram, it's your call. But we won't blame you if you decide to not go through with it for religious reasons.

However, the Enneagram is becoming more prevalent in the Christian faith. So, the question going forward is simply this: What has changed? Are people abiding by the words provided above?

Why is it becoming popular among Christians? It comes down to one thing: people want to know who they truly are. What is it that is missing in the Bible that allows people to reveal themselves?

The Bible as we understand may define people as the same in terms of who they are, how they look (i.e. - 'In God's eyes, we are all the same). Some Christian disciplines such as Unitarian Universalists are adopting the Enneagram.

The Enneagram may also be changing the face of the Christian religion as a whole. By this, we mean that the Enneagram may play a role in how someone can conduct a worship service. Those who conduct a worship service are considered leaders of the community.

Despite its pushback from many Christian disciplines, it seems to have benefited those who practice the Christian faith as a whole. They are deeply interested because it focuses more on themselves rather than how they can help others.

Some have used it as a way to enhance their faith in Jesus Christ. One Christian stated that the Enneagram helped her find her 'blind spots and pitfalls. She added that she thought she was self-aware of herself (but was proven wrong).

When there is power in learning your true traits based on your Enneagram type, those in the Christian faith may have the option of knowing what they are. In the future, the Christian faith will see more of the Enneagram in their local churches. But it will not progress without any pushback from those in the community.

The Enneagram and the Jewish Faith

Unlike the Christian faith, there is little to no evidence of the Jewish faith condemning or denying the Enneagram as far as its use is concerned. Even for something with no direct affiliation for a single religion, there are those in the Jewish faith who will use it to better themselves as human beings.

Despite its claimed origins from Judaism, clerics are laxer in allowing people to practice the Enneagram. Even Jewish religious centers and synagogues have hosted workshops and events related to the Enneagram recently. If you are interested in looking for an event related to the Enneagram, you may want to consult with someone who is among the Jewish community.

The Enneagram and Islam

"I seek refuge in Allah from Satan, the rejected one. In the Name of Allah, the Most Beneficent, the Most Merciful" -- *Verse 16:98 (Quran)*

Even those in the Islamic faith are looking for ways to better themselves both in their faith and otherwise. So, are there those who use the Enneagram while practicing Islam? The answer is yes.

They use it in a way where they recognize themselves as the person they truly are. When they recognize a negativity in their personality (i.e. - anger or stress), they will chant or pray it away. They see the Enneagram as a spiritual mentor.

They believe that the Enneagram has plenty of knowledge to which they seek. They use it to pray to correct their 'character flaws'. So rather than be cast away as some entity that threatens their religion, the Islamic faith uses it as a roadmap to become better people beyond their faith.

Is The Enneagram A Protest Against Religion?

Circling back to the Christian faith, many young Christians are more drawn towards the Enneagram compared to those much older than them. For this reason, there is a question as to whether or not the Enneagram was developed as a protest against religion.

As far as we know, it doesn't seem like it (unless said otherwise). In the meantime, the major religions have either embraced it or are in the process of doing so. If you are a member of a religious community, you may benefit from the Enneagram yourself.

And it can get to the point where you may lead your community in helping people use it to help them better understand themselves and uncover a new layer of themselves that has long been buried. Whether people decide to go along with it or deny doing so for religious purposes, that ball is in their court.

Final Thoughts

The Enneagram appears to have some ancient roots. However, its true origins are still debated even today. In modern times, many scholars have relied on the Enneagram to enhance their teachings. Even today, they are being taught in educational institutes.

The Enneagram has also been influential in most religious circles. The Jewish and Islamic faiths have utilized it as a spiritual guide to help them unveil their true selves (and unearth their personality types). However, the Christian faith appears to be coming around despite some protest and pushback.

The Enneagram has grown in popularity both inside and outside the religious communities. Thus, it has no other choice but to stick around for the years and decades that follow. Many will not embrace it, but others will in the interest of learning more about themselves.

Chapter 7: Cultivating Awareness

Awareness is one of the keywords that has already been thrown around in this book many times. But up to this point, we haven't touched on how you can cultivate it for yourself. You will learn how to use the Enneagram to grow that level of awareness that you are searching for in this chapter.

Awareness goes hand-in-hand with things like creativity. Without it, what's the sense in being creative? With awareness, people are more observant or even innovative.

Being aware of yourself allows you to gain access to other abilities such as being creative or innovative. The problem is a lot of people tend to lose their self-awareness. The reason why is because of fear.

Specifically, it's the fear of taking time out of our day to think about who we really are and what our true values are. However, the Enneagram will allow you to alleviate that fear. Thus, it will allow you to cultivate that awareness that a lot of us are searching for.

Let's talk more about awareness and how you can find it for yourself:

It Starts with Discovering Your Personality Type

Simply put, it all starts with your personality type. Once you are able to identify with who you are within the Enneagram, you will then discover who you truly are. From there, you become aware of it.

You will learn more about what your diminished traits are along with what drew you to become that personality type. You may be able to determine at what point you have developed some of the traits that make you who you are.

If they were developed in your childhood, do you still utilize them as an adult? Either way, answering this question will make you aware of whether or not such traits still exist.

Awareness and Creativity

As mentioned before, awareness and creativity go hand-in-hand. In fact, they are some of the basic human needs that we have. Without awareness, we have the inability to know ourselves better than anyone else.

Without creativity, we don't have a way to express our truths of who we truly are as a person. Many people assume that they are self-aware. The truth is, it's actually the opposite.

According to one Enneagram scholar, he stated that all people operate like machines. Specifically, we work in various mechanical patterns. Being self-aware is more like a cup of tea being spilled into the machines in order to throw off those mechanical patterns.

Without awareness, our creativity lacks direction. From there, it's a matter of whether or not we start something that expresses our true selves. Or worse yet, we don't have a starting point nor the confidence in creating something.

We feel like that even if we do create something, it doesn't seem real. Authenticity is what we're looking for. And self-awareness can help us find it. Creativity and authenticity are two key elements that can be generated from awareness.

In life, we tend to be unforgiving to ourselves and not know about it. We forget who we are, lie about ourselves, and thus lead us to destroy ourselves. One leads to the other.

Forgetting Ourselves

Forgetting ourselves is the first step towards self-sabotage. The one true remedy to this is being aware. Specifically, you want to be present physically, mentally, and emotionally. Focus on the real you rather than some manufactured version of yourself.

We tend to go through the motions and live life on autopilot. However, it is important to take a moment to ensure that we are present in the moment. We want to make sure that we are able to know ourselves and find the weak spots within our 'mechanical patterns'.

Lying to Ourselves

The second stage is lying or deceiving ourselves. At this point, we find ourselves in directions that are not the right ones. Imagine this scenario for a moment:

You walk down a path for miles on end. After a while, you come across a fork in the road. The path to your right is an endless path that is clear and goes to the horizon and beyond. Meanwhile, the road on your left is dark and covered in trees, bushes, and other vegetation.

At this point, you make a choice. Let's say you decide to take the clear path. Seems easy enough, right?

However, this is an example of what deceiving yourself will become. You take the clear path knowing it's an easy decision. But what you don't realize is once you reach the end of that path, you drop off of a cliff that suddenly appears out of nowhere.

We deceive ourselves into believing that the easy way is usually the best way. That the dark path is never one to travel. For this reason, whether we're aware of it or not, we are afraid of taking on the stresses and challenges of achieving goals and the like.

We are afraid of setbacks and failures. We are afraid of the unknown. So, we look for that 'easy path' that suddenly winds up becoming a deep drop to the bottom.

Rather than lie to yourself, you need to be honest with yourself. What really matters to you most? What do you really love?

Take the time to observe and dig into what you truly value most. What kind of impact do you want to make on this Earth so long as you are still alive? Stop lying to yourself.

Otherwise, this will happen...

Self-Sabotage

Self-sabotage is the result of failing to recognize that you are forgetting and lying to yourself. And yes, it also stems from a lack of awareness. What are the signs of self-sabotage other than what we've pointed out so far?

Let's take a look at some examples:

- You procrastinate or hold back on doing something because you fear that it won't meet your own standards (much less others)

- You turn down a project that you know will benefit you because you fear that you may not be good enough

- You don't 'sell' your talents and abilities that you know will benefit others because of something you fear

At this point, you may have already seen a pattern. Fear is the common denominator for self-sabotage. Fear and a lack of confidence will often go hand-in-hand with one another.

But knowing that you can cultivate awareness for yourself will allow you to be more in the know regarding the present. You will also be more aware of your feelings so you can identify how you truly feel and what the sources are for them.

Chapter 8: The Truth Is Simple and Beautiful

When we learn about ourselves through the Enneagram, we will feel a few things. At first, we may feel confused about our personality types. We may even protest by saying 'that's not who I am'.

But the truth is, your personality is who you are as a person. And the more you know about yourself, the better. Sometimes, the revelations may shock you.

You may have the personality of a certain Type, but you may be behaving in a way that is considered 'unhealthy'. We'll discuss the healthy and unhealthy traits of each type later on in this book. But the point of this chapter is that you will eventually learn about your true self.

The truth about you is simple and beautiful. You will be familiar with yourself in a way that you never thought was possible. But the beautiful thing about it is that you will soon learn how to embrace yourself and be able to live with your personality (albeit in the healthy sense).

This chapter will help you prepare for the big thing that lies ahead: finding out about your true Enneagram type. You may have found this out already, but still struggle to figure out how to handle it. But not to worry, we will help you come to terms with your true personality.

As we go further, let's share with you some things that apply to all Enneagram types. This will allow you to mentally prepare for what you may need to accept about yourself. Let's get started:

There will be a 'shock' to the system

Whether you know something about your alleged personality type or not, you may learn about the things that pertain to it and right away be surprised or even shocked. You may think to yourself that those behaviors and traits may be the polar opposite of what you do as a person. But the discoveries will unearth who you truly are as a person.

You will feel shocked at first. You may feel like you cannot accept the truth immediately. And that is normal. But rest assured, it will take time to process. It is important for you to consider taking the time to reflect and think about the actions (no matter how small they are) and see if they match up with your true personality.

You may not have known it or even remember it, but there may have been instances where your personality traits have been on display. And you may not have been aware of them. And that's fine.

To increase your awareness through mindfulness, you will know the truth

As you begin to build on being more mindful, you will become more aware of not just the things around you, but the truth about who you are. You will notice some of the lesser traits about yourself. And only you will recognize and acknowledge it in the slightest.

After you have discovered your Enneagram type, you may carry on with your day and express the traits that match your personality type to a T. But that shouldn't stop there.

You should also be aware that with your Enneagram type, there are ways to go about growing. Especially when it's in a personal or professional setting. Towards the latter half of this book, we will stress that each Enneagram type will have a unique way of taking care of themselves.

When you adopt personal growth practices, you will accept yourself

Simply put, when you apply the growth practices for each Enneagram type (as we will outline later on in the book), you will come to the realization that making peace with your true self is a lot better than trying to avoid it.

So instead of trying to resist or fight it, you become it. From there, you will be able to live a healthy and fulfilling life. You can also focus on making life much healthier by reducing stress and trying out things that may be outside of your comfort zone.

You want positivity in your life. At the same time, you want to deal with as little negativity as possible. The more positive you have over negative, you will be able to grow and maintain your lifestyle based on your Enneagram type.

There is no good or evil for your personality type

Later on in this book, we will be sharing with you the principles of the Enneagram. To give you a brief preview, one of those principles is that no Enneagram type is good or evil. Twos and Fours are not nicer than Eights and vice versa.

With your personality type, you may question yourself whether or not you are a good person. You may feel like your personality type may question whether or not your personality type makes you too nice or too rude. But rest assured, there are some traits and actions that you will act on based on your nature (even though you have the freedom to choose whether or not you can act on those actions yourself).

Acceptance is the best way forward

Accepting yourself for who you are is not giving up on something. It's a lot better than spending your life fighting the truth. Fighting it can lead to undue stress and thus prevent you from achieving your full potential based on your personal and professional growth.

Every Enneagram type has something positive to give to the world. There may be advantages and disadvantages. But if every type accepts themselves and sees the positive, they can easily get through their lives by leveraging their abilities.

Final Thoughts

At some point, you will learn the truth about yourself. You will learn more about who you are when you discover your Enneagram type. Even if you think you know your Type already, you may still have a way to go to learn more about yourself.

You may struggle with the truth at first. But fighting it is pointless. You have traits within your personality that you may have developed at a younger age. And those will stay with you for as long as you live.

Every Enneagram type has positives and negatives. But it is important for you to focus more on the positive traits while focusing on your own personal growth. When you grow personally, you will soon be able to accept yourself for who you are.

Your Enneagram type, no matter what it is, doesn't make you a good or bad person. It's something that defines you right down to the letter. And there is no shame in being that person that best defines your personality.

Chapter 9: The 3 Centers - Gut, Heart, and Head

Now, we are going to focus on the three centers that place a high importance on the Enneagram. We will be looking at the gut, heart, and head centers. You will get a deeper understanding of each center and how they relate to the Enneagram itself.

These centers are a point of contact that allows us to be present based on our sensations. You should also look at deepening your relationship with all three of these centers as well. What personality types are more focused on specific centers?

Which types are more focused on gut centers? Heart centers? What about head centers?

We will dive into that shortly. To better understand the Enneagram, it also includes being able to know these three centers. Already, we have discussed mindfulness and awareness as two of the biggest keys to unlocking the Enneagram code.

This is a very important chapter that we will dive deep into. We encourage you to pay close attention to this chapter since this contains key information that you'll need to note for future reference.

At this point, you may know your personality type or have yet to take the test. With that in mind, let's continue:

Overview of The Three Centers

The Gut Center

This is also known as the 'body center'. The gut center revolves around instincts (sounds fitting enough). One of the essential qualities of the gut center is based on the deep connection with that one quality that isn't recognized as much as it should.

You use your instincts to make better decisions. Your gut tells you to do this or avoid that. Your instincts will involve a sense of assertion and vitality.

Those who are considered Types 1, 8, and 9 are focused around the gut center. These personality types believe they don't have the ability to assert their wants and appear to have a lack of self-sense. For this reason, this leads them to be angry due to their inability to express themselves.

Their personality will attempt to create and nurture that sense of self. They want to influence those around them rather than the other way around. They want to find a way to motivate themselves while acquiring a sense of autonomy.

They will have a habit of carrying a lot of tension while creating walls and boundaries around themselves. They tend to become aggressive as a way to indicate that they are independent, and no one should control them. For this reason, they are more likely to resist change in any way, shape, or form.

Types 1, 8, and 9 have their own habits and idiosyncrasies based on the gut center. We will reveal these when we talk about each of these types individually.

The Heart Center

To put together the perfect analogy, the gut center is to your instinct as the heart center is to emotion. Makes sense, right? So, let's talk about the emotional sense of one's personality.

This center is focused around Types 2, 3, and 4. If healthy and balanced, they are using their emotions wisely. If unhealthy, then there is a clear imbalance that needs to be addressed.

These personality types may feel like they have lost their qualities. In its place, they believe that they feel like they are not enough to someone. They feel like their worth is lacking followed by a giant sense of shame.

Their personalities will look to compensate for these flaws by relying on things of the past. More specifically, they look to past events where they felt the best. They don't focus on the now as we are supposed to.

With this self-image, there is a false sense of self-value. And it also creates an environment where people are seeking approval and validation. Those who seek approval and validation are those who lack confidence.

Personality types are those who are considered nurturers. They care more about others than themselves to a certain extent. The other personalities focused on this center focus on themselves in the context of improving themselves and finding a sense of accomplishment.

Self-image both inwards and outwards are the two things that these personality types tend to focus on. If your inner self speaks negatively, then you will act it out externally. That is why it is important to make the vital changes to your mindset. Rather than live in fear or feel like you are worthless, make it known to yourself that you are enough no matter what.

The Head Center

The head center involves thinking. If you are healthy and balanced in this regard, you will be able to acquire sharp insights and an abundance of ideas. The mind is one of the most important parts of your body.

Personality types 5, 6, and 7 hold their minds in the highest regard. Their one true goal is getting connected to it in the best way possible. The mind is a source of guidance and confidence.

The mind also produces our ability to perceive, observe, and understand things. One of the common issues with these personality types is the lack of inner guidance that points them in the right direction. Because of this, their self-confidence suffers, and they feel that their inner support is sitting on quicksand rather than solid ground.

As a result, these personality types will look for confidence and security through any possible source. They will even put together a strategy on how to acquire it and where they can find it. However, their fear tends to hinder this and therefore amplifies any insecurities and anxieties that currently exist.

Some of these personality types may develop bad habits such as overthinking, analysis paralysis, and preoccupying themselves with things that they believe will distract them from the real issues.

Sometimes, in order to improve in this area, they should consider the idea of disconnecting themselves mentally from what could be triggering all the anxiety and stress. This will allow them to focus on what truly matters most.

Final Thoughts

Now that you are aware of the centers of the Enneagram, it is important that you keep them aligned. This can be done through regular practices of mindfulness. There are Enneagram types that are corresponding to specific centers based on various feelings.

Type Twos are located in the heart center based on feeling-based traits while Type Fives are more of a head center type because they use their logic rather than feelings.

Chapter 10: The Nine Faces of The Soul

Now, we will be unveiling the nine faces of the soul based on the Enneagram. Specifically, we will not unveil each of the nine personality types that consist of the system itself. If you have yet to know about your personality type, consider this a preview of the test that you will be taking on the next page.

If you have read books on the Enneagram, you may be familiar with these nine faces or types. But we will provide you with our own insights regarding each personality type so you may have a good idea of what you might be. We will begin by starting with Type 1 and then working our way up to Type 9.

As you read through each type, you will probably identify some of the characteristics you may have. Take note that it may match your potential personality type. You may be drawn to one already and may be looking for confirmation.

Meanwhile, we will also be looking into the religious connections of the Enneagram. We will talk about it from both a Christian viewpoint as well as from other religions.

With that said, let's get right into this portion of the book:

From the Perspective of Christianity

From this angle, we will discuss two things: your true self and your false self. Let's break down each one:

Your True Self

Your true self is who you really are. It is your absolute identity. It is who you are in the eyes of God.

You may feel like you are immortal and can live for as long as possible. Your true self is connected to what is known as the 'Great Self' or the 'Christ self'.

Your False Self

This is known as your relative identity. This is the kind of identity that is created by you and you alone. Unlike the true self, this one will eventually change into something different and 'die'.

Your false self is someone who is considered fragile or needy. It's based on the false rather than the true. You may be putting up a front, exuding an outward appearance. But nobody will know what really goes on underneath.

As the old saying goes, there is more than meets the eye. Furthermore, we have to look at the conscious versus the subconscious. Whether you know it or not, 97 percent of your unconsciousness will show while the remaining three percent will be based on what you are doing consciously.

To the trained eye (i.e. - the people who know how to 'read people'), they can spot the unconscious actions of a person. They'll know the difference between who is being authentic and who is putting on an act to compensate for something. Furthermore, the way you behave is based on your conscience.

Meanwhile, your unconscious consists of your personality, motivation, defenses, anxieties, and fears. At this point, our goal here is to unearth what is buried under the surface. To get in touch with your true self while shedding your false self at the same time.

The Enneagram Types

Now, it's time to unveil each Enneagram type and their core personality types. These nine personality types are unique based on certain behaviors. As you go through each one, we will explain what makes them what they are.

We will provide you with an overview of each type. Later, we will go much deeper into them and discuss elements such as their behavior, their strengths, weaknesses, and so on.

Let's start with the first type:

Type 1

The first personality type is known as 'The Reformer'. Ones are the types of people who tend to be on a mission. Specifically, it is a mission to make the world a better place from their own perspective.

They will rely on whatever degree of influence they currently possess. As they carry out this mission, they will face adversity in many forms. Of them all, they will face moral adversity.

They are firm believers of achieving higher values. But these higher values are not acquired without great sacrifice. Ones are the types of people who perform great things at the behest of a 'higher calling'.

You may have a promising career that will make you prosperous and allow you to live a comfortable life. However, there is an event or some kind of threat to a greater good that has triggered you to take action (to the point where sacrificing a seemingly prosperous life is justifiable). Their actions in doing so may inspire others, even in high numbers.

As we dive deeper into Type One later on, we will unveil some examples of famous Ones who have made their sacrifices for a greater good. Some of them have done so, even though it may have resulted in their own demise.

Ones are people who have a strong sense of purpose. They also feel the need to justify their actions to both themselves and other people. Meanwhile, they also ponder on the consequences of said actions.

Ones are true activists whose goal is to look for a rationale that is acceptable and therefore justifiable enough for what they feel must be done. They want to stay as true to their principles as humanly possible. Using their convictions and judgments, they have the ability to control themselves and their actions.

For this reason, Ones will resist the urge of what their instincts tell them. They may not express them freely nor give into them at a conscious level. This will result in issues that may include aggressive behavior, resistance, and repressing their true feelings (at the start).

Though self-controlled, their anger might be justified. The reason being is those who feel that they are in control are angered by those who want to control others. It's like a passenger sitting next to you in a car suddenly reaching for the wheel and jerking it in a specific direction.

When it comes to their passions and desires, Ones are the kind of people that tend to keep a lid on them. They are storing them in a pot that tends to be boiling. And that 'boiling' is about to reach the top (even to the point where it can slowly leak from the pot).

However, Ones are known perfectionists. They are strict with themselves in every way possible. They will justify this perfection with themselves and others. However, their intent on being perfect can create their own chaos.

For this reason, Ones may be in a constant battle with their inner guidance. Therefore, the trust in themselves may depend on the day. Some days they will trust themselves and other days they will not.

However, Ones are on a mission to achieve a greater good. And they want everything to go smoothly or it is considered a failure. As perfectionists, they place little on errors (even in the slightest).

Type 2

Twos are known as 'The Helper' and rightfully so. They are known for helping other people whether they are healthy themselves or not. Twos want to be viewed as such by other people.

They have a tendency to be generous and will go out of their way to make others feel important (especially when helping out other Twos). Twos are loving people and they deeply show concern for others genuinely. They feel the need to warm their hearts and the hearts of others (making them feel worthwhile in the process).

Of the things that Twos value the most, they are love, closeness, friendship, family, and sharing. If healthy, they are helpful, generous, considerate, and loving. For this reason, people are drawn to Twos. The good feelings will work like a magnet.

Other people will feel the mutual appreciation they share with Twos. At the same time, these other people are able to see the positive qualities that they otherwise would never see themselves. The people who are greatly impacted by those are those who may have grown up without a stable family (that is not to say everyone who is impacted by Twos has that).

Why are they viewed as the 'good parents' that people wish they had? It comes down to what the Twos have. This includes seeing someone for who they are, understanding them with compassion, using infinite patience to help others, and willing to reach out at the right time.

However, Twos may see their inner development covered by the following negatives: self-deception, pride, and a penchant for being over-involved in the lives of others. At the same time, they may tend to manipulate others to get what they want (which is contradictory to who they are). However, their greatest fear is the feeling that despite all the work they put in with their love and compassion, worthlessness is what stands in the way.

They feel like they have worked so hard and have been paid so little. And for this reason, it triggers Twos to become angry or even resentful of other people. They can often accuse others of denying or even resenting them for being the kind of person they truly are.

Twos are those who will take care of others and treat them as if they were their own. They open up their hearts and their homes to others. A Two can certainly be the pillar of a community (especially in times of war and peace).

As we dive deeper into how Twos behave, we will share with you a story of how a military mother opened her home to the children of the servicemen who were fighting in World War II.

Type 3

Next, we take a look at the Threes. These are known as 'The Achiever'. Simply put, Threes have the true ability to do great things.

Because of this ability, they are often looked to by others for inspiration or even as mentors. When healthy, Threes feel a sense of accomplishment knowing that they can work on themselves while making significant contributions to the world. They also motivate others to do the same and hammer out their own personal achievements (i.e. - as a mentor).

Threes are usually the ones who are considered the most popular by their peers. In their schooling, they were elected 'class president' or even 'Homecoming King/Queen'. To an extent, they are seen as leaders rather than followers.

Threes are considered to be well-liked by their peers and are usually successful. This is due to their high levels of confidence and their ability to develop their talents. They are usually considered role models by younger peers.

Their success will further build on their own self-development. If done right, their investments on their own will yield favorable returns. They know what it takes to be the best.

Threes are known for making sure that their successes are known. They also want their success to be tied to their social circle, their families, and their personal culture. Measurements of success may depend on the family.

One family can base success on the house they live in, the car they drive, or other symbols that reflect on their status. Some will often use values and ideas as a measurement of success as opposed to possessions while others will consider academic achievements (i.e. - Harvard or Yale over Stanford or UCLA). Meanwhile, some may look at success depending on which line of work a person is in.

Specifically, this line of work is usually public centric such as politics, acting, or modeling. Family culture may also play a role in success. For example, a family that is deeply Christian may view a member of their family as successful if they were a member of the clergy.

One of the things that a Three strives to avoid is to become a 'nobody'. They will not accept anything less than a 'somebody'. Threes will do what they need in order to receive praise and positive feedback and attention.

They learn to recognize such activities from their parents or their older peers (like an older sibling or schoolmate). From there, they can focus their energies on excelling in the activities they are interested in. They also develop a personality that tends to attract other people or even impress others with little to no effort.

It is true that people need encouragement, attention, and affirmation of their values in order to grow. Threes are the prime example of why this is true. They don't believe in buying their way through success, but rather do so to gain power and independence.

The reason is due to the fear of feeling empty and worthless. Threes that are not given the attention and the feeling of accomplishment associated with success will make them feel like they are invaluable. In short, they will feel like they are a 'nobody'.

Threes may alienate themselves to the point where they may lose focus of what they truly want. They may also lose sight of their true feelings and interests. As a result, they can fall victim to lying to themselves, believing the lies of others, and the like. If unchecked, they will even lose their heart's desire or intentionally abandon it.

Threes are not much the 'feeling' type. They express themselves based on the actions they take. As for their feelings, they usually put them away in a box, so they don't get in the way of what they want to accomplish.

Threes believe that if emotion comes between them and the goals they strive to achieve, it will lead to such things like second-guessing themselves. They will ask themselves sometimes if they are doing something and getting nothing in return. And those questions are based on how they feel compared to how they really think.

Threes may seem to live up to other people's expectations, leaving them to ask another question: 'What do I really want?' Most of the time, Threes don't always have the answer to that question. Their focus on their success and the like may have clouded some of their personal wants in life.

Type 4

This is 'The Individualist'. Fours are the kind of people who maintain the identity as being different from the rest. For this reason, they feel like no one can understand them or love them enough.

Fours are the types of people that view themselves as talented or possess some kind of gift that not many people have. Another thing that makes them unique is a flaw or disadvantage. But of the personality types so far, Fours are the most aware of their strengths and weaknesses.

If there is one thing that Fours will never do, it's lie to themselves. Whatever they are feeling, they own it. They don't whitewash or deny it.

They make the effort to rationalize their feelings. And they are not afraid of viewing themselves for who they truly are. Simply put, they may not care what others think.

So, could Fours be naturally confident? That may be a possibility. You may even need to improve your confidence levels.

When healthy, Fours are usually willing to reveal things about themselves. It doesn't matter if it's a high point or a low point in their life. They do this without shame and show no fear in opening themselves up to others.

Fours are known to 'suffer quietly'. Because of this, they may still feel pain even though one can assume that they are impervious to it. While some may feel pain in a much greater magnitude, Fours will still be able to feel it, but it may seem 'numbed down'.

Fours will usually say that something will be missing. The real issue for them is figuring out what exactly that missing thing is. Some may say power, others will say their easy ability to socialize with others. And despite their possible natural ability to be confident, there is the possibility that self-confidence may be the missing piece.

Fours will recognize some parts of their self-image and be unsure about them. They feel like their identity may be lacking and unclear. They may feel like they are not being their true selves.

Fours will usually have an issue with their self-image and self-esteem. For this reason, they will cultivate a false self. In other words, they are building their imaginary selves and will try to live that out. However, reality will come crashing down and remind them of their real selves.

One of the recurring themes of Fours is trying out 'different identities'. They will try to focus on different styles of clothes to wear, change up their qualities or preferences, or even figure out what qualities are attractive to others. Underneath it all, they are still struggling to find out their true selves.

Given their individuality, defining it is the most difficult part. They want stability like the rest of the world. At the same time, they may be holding on to feelings of the past.

On top of that, Fours may also be holding on to feelings of people that have wronged them. Fours may be the kind of people that can easily hold a grudge against someone.

Type 5
Fives are known as 'The Investigator'. They are the types of people who are always searching for the 'why'. Why does something exist?

Why is something the way it is? These are the kind of people who want to know how the world works. It doesn't matter if it's the smallest element that makes up the Earth itself.

Fives are deep diggers. They are pursuing more knowledge compared to the rest of the world. At the same time, it could be used as a deep insecurity regarding their ability to function in the world (albeit successfully).

They will usually engage in activities that will help them build their confidence. One such activity is anything that boosts their knowledge. The more they know, the more confident they are.

To Fives, a day without learning something is a subpar day at best. Learning even the most trivial of things will be one of their most fulfilling activities. There will be a time when Fives will step back and go to a part of their mind where they believe they are highly capable.

They tend to retreat to their mental comfort zone and figure things out before they step back out again. Fives are thinkers. They will always contemplate and observe, even if it's the littlest of things.

It can be something like the weather outside, observing what's going on in their backyard (while taking notes) or even the sounds of a musical instrument. Of these Types, we believe that Fives can amplify these abilities by simply accessing their mindfulness.

When mindful, Type 5's will have an even sharper ability to observe and use their brains. It's like using a powerful weapon only for a greater good (as opposed to a weapon of mass destruction). Once they observe and make notes, they will report their findings and the like to people who may be interested in knowing about it.

When they come across new information, Fives are like children on Christmas morning. They will verify their observations and find out whether their predictions or hypotheses of things are right or wrong.

When it comes to familiar things, Fives have no interest. They are the ones looking for the things that are considered unusual, overlooked, absurd, and the things that are hidden in plain sight that no one else sees. They fine-tune these abilities as a way to be independent from others (in terms of how they think) while boosting their confidence in developing a unique skill that not everyone has.

Fives will have at least one area of expertise. It may be enough for them to know they can connect with the world in a certain way. They are not the 'do-it-all' types.

Their motto is 'I will find something and be really good at it.'. They possess the mindset of wanting to be the master of one. It doesn't matter if it's a certain martial art discipline, a genre of writing or music, or any one thing.

They are able to meet challenges thrown their way. What seems to be mere distractions to others, Fives can sense them well off and can find a way to dodge them. Not all Fives are considered academics or the like (and simply do not need a Ph.D. to be masters at what they want to be).

They use their intelligence to their advantage and are often resourceful. When they are at their happiest, they pursue their area of mastery with such unmatchable vigor. And eventually, that hard work will pay off multiple times over.

Socially, Fives are not dependent on validation. Fives may have ideas that they can share with others. If others readily agree with them, Fives will seem to think that what may seem like a unique idea may have been brought up before (and in many variations).

Some of history's most famous people are Fives. We will unveil these recognizable names in their own special section when we discuss more in-depth about Fives. But in the meantime, let's discuss some of the issues that Fives can face.

Fives may run into problems that may be self-defeating. That's because they are focusing on things that tend to distract them rather than the practical problems that lie before them. They may have anxieties that will cause them to willfully disconnect from them.

These anxieties may include but are not limited to their ability to develop relationships, inability to get a job, and so on. Fives want to do something where they feel like they can thrive and feel much more competent than outside of it. Even though they focus on one single thing, their basic insecurities and the like continue to become a glaring problem.

While they may feel like they know a lot about their discipline, they may fall short in some ways. For example, a Five who is a master at making art that will yield them commissions that earn them thousands of dollars may have a terrible time handling their money. They can spend that money as fast as they earn it.

They fear that they may never solve their money issue and could eventually find themselves drowning in debt. Furthermore, they could lose everything. All it takes is learning how to reign in that fear and alleviate it by taking a certain action.

Type 6

Sixes are known as 'The Loyalist'. These are the people who will stick to their beliefs, their friends, and their family. When 'the ship' sinks, they go down with it.

They value relationships greater than anyone else. But their loyalty goes beyond that. They are also loyal to certain systems, ideas, and beliefs. And there may be nothing anyone can do to influence them to make a change.

Even if those ideas and beliefs are questioned, Sixes hold the line. As for the status quo, some Sixes go along with it and others won't. The main reason for the latter is because those ideas and beliefs may go against said status quo.

They will fight for their beliefs tooth and nail if it ever comes down to it. They will defend their families, friends, communities, and others if they believe it is necessary. And they will do so with such tenacity that others will feel like they are playing tug of war with a wolf rather than a poodle.

Sixes are considered loyal to the point where they do not want to abandon others or leave them without support. Despite their basic fear of leaving one behind, they also contend with self-confidence issues. They believe that they may not have the abilities or resources to handle their own challenges.

They may rely on their allies, their beliefs, or any external support sources as keys to survival. If those structures do not exist, they are created. They also tend to worry a lot. This includes the worry of repercussions of a potential bad decision.

The important decisions they can make may not be the best. So, it comes down to the lesser of two evils. What could soften more of a blow?

They want to avoid being controlled by others. At the same time, they fear taking responsibility for something that might hurt them in the long run. They feel like they are 'in the line of fire'.

Sixes know well about their anxieties and are looking to build walls to keep them out. If they feel that they have enough support, that will give them enough confidence to move forward. Without that support, they will have increasing amounts of self-doubt and their anxiety over time will grow.

The anxieties that will build up won't have a label to them. At the same time, they feel like they can trust someone without hesitation. They will do everything they can to ensure that they continue to associate with the people who they trust most.

Most Sixes see themselves traveling back and forth between one influence and the next that impacts them greatly. This can stop when they get a hold on their inner guidance. They also tend to find themselves on either side of the coin.

They can provoke or defend someone, fear or courage, bully or be bullied, and so on. Sixes will try to create a sense of safety without paying close attention to their own insecurities (albeit their emotional ones). However, it is possible for them to acquire inner peace even if uncertainties still hang around.

Type 7

Sevens are known as 'The Enthusiasts'. And they live up to the title for sure. Their approach to life is with optimism, curiosity, and adventure.

They see the world as a big place where they can look around and indulge. These people are not afraid to be bold in terms of their pursuits in life. To describe them in one word, it's 'spontaneous'.

They can take road trips on the fly, make decisions without giving themselves enough time to think it over, and so on. Sevens do not consider themselves smart or studious. But that isn't to say that all Sevens are not intelligent.

There are Sevens who are intelligent for sure. They can also be verbal about it. Their two major abilities are being able to brainstorm and come up with ideas while synthesizing and processing information.

Brainstorming and coming up with ideas is like drugs to them. They can't get enough of it. And it may get to the point where they are addicted to coming up with ideas.

Once those ideas are formed, Sevens will test them vigorously to determine whether or not they will sustain or fail. Sevens are fast learners, quick, and mentally agile. And this will help them suck in plenty of information about every possible detail.

For this reason, they can learn new skills and be able to put them to good use quicker than anyone else. These skills usually involve mind-body coordination and dexterity. Skills such as typing and playing certain sports are prime examples.

Sevens are considered 'Renaissance people'. However, their voracious hunger for learning can also become an issue for them. Specifically, they are left with an arsenal of abilities and skills. They have more knowledge than they know what to do with it.

And therein lies the problem. They are stuck between multiple choices. Can they pursue one area of knowledge or will they attempt to do anything and everything they physically and mentally can?

Doing it all is certainly risky. And Sevens know this (hence their struggle). Sevens are usually not in touch with their inner guidance.

Because of this, Sevens will have a deep level of anxiety that is on part with the anxiety both suffered by Fives and Sixes. However, Sevens have two different coping mechanisms. The first one is keeping their minds busy constantly.

This is basically them retreating back to their natural comfort zone of sorts. They feel that as long as they keep their minds busy, their anxieties won't be as prevalent. They will get something done no matter how long it takes.

The second way that Sevens cope is by way of 'trial and error'. They will try new things and experiment. They don't care about the mistakes they make.

They will try something and make changes if necessary. Again, they don't care about the timing. They will try everything under the sun until they see a positive result.

When it comes to decisions, Sevens may want to strive for 'all of the above'. For example, a Seven would rather explore much of Europe rather than visit a single country. They would rather explore France, Germany, and Austria in addition to the United Kingdom.

Sevens want to tend to their pursuits as fast as possible (or whatever provides them with more freedom and happiness). For this reason, their decision-making will be regrettable. And that can lead them to feel anxiety and other emotions.

Furthermore, they will face the prospect of dealing with limited resources. And that can make things worse in both the health, relationship, and financial sense. But nevertheless, Sevens are highly optimistic and usually happy.

Type 8

Eights love taking on challenges (and rightfully so). For this reason, they are known as 'The Challenger'. They never met a challenge that they would turn down.

Personality-wise, Type 8s are typically charismatic people. And they are willing to focus on various endeavors that will allow them to invest their own time in. Type 8s are people who want to build things.

Whether it's a company, planning something on a major scale or even leading a household, Eights believe they are capable of such challenges. That's because they possess an immense amount of willpower and feel most alive whenever they take on challenges.

Eights have a mission to 'leave their mark' on the world before they die. Meanwhile, they want to leave it better than when they found it. They know that such things will take a lot of characteristics including strength, persistence, and endurance among others.

Eights are the kind of people that do not want to be controlled. And they will make sure that nobody will have power over them. They will sniff out and eradicate the threats if and when necessary.

Simply put, there is no Eight in the world you will ever find that is a pushover. You have a better chance of winning the lottery than finding an Eight who is willing to be a doormat for someone. As far as power is concerned, Eights are more apt to retain as much of it as possible.

Eights are leaders. They are the generals, the CEOs, the World Leaders, the matriarch or patriarch of the family, and more. The common denominator is being 'in charge'.

Eights are considered to be individualists in their own unique way. They are independent and will not submit to anyone's will. They will not submit to what is considered to be social convention.

They do not care if there is shame or consequences that stem as a result of their actions. They know what people think of them and it will not deter them at all. If anything, they will continue doing what they do with a high level of determination.

That determination may even intimidate others. Eights may fear physical confrontation with someone. Specifically, that someone will feel threatened by the Eight and their fears and insecurities have reached critical mass.

However, Eights are tough enough to withstand such physical punishment. Even though they may fear emotional pain, they will use physical strength to their advantage as a way to protect themselves and others.

When Eights work hard, they may lose emotional contact with those important to them. This includes close friends and even members of their family. Eights may not seem to know why there is tension between themselves and those important to them until they figure it out.

Once they do, Eights will feel like they have been misunderstood. As a result, they may disconnect themselves from their inner circle, even people as a whole. They also have a fear that they may feel harmed or rejected in some way.

When healthy, Eights are the most resourceful people fueled by an attitude that allows them to rise above any challenge. Their drive is second to none.

Type 9

Lastly, we'll be taking a look at the Ninth and final Enneagram type. Nines are 'The Peacemaker'. These are the people who are considered to be spiritual seekers.

Their mission is to maintain inner peace while making sure that the world itself achieves its own peace and harmony. Nines are perhaps the most grounded of the Enneagram. And they tend to be personally magnetic people and possess elemental power.

Meanwhile, they are known for being out of sorts in terms of their instinctual energies. Because of this, Nines will rely on their emotional fantasies (which also risks them for being mistakenly identified as Fives or Sevens by those who know the Enneagram). Nines are located at the crown of the Enneagram and possess such strengths of the other Types.

They possess at least one characteristic from Eights, Sevens, Sixes, and beyond. Nines are individuals who must assert themselves. Otherwise, they may operate in the background and try to chase their 'daydreams'.

Nines are the kind of people that look at the bright side of life. And that allows their peace of mind to be undisturbed. They are accepting of the fact that there is a light side and a dark side to things.

Arrows and Wings

Already, we have touched on the Arrows and Wings briefly. As you may recall, the wings are based on the numbers adjacent to your personality type.

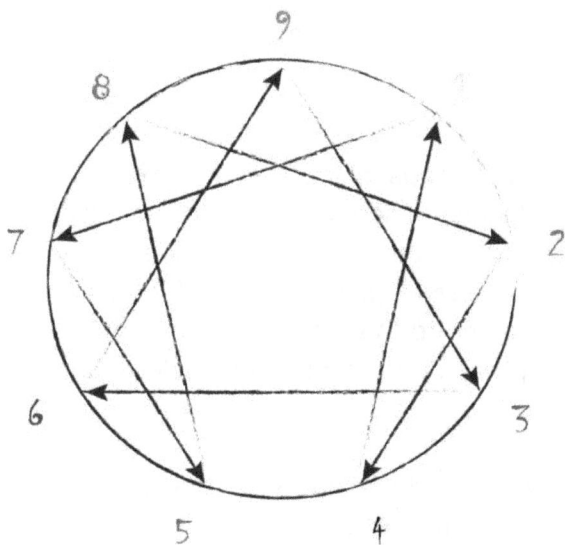

For example, a Type 9 will have Types 1 and 8 as its wings. The wings are designed to complement your type and add important elements. Sometimes, those elements will be contradictory to your personality type as a whole.

There is a theory stating that your personality type is supported by one wing or the other. This has triggered debate as to whether or not each personality type is allowed to have one or two wings. The reason being is because some personality types have a 'dominant wing' that compliments their true personality while the other contradicts it.

Regardless of type, some will have both wings while others will have a dominant wing. This varies from person to person. Meanwhile, some will report that over the course of time, their 'second wing' will develop based on their use of the Enneagram.

Arrows

There are two kinds of arrows that exist: the arrows of growth and stress. There are specific numerical sequences based on each of these arrows and the direction they are going in. To better explain this, see the diagram above. (If you are listening to this book in audio format - be sure to download your PDF version of the book so you can see the diagram).

Let's show you which arrows are which based on the directions they are going in:

The Arrows of Growth

Do you see the arrow from 1 to 7? How about 2 to 4? These are the arrows of growth.

The numerical sequence is as follows: 1-7-5-8-2-4-1 and 9-3-6-9. Let's say that your Enneagram type is Type 2. Therefore, your direction of growth is 4.

If you are considered a healthy 1, you will behave in accordance to how a Type 4 will act. Therefore, the arrows will be based on positive actions that will be responsible for radical changes in your life.

The Arrows of Stress

These arrows will represent how you will handle things under pressure. Circling back to the example of a Type 2, your direction of stress is a Type 8. This means that when you are stressed or under pressure, your behavior will be based on the way an unhealthy 8 would act.

These arrows represent negative actions. If unrecognized, you will suffer what may be unfavorable effects that will not only hinder your growth but may also affect the morale and well-being of those around you.

Vices, Virtues, and the Enneagram

Based on the nine types of the Enneagram, they can be matched with the following vices and virtues. These vices are mostly based on the 'deadly sins' as outlined in the Bible. Before we unveil which type is tied to each, let's take a look at the following vices and virtues:

Vices

- Lust
- Anger
- Envy
- Gluttony
- Sloth
- Greed
- Pride

Virtue

- Chastity
- Patience
- Kindness
- Temperance
- Diligence
- Charity
- Humility

As you can notice, vices and virtues are the opposite of each other. So, which of the root sins are matched with each Enneagram type? What about the virtues associated with it?

Let's have a look:

Type 1: Anger/Patience

Type 2: Pride/Humility

Type 3: Deceit/Truth

Type 4: Envy/Kindness

Type 5: Avarice/Non-attachment

Type 6: Fear/Courage

Type 7: Gluttony/Sobriety

Type 8: Lust/Innocence (Chastity)

Type 9: Sloth/Action (Diligence)

Final Thoughts

At this point, you are now aware of all nine of the Enneagram types. You also have a brief overview of each one based on specific characteristics, fears, anxieties, and the like. You may have a good idea of which type you are drawn to the most.

We must do our best to find our true selves while shedding our false selves at the same time. That is the point of the Enneagram. Most of us are buried underneath the falseness of what we try to put up.

Another thing to understand is how the wings and arrows work. Your wings and growth arrows will help you immensely. Meanwhile, your stress arrows will give you a glimpse of how you handle stress and pressure.

And now, we will get to the part many of you have waited for. Next, you will be taking the Essential Enneagram Test. The next pages will be very important.

And we ask you to not skip through it. You are to take the test as instructed and you will soon find out your Enneagram personality type.

Chapter 11: Essential Enneagram Test Instructions

The following is a test that will help you identify your Enneagram type. Before going any further, we will be going over instructions that will allow you to take the test correctly. We place a high premium on accuracy, so this test will need to be answered truthfully.

Now, the instructions:

This test will contain nine different paragraphs. Each paragraph will describe each of the nine different personality types of the Enneagram. These are simple, easy-to-read paragraphs that will provide you with an overview of each type. These paragraphs should not be confused for any descriptions of anyone's personality.

Read the descriptions and choose three paragraphs that are considered the best fit based on yourself. Be sure to select them honestly.

After choosing your three paragraphs, you will need to rank them from one to three. Mark a one next to the paragraph that best relates to you, followed by a two to a paragraph that is next most like yourself, and a three next to a paragraph that is third most.

Remember, there are nine paragraphs that may describe you to an extent. The key here is to select

three paragraphs that are like you the most. Be sure to consider every paragraph as a whole instead of each sentence.

Choosing a paragraph may not be easy to do. For this reason, you can consider which description or paragraph someone may choose for you (specifically someone close to you like a spouse or family member). Or ask yourself which pattern would fit you best in your younger years (assuming you are older than your teens or twenties).

The Paragraphs

Note: Each paragraph will be labeled 'Paragraph A through I'. Go through each one thoroughly. Do not choose a paragraph until reading through them all. If you read one that appears to resonate with you the most, make a note (Ex: 'Check back Paragraph A'). After reading through all paragraphs, go back to the ones that stand out the most. If you have chosen three, rank them from 1 to 3 as instructed earlier.

Paragraph A

I approach things in a way where it's 'all-or-nothing'. This includes the issues that matter to me a lot. I hold a lot of value in being strong, dependable, and honest. What you see in front of you is what you will get from me. I will not trust other people until they prove themselves otherwise. I appreciate it when people are being direct with me. At the same time, I know right away as to whether not someone is lying, being deviant, or trying to be manipulative. I find it difficult to tolerate weakness in other people unless I have a better understanding as to why they have it or if they are trying to do something about it. I also find it difficult following directions or orders that are from an authority figure that I do not respect or agree with. I tend to take charge of myself and I'm better for it. I am not afraid to express my feelings when I'm angry. I am always willing to defend and stand up for my friends and family, even if they are facing some kind of unjust treatment. It is to my understanding that I may not win every battle I find myself in, but I am aware that I have been in similar situations.

Paragraph B

When it comes to correctness, my internal standards are high. I make sure that I live up to those standards every day. I don't find it difficult to see what is wrong with things and I find a way to see how they can be improved. In the eyes of others, they view me as someone who demands perfection and is overly critical. What they don't realize is that I find it difficult to ignore or accept things that are not done correctly. I take pride in being responsible for doing something and make sure that it's done right. Sometimes, I harbor feelings of resentment. This stems from people not trying to do things correctly or when they act irresponsibly or unfairly. I would much rather conceal that feeling as opposed to expressing it openly. My personal philosophy is work over pleasure. I live by that to the point where I subdue any desires to seek pleasure in order to get something done.

Paragraph C

I am someone who is aware of the different points of view that exist. Especially when it comes to certain topics. I am someone who may be indecisive on such a point of view because of my ability to see the advantages and disadvantages of every side of the argument. However, I do my best to help others resolve a problem despite their differences. Furthermore, I become more familiar with someone's positions, priorities, and agendas and focus more on those than my own. So, it is not uncommon for me to get distracted or go off course in terms of my own tasks and priorities. For this reason, my attention is usually invested in tasks that are trivial or unimportant. I struggle to find out what is actually important. I go along with what other people want and avoid conflict in the process. Most people see me as someone who is pleasing, agreeable, and easygoing. However, it takes a lot for me to get angry (almost to the point where I directly express it). I want to live my life with a sense of comfort, harmony, and acceptance.

Paragraph D

When it comes to the feelings of others, I am sensitive to them. Even if I don't know someone, I can see and probably know what they need. To be aware of someone's needs, their pains, and their sadness, it becomes a source of frustration for me. Because I feel like I am unable to do as much as I can as I intend to. Giving of myself is like second nature. There are times where I wish I could say 'no'. But I don't because I focus more about caring for others, even to the point where I don't care for myself. When people think that I am trying to manipulate them or accuse me of ulterior motives, this hurts me greatly. My mission is to understand them and help them. I want to be viewed by others as someone who is a good person or warmhearted, even if many people do not appreciate or take that into account. At times, I can become very emotional or demanding. I take pride in maintaining good relationships and I will do whatever it takes to make them happen.

Paragraph E

The one thing that motivates me greatly is being the best at what I can do. In the past, I have received plenty of recognition for my achievements. I am known for getting much done and I manage to succeed in whatever I set my mind to. I believe that my value is based on what I have accomplished and the recognition that I get from it. Therefore, I strongly identify with what I do. If there are things to do, I will find a time to get it done if there is time available. For this reason, I often find myself setting aside any opportunities for feelings and self-reflection. I find myself always doing something, because sitting around and doing nothing is pointless. When people are not using my time wisely, I lose patience. If someone is completing a project at a slower rate of speed, I am tempted to take over and get it done at a much faster rate. I want to appear on top of the situation, whatever it may be. I see myself as a team player even though I have a personal drive to compete with others.

Paragraph F

To best describe myself, I am quiet and analytical. I am someone who needs time to myself compared to others. I tend to be observant and interest myself in seeing what's going on. The last thing I want to do is be involved. I don't appreciate it when people demand a lot from me or expect me to know something or even express my feelings. I do get in touch with my feelings whenever I am by myself, but not when I am in the presence of others. When it comes to past experiences, it's a lot better reliving them than going through the actual thing. When I'm alone, boredom is seldom existent because my mental life is active. I protect my time and energy in an effort to live a life that is simple, self-sufficient, and free of any complications.

Paragraph G

My imagination is vivid, even when it comes to what could be a threat to my safety and security. I find it easy to spot potentially dangerous or harmful threats. I may fear it as if it were already happening. Every time, it comes down to two choices: either I avoid danger completely or take it head-on. On the other hand, my imagination will lead to ingenuity and develop a sense of humor that may be viewed as slightly offbeat. When it comes to life itself, I want it to be certain. I harbor doubt for people and the world around me. I can be able to see the shortcomings of someone if they put them forward. Because of this, people will view me as astute. I am often suspicious of authority and do not wish myself to be seen as such. I can see the wrong in generally held views and I often side myself with the underdogs. After I've committed myself to something, I stay loyal to it for as long as possible.

Paragraph H

I am optimistic. I am also someone who enjoys doing things that are new and interesting. My mind is very active and has a tendency to move back and forth between one idea and another. I try my best to get a picture of how these ideas all fit together like a puzzle. When I am able to, I am very happy. I like to work on things that I am interested in and place a lot of energy and devotion into them. When it comes to tasks that are tedious or repetitive, I find it difficult to stick to them. I want to be at the beginning stages of a project or during the planning phase. The latter gives me the opportunity to consider various options. After exhausting such interests, I find it difficult to stay with it. Because I have a growing desire to move onto something else that has actually captured my interest. If I am feeling down, I want to shift my attention to something that I consider pleasant. I have a belief that people are entitled to live a life of enjoyment.

Paragraph I

I am someone who is sensitive and harbors intense feelings. Most of the time, I feel misunderstood and lonely because I am different from everyone else. The way I behave may be considered dramatic in the eyes of others. Because of my oversensitivity and over-amplification of feelings, people have criticized me for it. I often find myself having trouble appreciating relationships since I have a tendency to want what I know I cannot have while having disdain for what I currently have at the moment. My search for emotional connection has been with me for as long as I have been alive. I am void of emotional connection, which has been the source of feeling melancholy and depressed. I sometimes ask myself why other people have more than what I have, including happier lives and better relationships. I live in a rich world where emotions and meaning reign supreme.

Choosing Your Selections

Now, it's time to choose which paragraphs are your first, second, and third choice. Circle the lettered title of the paragraphs that best fit you:

First Choice: A B C D E F G H I

Second Choice: A B C D E F G H I

Third Choice: A B C D E F G H I

After choosing your paragraphs, we will move on to reveal which paragraph is matched with the corresponding Enneagram types. These will be noted in a separate chapter to ensure that you didn't skip ahead or 'cheat' on the test.

Feel free to review each paragraph as many times as possible before choosing the best three that stand out. Once you have them, continue to the 'Linking to Types' Chapter.

Chapter 12: Linking Test Results to Types

Note: DO NOT proceed beyond this point if you have not taken the Enneagram test in the previous chapter.

If you have completed the Enneagram test, we will be linking each paragraph to the corresponding personality types. By now you should already have your top three paragraphs chosen. Your Enneagram type will be based on your first paragraph choice.

Once you find out about your Enneagram type, you will probably be interested in learning more about yourself. You might even learn something new. You may have chosen your paragraphs based on what you already know about yourself as well.

Let's get right to it and review each paragraph, followed by the personality types that are linked to it:

Paragraph A

"I approach things in a way where it's 'all-or-nothing'. This includes the issues that matter to me a lot. I hold a lot of value in being strong, dependable, and honest. What you see in front of you is what you will get from me. I will not trust other people until they prove themselves otherwise. I appreciate it when people are being direct with me. At the same time, I know right away as to whether not someone is

lying, being deviant, or trying to be manipulative. I find it difficult to tolerate weakness in other people unless I have a better understanding as to why they have it or if they are trying to do something about it. I also find it difficult following directions or orders that are from an authority figure that I do not respect or agree with. I tend to take charge myself and I'm better for it. I am not afraid to express my feelings when I'm angry. I am always willing to defend and stand up for my friends and family, even if they are facing some kind of unjust treatment. It is to my understanding that I may not win every battle I find myself in, but I am aware that I have been in similar situations."

Linked Enneagram Type: Eight (8)

Eights are born leaders. And there is no doubt that they will hold a lot of value in terms of strength, honesty, and reliability. At the outset, an Eight will trust nobody until that person has worked hard enough to earn it. Eights are unafraid to show their feelings and share their thoughts about things. They exemplify the qualities of a true leader. They would rather be the authority than follow it.

Paragraph B

"When it comes to correctness, my internal standards are high. I make sure that I live up to those standards every day. I don't find it difficult to see what is wrong with things and I find a way to see how they can be improved. In the eyes of others, they view me as someone who demands perfection and is overly critical. What they don't realize is that I find it difficult to ignore or accept things that are not done correctly. I take pride in being responsible for doing

something and make sure that it's done right. Sometimes, I harbor feelings of resentment. This stems from people not trying to do things correctly or when they act irresponsibly or unfairly. I would much rather conceal that feeling as opposed to expressing it openly. My personal philosophy is work over pleasure. I live by that to the point where I subdue any desires to seek pleasure in order to get something done."

Linked Enneagram Type: One (1)

Just by reading this paragraph alone, it's the words that can be said by someone who is a perfectionist. So, linking this paragraph to Type One was obviously a no-brainer. Ones are those with superhuman vision that allows them to see the slightest of imperfections. Once they see it, they can find ways to fix them. When Ones want something done, it needs to be done right. They will never settle for anything less than the best. 'Good enough' is not 'good enough' for them. What some see as 'passable' is an atrocity in the eyes of a One.

Paragraph C

"I am someone who is aware of the different points of view that exist. Especially when it comes to certain topics. I am someone who may be indecisive on such a point of view because of my ability to see the advantages and disadvantages of every side of the argument. However, I do my best to help others resolve a problem despite their differences. Furthermore, I become more familiar with someone's positions, priorities, and agendas and focus more on those than my own. So, it is not uncommon for me

to get distracted or go off course in terms of my own tasks and priorities. For this reason, my attention is usually invested in tasks that are trivial or unimportant. I struggle to find out what is actually important. I go along with what other people want and avoid conflict in the process. Most people see me as someone who is pleasing, agreeable, and easygoing. However, it takes a lot for me to get angry (almost to the point where I directly express it). I want to live my life with a sense of comfort, harmony, and acceptance."

Linked Enneagram Type: Nine (9)

As Nines are the peacemakers, they see things from different angles. Their mission is clear: to get disagreeing sides to come to a common conclusion. No matter how difficult it may be, Nines will spend as much time as they can to conjure up a solution that will satisfy all parties, not one. Nines may wield considerable power when it comes to negotiation. Nines may even have the ability to mediate a situation with a level head. They want people to work together despite disagreements. They serve as the perfect wing to an Eight (especially in the business world where negotiations are always standard procedure).

Paragraph D

"When it comes to the feelings of others, I am sensitive to them. Even if I don't know someone, I can see and probably know what they need. To be aware of someone's needs, their pains, and their sadness, it becomes a source of frustration for me. Because I feel like I am unable to do as much as I can as I intend to. Giving of myself is like second nature. There are times where I wish I could say 'no'. But I

don't because I focus more about caring for others, even to the point where I don't care for myself. When people think that I am trying to manipulate them or accuse me of ulterior motives, this hurts me greatly. My mission is to understand them and help them. I want to be viewed by others as someone who is a good person or warmhearted, even if many people do not appreciate or take that into account. At times, I can become very emotional or demanding. I take pride in maintaining good relationships and I will do whatever it takes to make them happen."

Linked Enneagram Type: Two (2)

This is a paragraph where it was clear which Enneagram type this belongs to. Twos are the helpers. And they will make it their mission to put others before themselves. Granted, there will be people who will accuse Twos of having ulterior motives. Mainly because those people may have trusted someone only to be 'burned' in the end. Circling back to the paragraph linked to the Eights, they have a hard time trusting someone at first until they are proven otherwise. Thus, Twos may take this distrust personally. And as you can probably notice, the Stress arrow is pointed from Two to Eight.

Twos may alleviate the stress of Eights using their power to help them. Therefore, in order to gain the trust of Eights, the Twos will need to stay true to their intentions and their abilities. While Eights can set up a deal, Twos will stop at nothing to help them close it.

Paragraph E

The one thing that motivates me greatly is being the best at what I can do. In the past, I have received plenty of recognition for my achievements. I am known for getting much done and I manage to succeed in whatever I set my mind to. I believe that my value is based on what I have accomplished and the recognition that I get from it. Therefore, I strongly identify with what I do. If there are things to do, I will find a time to get it done if there is time available. For this reason, I often find myself setting aside any opportunities for feelings and self-reflection. I find myself always doing something, because sitting around and doing nothing is pointless. When people are not using my time wisely, I lose patience. If someone is completing a project at a slower rate of speed, I am tempted to take over and get it done at a much faster rate. I want to appear on top of the situation, whatever it may be. I see myself as a team player even though I have a personal drive to compete with others.

Linked Enneagram Type: Three (3)

This paragraph screams Three right from the beginning. Achieving something is an addiction to them. After they complete one thing, they move onto another. It's what makes them happy. It's part of their identity. Threes are those who have achieved great things even at a young age.

Into their adult years, they want to keep the momentum going. Otherwise, they may slip through the cracks and end up being 'cogs in the machine'. As a Three, you may be measuring success depending on several factors. These factors are based on beliefs, culture, and the like. They know what they want, and they will find a way to get it (even if they have to work even harder). When it comes to compromise, it may be difficult for them to come around (as the stress line from Three goes to Nine). Eventually, they will be willing to cooperate and hammer out a solution since they are keen on accomplishing something rather than nothing.

Paragraph F

"To best describe myself, I am quiet and analytical. I am someone who needs time to myself compared to others. I tend to be observant and interest myself in seeing what's going on. The last thing I want to do is be involved. I don't appreciate it when people demand a lot from me or expect me to know something or even express my feelings. I do get in touch with my feelings whenever I am by myself, but not when I am in the presence of others. When it comes to past experiences, it's a lot better reliving them than going through the actual thing. When I'm alone, boredom is seldom existent because my mental life is active. I protect my time and energy in an effort to live a life that is simple, self-sufficient, and free of any complications."

Linked Enneagram Type: Five (5)

When 'The Investigator' is at work, they do it quietly. Because they need to focus. Plus, they do it better when solo. They have observation skills that are unrivaled. Their lack of involvement further enhances their role as the Investigator because the slightest hint of it may cause them to develop some kind of bias. They are independent (as are you) to an extent when it comes to your findings. Your feelings are often expressed when no one is around.

However, you are always hard at work figuring out things like why something exists or how something in particular functions. You're never bored with things because you always have something to do.

Paragraph G

"My imagination is vivid, even when it comes to what could be a threat to my safety and security. I find it easy to spot potentially dangerous or harmful threats. I may fear it as if it were already happening. Every time, it comes down to two choices: either I avoid danger completely or take it head-on. On the other hand, my imagination will lead to ingenuity and develop a sense of humor that may be viewed as slightly offbeat. When it comes to life itself, I want it to be certain. I harbor doubt for people and the world around me. I can be able to see the shortcomings of someone if they put them forward. Because of this, people will view me as astute. I am often suspicious of authority and do not wish myself to be seen as such. I can see the wrong in generally held views and I often side myself with the underdogs. After I've committed myself to something, I stay loyal to it for as long as possible."

Linked Enneagram Type: Six (6)

At first, you would think that this paragraph was fitting for another Enneagram type. Even though we encouraged reading the full paragraph rather than picking it apart by each sentence, the loyalty part is what seals it. Sixes are loyal to those who are important to them. And their ability to spot the threats will prepare them for their strong defense.

They will try to avoid danger as possible. But if there comes time to take it head-on, they will try and be prepared.

Those who consider themselves loyal will refuse the opportunity to become authority. But if the conditions are right, they will stick with an authority figure that they respect immensely.

Paragraph H

"I am optimistic. I am also someone who enjoys doing things that are new and interesting. My mind is very active and has a tendency to move back and forth between one idea and another. I try my best to get a picture of how these ideas all fit together like a puzzle. When I am able to, I am very happy. I like to work on things that I am interested in and place a lot of energy and devotion into them. When it comes to tasks that are tedious or repetitive, I find it difficult to stick to them. I want to be at the beginning stages of a project or during the planning phase. The latter gives me the opportunity to consider various options. After exhausting such interests, I find it difficult to stay with it. Because I have a growing desire to move onto something else that has actually captured my interest. If I am feeling down, I want to shift my attention to something that I consider pleasant. I have a belief that people are entitled to live a life of enjoyment."

Linked Enneagram Type: Seven (7)

By reading the paragraph alone, you can tell that it's filled with such enthusiastic energy. Fittingly enough, this paragraph is linked to Type Seven (and rightfully so). It's no surprise that Sevens will move on to other interests once they get tired of another. It will feel like you are doing the same thing over and over again. And repetition is not as exciting after an amount of time passes. Enthusiasts want to be in the thick of it all. Especially when it comes to planning everything right down to the letter. When an idea pops up in their head, they will incorporate it into the plan. But not before they test it out first.

Paragraph I

"I am someone who is sensitive and harbors intense feelings. Most of the time, I feel misunderstood and lonely because I am different from everyone else. The way I behave may be considered dramatic in the eyes of others. Because of my oversensitivity and over-amplification of feelings, people have criticized me for it. I often find myself having trouble appreciating relationships since I have a tendency to want what I know I cannot have while having disdain for what I currently have at the moment. My search for emotional connection has been with me for as long as I have been alive. I am void of emotional connection, which has been the source of feeling melancholy and depressed. I sometimes ask myself why other people have more than what I have, including happier lives and better relationships. I live in a rich world where emotions and meaning reign supreme. "

Linked Enneagram Type: Four (4)

Fours tend to be individual and unique in their own way. Hence the reason why they may have difficulty with appreciating relationships. That's because they are usually different from everyone else. For this reason, these inabilities to connect with others will only make a negative impact on them (especially emotionally). They want someone that is equal to them. Their search for happiness often comes up short. They have no problem expressing their feelings in the best way possible. And it comes as no surprise that Fours will use their creativity as a chief way in doing so.

Where to Go from Here

Now that we have connected the paragraphs from the test to each Enneagram type, we will move forward with a detailed explanation of each type determination and how to understand them. It is important that we as people must better understand ourselves by getting to know more about our Enneagram type as humanly possible.

We will also talk about how you should proceed with your newfound Enneagram type without getting into too much detail (since we will be covering them much later on in the book). Now that you know your type, you're about to delve into parts of the book where you will deeply understand yourself.

How does your Enneagram type behave in a professional setting? What about relationships? How will you use it to improve in areas of your life?

We will discuss this in due time. At this point, we have cleared a major hurdle. Now that you know your type, it's time to make a commitment to yourself right now.

It's time to make a promise that you will use the power of the Enneagram for a greater good rather than a weapon of mass destruction. Performing the latter will only make things worse. We are here to help build people up for the better.

If you are willing to do this, proceed to the next chapter.

Chapter 13: Understanding the Type Determinations

Now that you have a grasp on what your Enneagram type is, it comes down to understanding the type itself and why the paragraphs from the test link up with them. The paragraphs were written as clear and easy to understand as possible. At the same time, they were written in a way for people to think about themselves and determine whether or not the paragraphs fit them or not.

Assuming you've read them all entirely, you would have arrived at one of two conclusions: 'This sounds a lot like me' or 'this isn't me at all'. Some of the paragraphs were a clear interpretation of which Enneagram type it was linked to. And you might have already known about your type but needed to take the test to confirm.

When it comes to type determinations, we talk about the probability of how your first paragraph choice is more apt to be your personality type. The other two, your second and third paragraphs, are considered alternatives for your first choice. We will also be talking about your arrows, wings, and security types.

You will learn more about your Enneagram type later on based on certain practices you need to follow, their key features, and how you can use them in various areas of your life such as your professional life and your relationships with others.

Since we will be covering all nine types, you can start by skipping to the Enneagram type based on the first paragraph you chose on the test. If you like, you can then find the Enneagram type that is based on your second and third paragraph choices. Let's begin with the Type Ones:

Type One

The Reformer

Center: Gut

Basic Fears: Viewed as evil or corrupt

Basic Desire: Seek balance and integrity to preserve an image of good

Wings: 9-2

Growth Arrow: 7

Stress Arrow: 1

Type Ones Explained

Type Ones are the kinds of people who consider themselves to be ethical. Knowing what tasks are considered right or wrong are their strong suits. These are the people who usually teach other people. Other ones are usually advocates and crusaders.

Regardless, they share a common goal: to change something for the better. While that is their mission from the start, they have a fear of making mistakes. Hence that is why they are considered perfectionists.

For this reason, they are meticulous in their planning. And they will make sure that nothing is overlooked. They are orderly and well-organized. And they uphold high standards.

Not surprisingly, perfectionists may have an issue in regard to their patience. If something is slightly out of the ordinary, it can anger them. They also hold some kind of resentment for those who feel that good enough is indeed good enough.

In terms of how things are accomplished, they hold quality in the highest regard. They want to finish in first place rather than say fourth place in the race. They want to strive for the A grades and will settle for no less (i.e. - a B+).

Because of their affinity for being perfect, people may view them as evil. Especially when a One is not satisfied with anything that may be considered a less than 'A+' effort. For Ones, this throws their intent to be viewed as good right out the window.

The wings of a One are the Nine and the Two. Let's take a look at them:

Type One/Wing Two (1w2)

The Two wing is considered to be the advocate for the One. Twos have a willingness to help others.

They will put in a good word and fight for the One's intentions and accomplishments. The Ones may have a hard time proving themselves that they are not as bad as people think because of their strive for perfection. So, it would be the responsibility of the Twos to be a third-party observer.

In other words, Twos will provide glowing testimonies of a One and explain why they want things done a certain way. Twos will go out of their way to make sure that nobody writes off Ones as arrogant, cruel, or just plain mean. They believe that perfection is a lot more durable compared to something that is considered 'decent' in performance.

At the same time, Type Ones/Wing Twos are striving for change. Ones will oversee the entire mission and make sure it goes according to plan. Meanwhile, the Twos will carry out its message and inspire others to join them in their cause for the better.

Type One/Wing Nine (1w9)

Meanwhile, we take a look at the Nine-wing. Nines are considered idealists. More specifically, they may be more optimistic in nature. They know that change will soon come.

Type One/Wing Nines are those who strive for change using methods of teaching. They are willing to listen to other viewpoints in the process. They explain why such change is good, even if there is some kind of pushback from it.

Seeking awareness and understanding of the world around them is what a 1w9 does. At the same time, they tend to make choices that are more rational and objective. They believe in something that is considered right and they tirelessly pursue it.

Growth Arrow: 7

One of the ways Ones can grow into something better is by adopting the higher qualities and behaviors that Sevens have. Sevens are enthusiastic. When a One looks to make changes in the world, they should do it with such excitement and enthusiasm that they will do whatever it takes to get the job done.

They are spontaneous when the opportunity presents itself. More often than not, they are reactive to the surprises life throws their way. Their ever-present inner critic will usually sit back and relax for a bit, thus allowing Ones to enjoy the moment.

Furthermore, they are willing to consider various ideas and opinions. This is valuable considering the fact that Ones want every plan they conceive to come together perfectly. It's a matter of which opinion or idea that fits better.

Ones will adopt a Seven's willingness to learn something new. They know that if they learn about something that pertains to their goals, they know that they are much closer to that 'someday' when the mission will be accomplished. Furthermore, there is newfound joy among them.

Stress Arrow: 4

With the stress arrow pointing to Four, Ones will typically adopt the lower qualities of Fours. For example, Ones may feel sadness at times. Typically, because they are imprisoned by the burden that is their perfection.

As a coping mechanism, they will often imagine themselves in fantasies and daydreams. They find themselves in a place where everything is perfect. But perfection itself doesn't really exist.

In order to see it better, Ones will have a tendency to withdraw themselves from others. And this may be a good thing. If surrounded by others, they may show envy and resentment for other people.

They will express their feelings in the most dramatic sense. And it may be hard to deal with for some people. Meanwhile, Ones may assume that nobody will understand them.

Type Two

The Helper

Center: Heart

Basic Fears: Being unloved or unwanted

Basic Desire: To feel loved

Wings: 1-3

134

Growth Arrow: 4

Stress Arrow: 8

Type Two Explained

Twos are motivated by love. There may be a reason why that is. It may have been that you could have not received it at a young age for one reason or another.

You could also have a childhood filled with loving family members and learn how to spread it yourself. You go out of your way to help others even if it means dropping everything that you're focused on. They are natural people-pleasers and would want nothing more than to be closer to others.

Twos are high in empathy, so they do their best to feel what others are feeling. Selfishness is the last thing they ever want to deal with. Their love for others is unconditional.

Their generosity is ongoing, whether people notice it or not. Their good-natured behavior is what draws other people to them. However, because of this willingness to help others and be generous, it may attract the wrong people.

Besides the point, Twos are the kind of people who are looked at as the parent someone never had. In fact, if Fours are looking for someone willing to give them an emotional connection, Twos may be the perfect match for them. So, a Four could feel loved by someone who is known for giving it freely like a Two.

Aside from their loving nature, there is a dark side to those who are Twos. Typically, they may act in a way that is considered to be intrusive or possessive. As if they have the right to know how people are doing.

Certainly, they are willing to help others. But there may be times where they could unknowingly cross boundaries and may be prying for a little more than they should. As such, Twos may need to know how to honor such boundaries in order to better themselves as people.

Type Two/Wing One (2w1)

Those who are considered 2w1 are those who take on the role of caretaker. This is where their ability to serve others comes into play. Their reward for doing so obviously is love and appreciation from others.

These are people who live to serve while creating betterment within the world around them. They see the needs and feelings of others and will do their best to make them feel good. They are mostly sacrificing their own needs and self-interests, which may come back to haunt them later on in life.

Even though they feel like they are doing good, there are those who may be critical of it. For example, critics of a 2w1 may often accuse Twos of being approval-seeking or having ulterior motives. As such, persons like Eights are susceptible to being critical of Twos.

The main reason stems from the Eights struggle with trusting others. We cannot blame Eights for not trusting anyone UNTIL there is a reason to do so. But when there is distrust being voiced towards Twos, the latter feels like they are not doing enough to gain such trust.

Furthermore, 2w1 will strive for perfection in the same way Ones do. The characteristic that a 2 draws from the One wing is knowing what's best (or at least thinking that). In times of stress, their ability to help others is an imposition on people.

It can get to the point where a Two will try and tell others what to do and how to do it correctly. They may seem like they are right. But the reality is that Twos are trying to control the lives of others and not their own.

For this reason, Twos may rub others the wrong way. And that could even stoke the fears of being unwanted or unloved. Again, Twos need to know the boundaries in order to avoid such fears from becoming reality.

As for other unhealthy traits, Twos may subject themselves to neglecting their health. That is why Twos need to step back and spend time working on themselves both physically and mentally. It is fine to take care of others, but you need to know where to draw the line.

Type Two/Wing Three (2w3)

This personality type is known as the host/hostess. Compared to 2w1s, these Twos are more social and even excellent with humor. Their feelings and the way they act on them will be like second nature. They acquire security by way of starting and nurturing as many relationships as possible.

Since they tend to be more social, they have no trouble being people pleasers. And they will do it a lot easier compared to their One wings. Naturally, they are charismatic but can be chatty.

Simply put, they are pleasant people to be around. So, you may find it not surprising that you draw people in like a magnet. They are more of the host or hostess type and are not so much caretakers.

Under stress, a 2w3 may behave the polar opposite. They may act arrogant or authoritarian. They may even burst out in anger without warning. They also may seem sensitive to criticism (which is common amongst Twos as a whole).

They see criticism as the needle to the balloon filled with the air of pride. One 'prick' of the needle and it slowly deflates or suddenly pops. Like 2w1s, they may lack self-awareness to the point where they may not even realize that they are ignoring the need for self-care.

Growth Arrow: 4

Simply put, Twos and Fours may be the best match of the Enneagram so far. They share a common need for warmth and connection. And they are willing to help out one another if both are behaving in a healthy manner.

Twos and Fours will usually share mutual trust. If a Four needs to express their actual feelings, they seek safe haven in a Two. They will place more trust in Twos considering the latter's ability to listen and to accommodate if needed.

Obviously, Twos bring their warm, considerate nature to the table. Meanwhile, Fours will bring their sense of humor, creativity, and emotional honesty as part of the deal. Twos will appreciate Fours in plenty of ways (and Fours will thrive on that appreciation that they have searched for).

Twos may have patience to an extent. But they need to be aware of how moody Fours can be. Aside from Eights being critical of Twos, do not rule out Fours doing the same. They may be critical of Twos under the guise of being 'fake'.

Some Fours may resent the idea of love. But that doesn't mean all Fours will reject it. But through it all, Twos and Fours are the perfect combination for friends and colleagues as opposed to romantic partners (especially when Fours tend to be highly emotional).

Stress Arrow: 8

Twos and Eights have a stark difference from one another. Both of them operate on different value systems. To dig even deeper, it comes down to their attachability with people.

Eights are unsentimental when dealing with people and various situations. Twos, on the other hand, are highly attached to others. Twos have more empathy while Eights have an independent and direct demeanor.

Twos see different points of view, while Eights are more focused on their self-interest. The list goes on and on. Yet one of the glaring differences that you will see amongst Eights and Twos is how they deal under stress.

Twos will have that possessive, self-sacrificial behavior. Meanwhile, Eights are hard-hearted and will become confrontational if such a situation warrants it. In relationships with Eights, Twos may be susceptible to codependency, which can be unhealthy for both from a mental standpoint.

Specifically, if an Eight is behaving badly, Twos' will profusely apologize. And because of that, it enables Eights to continue traveling down a path where being anti-social and self-destructive can be the norm.

Because of Twos nice, accommodating demeanor, it can get to the point where Eights will resent them. Meanwhile, Twos will lose respect for Eights because of the latter's potentially domineering and cruel behavior.

If Twos and Eights somehow end up in romantic relationships, they may not be as durable. A breakup won't happen quickly, but it's like a dilapidated building waiting for itself to implode.

Oftentimes, they may argue with each other because of their different viewpoints and values. But what about the good that Twos and Eights bring to each other? Can they at least focus on the good qualities?

Sure enough, they do share commonalities. Both Twos and Eights are driven by action. They each have a common goal to make a personal mark on the world around them.

Eights have a soft side, but a Two can certainly set the stage where it can be brought out more openly. They both have the ability to provide, protect, and nurture at the expense of their own needs. Eights and Twos can be each other's strongest supporters when they are at their healthiest.

Type 3

The Achiever

Center: Heart

Basic Fears: Being worthless or seen as a 'nobody'

Basic Desire: Feeling valuable or seen as a somebody

Wings: 2-4

Growth Arrow: 6

Stress Arrow: 9

Type Three Explained

Threes are amongst the most ambitious of all the personality types. They know their accomplishments and they thrive on the recognition they receive for them. To be well-known for something, they feel like the world can see them.

They tend to work hard and will often be competitive in nature (even if they are team players). At the end of the day, they hold a lot more value over individual accomplishment over team effort. When it comes to solving problems, Threes will be more diplomatic and will try to find a solution. Because of their successful endeavors, Threes can assume the roles of leadership and authority much easier than most. They are captains of their school sports team, student government leaders, and so on.

One of the most famous Threes on a long list of famous persons (who we'll discuss later on) had so many achievements by his senior year of high school, that the principal actually barred him from running for class president. But that didn't stop him from becoming President of the United States some thirty years later.

Threes are usually developed from a young age. They are usually the ones who are by default the 'popular kids'. They achieve tasks like being elected class president or 'Homecoming Queen' during their school years.

But what about after they graduate high school? That's where the challenge begins. When Threes are thrust upon a new environment, they feel like a small fish in an even larger pond. That's when they realize that hard work and dedication are what it takes to keep the momentum of success going.

The fear of feeling like a worthless 'nobody' might drive them to do this. Their feelings about it are never expressed to anyone because they have a habit of putting them in a box. While they may not show their emotions to those around them, they may do so in private.

Despite being successful in their past, they are now wrestling with the question of "what do I want now". They never asked this question themselves growing up since they had been riding the waves of success. And now, the reality of putting more effort into it begins.

Type Three/Wing Two (3w2)

Threes with a two wing are the ones who may fear failure the most. For this reason, they try to work their hardest by setting and achieving their goals. Because of this intense focus, they may feel like they are unworthy of being loved by someone.

Admiration and acceptance are what they seek. Certainly, they have received it through their accomplishments. But The Enchanter as they are called is focused on the people who are watching them achieve their goals.

They act as if they are the main character of a movie that people are watching in real-time. And they want to put on the performance of a lifetime. They are ambitious in their goals and will focus on their appearance more than anything.

This is easier to do considering that they are self-confident. Plus, they have a high level of self-awareness. Their role as an 'enchanter' makes them well-liked and easy to connect with people (which is a clear trait that Twos possess).

Though they focus on self-image, a 3w2 may focus too much on it at times. And it might get to the point where they may veer off course a bit. Even though they are successful, they ask for others around them to be successful themselves.

They have little patience for those who do not pull their own weight. While they may be accepting of failure from others, that acceptance will not come easy for them. At the same time, they will drive themselves to be more competitive and even possessive (the latter being a negative trait of Twos).

Their competitiveness can get to the point where they could 'mow' anyone out the way. In other words, the risk of burning bridges with the longest known or best of friends is present.

Type Three/Wing Four (3w4)

Threes with a Four wing are known as 'The Expert'. Like 3w2, they too are afraid of failure. And they will stop at nothing to become more successful in their own right.

They will focus on their careers much more often than others. For this reason, they will do their best to seek validation for all of their hard work and success. Experts will usually adapt to newer environments and often will change their behaviors and personalities just to 'blend in'.

For the most part, 3w4s are excellent communicators. But sometimes, their communications may get lost in some misunderstandings. And they will feel like they have deceived people.

They do have the ability to think and process their thoughts internally. They almost never express them to others. That's because they have the ability to restrain themselves and be in more control.

Because of their hard work and dedication to their careers, they pay a lot of attention to the tasks at hand. They also know where they are growing and where they need to improve. Because of their drive for constant improvement, they also have an easier time connecting with others (even if there is a motive of getting what they need).

While their focus on their professional life is admirable, there can be a time where too much focus is unhealthy. In situations where they are stressed or under pressure, 3w4 will often suffer episodes of self-doubt. If they lose or deal with disappointment, 3w4 will have a hard time dealing with it.

They can be moody at times as well. They may be confident in their abilities to the point where others may say that 3w4s may be too confident. You can be confident in your abilities but knowing where to draw the line is key.

A 3w4 must be aware that things can and will go south at any time. Loss and disappointment are part of the process. They must learn to embrace it rather than let it consume them.

Because of their superior focus on the tasks at hand, they would rather keep meetings with others short and sweet. When communicating, they want you to get to the point quickly. 3w4s place a high premium on time and they would appreciate it if no one wasted it.

Growth Arrow: 6

Threes are achievers and Sixes are loyalists. When the two join forces, they know that they can achieve anything from start to finish. Sixes will finish what they start.

Both are hardworking, energetic, and optimistic. They are strong communicators that connect with people and know that success will be assured. If there ever was an example of a winning team, Threes and Sixes can beat the pants off anyone.

It makes sense that a Three's growth arrow is Six. Sixes will provide the support that Threes look for. And they will feel like the Sixes are going out of their way to validate their success and give them support for future endeavors in advance.

Sixes know that Threes aspire for something greater. And they will see to it that it will happen. Even though they can work as teammates, they become even stronger individually. However, there may be issues between the two.

Both Threes and Sixes tend to be workaholics. On top of that, they each are willing to put their feelings aside. For this reason, if something they are working on hits a snag, their inability to communicate about feelings may exacerbate the problem.

The momentum comes to a grinding halt and things get a little uneventful and boring. Threes and Sixes have different coping styles. And it can get to the point where it can frustrate each other.

But nevertheless, they will find a way to press on and move forward with completing whatever goal they set out to do.

Stress Arrow: 9

They say 'too much of a good thing' can be bad. That statement is true. Threes and Nines are an example of the two positive qualities coming together and potentially leading to something bad. In this instance, there may be too much comfort or stability to the point where complacency sets in.

Because of this, whenever conflict arises, it's like a massive earthquake jolting them out of that state. From there, the questions about the status quo and the routines they perform will become more difficult to task. Nines won't even bother talking about conflict for fear that it may implode the relationship.

Likewise, Threes don't want to express their emotions in regard to conflict. However, they also worry about rejection whenever they do complain. They fear that Nines won't care to acknowledge it.

Nines want peace and nothing more. The slightest bit of conflict may disturb it. Especially the slightest of complaints from a Three.

On the other side of the coin, Nines tend to provide plenty of encouragement and support to Threes. Thus, Threes have a support system that benefits them from both their Six and Nine counterparts. This will be enough to drive them to achieve greater accomplishments than ever before.

However, Threes must learn not to get complacent. And they must come to the realization that no one may care about their complaints, even if they are trivial. If they have something to complain about, their first task would be to do something about it themselves.

Type Four

The Individualist

Center: Heart

Basic Fears: No Identity

Basic Desire: Creating their own identity

Wings: 5-3

Growth Arrow: 1

Stress Arrow: 2

Type Four Explained

Fours are by far the most sensitive and reserved of the Enneagram. They are moody and self-conscious. And they make no bones about expressing their emotions and how they truly feel.

They may seem like they are dealing with issues of self-pity, melancholy, and depression. Beyond that, they are willing to create an identity for themselves that can be viewed as positive. For one, they can harness their emotions and feelings in the form of their creativity.

When Fours put their creativity to good use, they do an excellent job of it. They put their heart, soul, and emotions into their work. They see their creativity as an opportunity to express their feelings without saying a single word.

They want nothing more than to express themselves and who they are in the best ways possible. Fours want to maintain their moods and feelings while surrounding themselves with beautiful things. But most importantly, they want someone who can pull them out of the deep dark hole that they seem to trap themselves in.

As they search for their true identity, they will try on many different hats. They may have different preferences, attractive qualities, and everything in between. Despite this, they still wrestle with the uncertainty of what they want in their identity.

Fours want to be true to themselves. But sometimes, when trying out these new identities, they may not seem like the case. And that can lead them to feeling disappointed all the time.

For their part, Fours must come to the realization that their story is not a negative one. But the negativity of it all is only the beginning of something better.

Type Four/Wing Three (4w3)

Fours with a Three Wing are known as The Enthusiast or the Aristocrat. Despite four and three together making seven (also known as The Enthusiast), is quite the coincidence. But we digress.

The biggest fear a 4w3 has is they may feel insignificant to the world around them. The reason is they have a habit of distinguishing themselves from the rest of the world. They seek a personal and unique identity, despite their intent on being different from the rest of the world.

They want to be remembered as the kind of people who were one of a kind. The person that no one duplicated. They want to engage with other people while maintaining such an identity.

4w3s will usually be more in tune with themselves compared to others. While they have their feelings, they will understand the feelings of others as well. They can use that to express their creativity as well.

They want authenticity and genuineness in their life, and they will provide it at such consistent levels. In other words, while they care more about their own uniqueness, they don't ignore the others around them.

In difficult times or under stress, they may react emotionally. At the same time, they may possess a negative quality from Threes such as focusing too much on their self-image. This focus may be intended for gaining approval from other people.

Those who want to become their own identity may seek such approval from others. They ask, 'what do people think about my individual identity'?

Type Four/Wing Five (4w5)

4w5s are considered The Free Spirit and rightfully so. This exudes strong individuality on their part. However, they may be afraid that their impact on the world will be non-existent.

Despite their reserved demeanor, they want recognition and admiration like the others. Yes, they want their own unique identity. But there may be times when a 4w5 will need to pull it back a bit and determine whether or not that the identity they seek is in match with their true selves.

Free spirits are intelligent and have excellent creativity. They may be considered loners given their willingness to withdraw from others and be reserved about themselves. One of the biggest qualities that they adopt from Fives is trying to understand how things work.

Fives often search for understanding and answers about how and why things work when they are alone. 4w5s do the same when it comes to the world around them. Meanwhile, they figure out what they can do to make an impact on the world without compromising their own identity.

Certainly, they are intelligent, but they fear that they may know less than they thought. In order to stay true to themselves, they want to confirm that they know things to the best of their knowledge rather than less. However, they are better at connecting with themselves rather than other people.

Even though 4w5s try to understand the world around them, it becomes difficult for them to face real-world problems. This may stem from a habit of thinking too much about themselves most of the time. They also may have a problem dealing with authority because of their struggle to follow such rules and orders provided to them.

Growth Arrow: 1

Fours and Ones may have more in common than they realize. They want to bring good and beauty into the world. Fours place a high premium on the latter.

Fours will have no problem with Ones and their desire for everything to be perfect. When Fours want beauty around them, perfection is something they will want more than anything else. And that alone can make a relationship between Ones and Fours work.

Ones will bring true, value, and reason to the relationship. Fours will give Ones the go-ahead to explore and express the ranges of feelings and passions that the latter has. In return, Ones will help Fours in supporting their creativity.

While Fours are highly emotional, Ones will do their best to make sure that the former keep those emotions in check. Because of Fours' high level of creativity, they can easily connect with Ones on the top of the arts. They may appreciate different types of art.

But still, Ones and Fours will have their different viewpoints. Ones are objective while Fours are considered subjective. Idealism is the root of their difference. Ones may be idealistic about various causes, moralities, and issues concerning the world.

Meanwhile, Fours will have a more idealistic approach regarding their own lives. They care more about their lifestyle, their line of work, and who they want to love rather than the world around them. Borrowing from the perfectionism of Ones, Fours want nothing more than a perfect life for themselves.

Ones and Fours may view each other negatively because of their own personalities. Ones may see Fours as self-absorbed and overly emotional while Fours will see Ones as judgmental and insufferable.

With the good, the bad balances out. But nevertheless, Fours see that there are growth benefits with Ones.

Stress Arrow: 2

Fours are in search of their 'rescuer'. They look for someone to dig them out of the dark holes of their negative emotions and melancholy. Ideally, Twos being the helpers and lovers may seem like the perfect fit.

Unfortunately, the pairing of Twos and Fours may not be all that it cracked up to be. The two major reasons for this are the high level of emotions coupled with demands that often go unspoken. The amount of emotions involved may cloud their understanding of each other.

To simply explain it, Twos and Fours in a relationship would be like building a house over quicksand. Or building it over a sinkhole that is rapidly forming underground. The house will eventually implode and crumble (even without warning).

Fours will feel abandoned when Twos begin to focus on other people. They viewed such Twos as their rescuer. By default, they believe that they would be the primary focus.

Unbeknownst to Fours, Twos are on a mission to love and help others. So, a Twos' attention will consistently focus on one person to the next. When a Four accuses a Two of abandonment, the latter may view it as an insult.

More commonly, both types may be viewed as needy. The need for love and attention is what they crave, and they will stop at nothing to get it. But amongst the not-so-good springs the true good that Twos and Fours can share.

Twos and Fours trust each other to where they can share their feelings and emotions. Twos are generous, considerate, and outgoing. Fours will be able to use their emotional honesty to open up to Twos.

Fours will make the relationships more aesthetically pleasing while Twos will do their part by pitching in and doing their part in whatever capacity is necessary.

Type Five

The Investigator

Center: Head

Basic Fears: Feeling useless or incapable

Basic Desire: To be viewed as competent and capable

Wings: 6-4

Growth Arrow: 8

Stress Arrow: 7

If you ever question yourself why such things exist or how they work, that is completely normal. But for fives, they ask that question and find an answer for it beyond the surface. They will dig for every little detail that supposedly exists.

Type Five Explained

They focus on the littlest details that no one else sees (even if they are out in the open and in plain sight). Fives may seem like they have an extra set of eyes. Their observations drive to search for answers, and asking questions is in their nature.

Their pursuit for knowledge is ongoing. They wake up, pursue, sleep, and repeat. When it comes to their observations, they are mindful of what's going on (even if they haven't accessed their mindfulness yet). When they practice mindfulness regularly, those abilities heighten to a much greater level.

Knowledge and understanding are gold to Fives. They have an endless stream of ideas. And it may be possible for them to execute on those ideas without fear of them falling flat.

If such an idea were to fail, a Five wastes no time sulking about it. They figure out why the idea was bad or why it failed. They'll take what they observe and use it as a learning experience for future ideas.

When collecting evidence and ideas, Fives feel more prepared and confident about their findings. They want to retain all the information they have and take it with them wherever they go. However, this may pose a problem.

Whenever they have ideas, it's a matter of whether they go forward with it or not. When they do, they do it without fear. When they don't, they may question what might have been should they have carried out the idea.

Most of a Five's ideas may never see the light of day. This may be due to their fear of being viewed as incapable or incompetent. They can unveil their findings and the answers they may have as it can surely benefit someone.

Type Five/Wing Four (5w4)

For 5w4s, their greatest fear is being viewed as incompetent and helpless. For this reason, their pursuit for the answers and acquiring knowledge may be kicked into overdrive. They want to help others any way they can from an analytical standpoint.

They see their knowledge as a tremendous asset. And thus, they are known as 'The Philosopher'. They seek knowledge with such vigor and passion.

They also explore new and unfamiliar environments without fear or hesitation. Because they know that certain answers to their questions exist. Their curiosity runs wild.

5w4s function better by themselves. Especially when it comes to searching for fresh ideas, knowledge, and skills. At the same time, they may face bouts of loneliness at times.

Granted, they benefit from the key feature provided by Fours -- individuality. A 5w4 will thrive in working conditions when they perform the tasks alone. If working in a group, it's best to leave them alone so they can focus more and contribute with little to no interference.

A 5w4 will be more focused and attentive to the small details. They will also observe and understand them better than anyone. They will bring the small details that people overlook to light.

5w4 may be sensitive and spend a little too much time focusing on themselves. They may distance themselves from others to the point where loneliness is recurring. In terms of their thinking, doing so realistically or even practically may be difficult to do.

5w4s will communicate with others so long as there is a clear reason. They do not want to waste their time with unnecessary meetings. Furthermore, casual conversation is not their cup of tea.

Type Five/Wing Six (5w6)

This person is known as 'The Troubleshooter'. This is the kind of Five that will spot a problem and will find a way to solve it. Using the major trait of loyalty stemming from the Six, a troubleshooter will stay on the problem and never slow down on its quest of figuring out what causes an issue and finding the right kind of solution.

Like 5w4s, their fears are mostly the feelings of uselessness and being incapable. They know that there are plenty of problems that exist in the world around them. But they also know that with every problem, there will always be a solution (even if one doesn't exist yet).

Granted, they strive to be seen as competent and of good use. Their desire to solve problems will require them to learn new skills that can be beneficial to them most of the time. If it's a skill that will be useful in the long term, they will spend time crafting it.

5w6 are hard workers. When it comes to solving problems, they analyze them better than anyone else. While they are at it, they don't want anyone bothering them since they work better when alone.

Being practical and logical is something 5w6s do all the time. They stay focused, well-organized, and remain calm even in times of stress. That calmness will allow 5w6s the ability to solve problems with ease (especially when no one else is around).

5w6s hate it when someone is hovering over them when trying to solve a problem. They don't need an audience and they certainly don't want anyone in their ears talking to them when trying to figure something out. This can add on more stress to an already stressful situation.

To others, they may view 5w6 as people who are aloof, cold, and private. If they are uninspired by anything, it will be much harder to get them motivated or to even take action. As a 5w6, you want to be in meetings that are short, sweet, and direct to the point.

Growth Arrow: 8

Fives and Eights share the commonality of not wanting to be interfered with. They know each other's boundaries and will respect them a hundred percent of the time. On one side of the coin, an Eight may need answers to certain questions or solutions to a problem.

Who better for an Eight to rely on more than a Five? On the other side, Eights and Fives may be willing to have a debate on differences of ideas and opinions. Eights being the challengers that they are will waste little or no time challenging a Fives findings and ideas.

Even more so, they have a mutual respect for each other and enjoy a good thought-provoking debate and showcase of different ideas. Furthermore, Eights may see Fives as worthy advisors rather than adversaries. They want someone in their inner circle to help them dig deep for anything that may aid them in the long run.

However, Fives and Eights are different in some ways. Fives may focus more with their minds and mentality rather than their physical bodies. Eights on the other hand hold their physical abilities in the highest regard.

Their physical stature and energy is a tool that works in their favor. And they will use it to intimidate others or enforce their will. Eights may threaten Fives to the point where the latter will have no choice but to retreat at the snap of a finger.

Lower functioning Fives may even lose respect for Eights that tend to be over judgmental or even over-intimidating. Even though Fives will feel appreciated by Eights, they may even be terrified of them at times.

Granted, Fives and Eights will benefit from each other more often than not. But the key here is keeping the relationship between the two healthy.

Stress Arrow: 7

Fives and Sevens share a commonality: ideas. Sevens are more enthusiastic about pursuing and executing ideas (even to the point where they don't consider the consequences of the idea being a failure). They may not worry about the 'what ifs'.

When under stress, fives will tend to withdraw from people and even themselves. It can get to the point where they can become reclusive. This may annoy Sevens immensely.

Sevens want to do something whereas Fives may not want to by choice. If they feel like they don't want to deal with people, they will let them know about it. Sevens will feel like they are being demanding, pushy, or even needy whenever they want Fives to tag along with them.

Sevens may even express negative emotions to the point where Fives may simply cut them out of their lives. Trust and common ground may be hard to come by for Fives and Sevens. They may have their own ideas and beliefs, but they may be opposing one another and can clash constantly.

They will defend their positions until they are blue in the face. Tempers may even flare as a result. But it will usually be Sevens that can be the antagonist.

Amid the negative side of it all, both Fives and Sevens value their ability to think. They come in with an abundance of mental energy that is used to forge ideas. Fives may provide something a Seven may not have (and vice versa). Fives will bring more clarity and deeper insights to the table while Sevens will execute ideas and plans at a moment's notice.

Sevens are spontaneous while Fives want to plan it all out. Money-wise, Fives are frugal and will usually be smart with their finances. Sevens, on the other hand, not so much. Fives and Sevens can agree that life is short.

But the way they approach life is different. To a Five, it's to expect little. To a seven, try it all if such opportunities were to arise.

Type Six

The Loyalist

Center: Head

Basic Fears: No support or guidance

Basic Desire: Support and security

Wings: 7-5

Growth Arrow: 9

Stress Arrow: 3

Type Six Explained

Loyalty is something that Sixes hold near and dear to their hearts. And they will stick to something or someone for as long as they live. They will defend them with such bulldog tenacity that people will view them as defensive.

Sixes are the kind of people that will make excellent friends or even lovers. Granted, they are also the types of people that will value all kinds of relationships both in the personal and professional sense. As for the 'status quo', not all Sixes will go along with it.

The reason being is that a Six's beliefs may differ from the status quo. And they are ever loyal to said beliefs. Even though they are loyal to others, they expect it in return. This is why they fear abandonment from others.

They lack the inner resources that they need when life throws them a curveball. So, they rely on others to provide it for them. Sixes may not have the self-confidence in tackling complex problems unless they have a strong support system behind them.

They will build a network of people both in the personal and professional realm. But they feel like they are building this network like a house on quicksand. They question the structural integrity most of the time.

As for the important decisions, Sixes are put in a quandary. As much as they don't like making them, they also eschew the idea of having someone else make the decisions for them. The reason for this is because Sixes do not want to be controlled by other people.

Simply put, Sixes want stability in their lives. And they won't go on with it until they absolutely know for sure. Once they have confirmation that they can trust someone, they will reciprocate and live up to their end of the bargain.

When it comes to loyalty to others, they will take a side of the coin. Will they antagonize someone who has caused problems to someone close to a Six? Will a Six treat another person respectfully because the latter treated a member of a Six's family with respect?

Sixes can take one side or the other depending on the situation. And it is all rooted in their loyalty to a person or cause.

Type Six/Wing Five (6w5)

The 6w5 is known as The Loyalist. They have a penchant for protecting themselves and others. Even then, their fear of losing stability and guidance still exists.

They often seek support and guidance, preferably from people who are close to them. They work hard and are often intelligent. Their thoughts are often analytical and logical, a characteristic adopted from Fives.

The 6w5 possesses some of the Fives' strongest characteristics. This includes their ability to solve problems but from a practical standpoint. They want specific details when warranted.

As they figure everything out, they would want to focus on it without anyone surrounding them. They want to know more about things. Knowing what's on the surface may not be enough for them.

Aside from the positive characteristics, the 6w5 has some of the negative ones from Fives. This includes the habit of withdrawing from others even in stressful situations. They may even exude some kind of aloofness as well.

They may have a hard time getting a grip on negative thinking or expressing their emotions. The latter may be due to the fact that they are not expressing them in front of other people.

Type Six/Wing Seven (6w7)

Sixes are indeed loyal. Therefore, The Confidant as 6w7s are called are the kind of people that others will open up to. The fear of losing their support system does exist in this type of person.

These are people who care deeply about others. When it comes to projecting their feelings, they tend to use their sense of humor to their advantage. They are very social people and are dedicated to a cause that draws them in.

When it comes to commitments and promises, a 6w7 is guaranteed to stick to them. For this reason, many people may tend to trust 6w7s. And that will certainly give Sixes a better chance to build that support system they so desire (and further galvanize it in the process).

The more you keep your promises and commitments, the more people will trust you. And that is all the Sixes want to be aware of. But the truth is, the Sixes may be at war with themselves that may jeopardize that trust.

They may struggle with decisions that may be life-altering. And they may have doubts about themselves and others. When it comes to material possessions, Sixes may be loyal to them as opposed to other things.

In other words, the power of their loyalty may turn into a weapon of mass destruction. A 6w7 should not care more about material things as they depreciate in value over the course of time. What they need to understand is that relationships are the most appreciated asset that money can never buy.

A 6w7 will choose to stay loyal to their relationships with people. And as a result, the overall value will appreciate.

Growth Arrow: 9

Of all the stable relationships on the Enneagram, Sixes and Nines are perhaps one of the most stable. And that's good news for Sixes who want nothing more than stability. Yes, they have their differences.

But they certainly have their similarities. Specifically, they want security, stability, and autonomy above all else. Solid ground is what they want and nothing less than that. These are people who tend to be middle of the road when it comes to their values.

They are willing to be respectful of authority if they are considered subordinates. However, some Sixes can be rebellious. And it may be due to their obligation to stay loyal to a certain cause or belief that may otherwise allow them to compromise or go against it.

Sixes and Nines will get along swimmingly well. They could make great friends or lovers. They are simple and wish not to feel special in any way. They are also not demanding either.

However, Sixes and Nines may not voice what is on their minds. They may be stubborn about it. It's like two Elks locking horns in a battle for dominance, but it ends up being a stalemate. In situations where stress and pressure is in the air, Sixes and Nines often play a guessing game of what's bothering them.

Failure to express or disclose such frustrations will allow them to bottle it all up. From a physical standpoint, that is not the smart thing to do. Especially when such pent-up stress can harm their health.

However, Sixes and Nines need to trust one another and be open to what is bothering them.

Stress Arrow: 3

Sixes and Threes can work together just fine. But they also have negative qualities that run concurrent with one another. They tend to set aside their emotions since they have a common interest in completing tasks they set out to do.

Granted, Sixes can be dishonest with Threes and may even avoid their real feelings to them. Even though Sixes place a high value on trust, they feel that there is an opportunity to lie and potentially jeopardize a Three's trust. So, this puts Sixes in a predicament that they seem to can't get out of.

Sixes and Threes can get along together in a professional setting. They have a sense of getting things accomplished and will make sure that what they start will be finished.

Type Seven

The Enthusiast

Center: Head

Basic Fears: Pain and deprivation

Basic Desire: A fulfilled, satisfying life

Wings: 8-6

Growth Arrow: 5

Stress Arrow: 1

Type Sevens Explained

Sevens are perhaps one of the most extroverted of the Enneagram types. They are adventurous and take their curiosity to the next level. They live by the code of trying lots of things at least once.

Granted, one must know their limits. However, they have a zest for life. They are excited to see what each day brings them. And they are spontaneous at best.

They are fast learners, mentally agile, and quick to think. They can absorb a good amount of information. And they have a penchant for developing skills that will benefit their mind-body coordination. These activities include typing, playing a musical instrument, or even tennis.

Sevens may be the 'do-it-all' kind of people. Thus, it would be hard for them to just focus on one thing. They can keep busy in times of stress but may lose concentration depending on how stressed they really are.

Whenever they want to choose something, they would rather choose one of each. For example, if given the choice between vanilla, chocolate, or strawberry ice cream, a Seven may go bold and say, "all three". It's all about making the right choice anyway even if the other two were not.

Sevens are optimistic and happy. And they hold life to a high level of appreciation. Especially when they are healthy.

Type Seven/Wing Six (7w6)

The fear of missing out is common amongst Sevens. But no one fears it more than the Pathfinder (7w6). They search for happiness and value it to a high degree. The last thing they want to do is miss out on something exciting.

They think, but they are thorough in the thought process. Even in times of stress, a 7w6 will do their best to stay optimistic. They are sensitive to the feelings of others and are willing to be cooperative when asked.

However, they may be affected by other people's opinions. It may get to a point where they may question their confidence in themselves. Meanwhile, they struggle to focus under stress. When they have spent a vested amount of time in one interest, they will get tired of it after a lengthy period.

It is common for Sevens to get bored of something and have a desire to move on. And we cannot blame them for desiring change.

Type Seven/Wing Eight

A 7w8 is known as The Opportunist. And if opportunity indeed knocks, certainly a 7w8 will answer. Because if they don't, that's an opportunity missed.

A 7w8 will often think about what might have been. However, they do their best to seek out an opportunity that benefits them. They want to gain experience from it as well.

They are high in energy and always have a positive attitude among themselves. They are charismatic and highly confident in themselves. They are also self-assertive.

In stressful situations, a 7w8 is calm, cool, and collected. Especially when they are in a leadership position when such qualities are needed. However, they may come off as blunt and impatient in the eyes of other people.

They may place a high emphasis on their careers, thus risking them to miss out on the exciting things in life. Even though they have set plans, they may have a hard time following through with them. One can assume that an enthusiast may blow off a plan because something came up and their spontaneity decided to play a role.

Like a 6w7, they may focus on material things. And that might be risky enough considering that a Seven doesn't want to miss a thing. Sevens need to step back and see what is important as far as what life has to offer.

Growth Arrow: 5

Fives and Sevens have something in common. They love acquiring interests that become part of their identity. The only difference is that Sevens will dive into more of them compared to a Five, who wants to just focus on one thing at a time.

Nothing wrong with that at all. For a Five, they will bring a certain clarity of observation and inspire a Seven to go more in-depth with it. They respect each other's independence and ability to pursue an interest, whatever they may be.

However, Fives and Sevens may differ in terms of how they interact with others. Sevens may be more extroverted, which is a complete 180 from Fives, who will more often than not deal with people only in small doses.

Regardless, Fives and Sevens can agree on one thing: life is short.

Stress Arrow: 1

There is a glaring distinction between Ones and Sevens. And it can be described in one word: discipline. Ones tend to be disciplined and want to follow something a certain way.

Sevens on the other hand are the exact opposite. And nothing infuriates a One more than someone who is unorganized or inefficient. Then again, that's where that perfectionist trait comes into play.

However, Sevens can aid Ones in a way where they can provide the latter with plenty of energy to pursue their goals. Likewise, Ones will do their best to keep Sevens steady while helping them achieve the latter's goals. Ones place a premium on consistency and reliability, something a Seven may be lacking at times (especially when they jump from one interest or goal to the next).

Type Eight

The Challenger

Center: Head

Basic Fears: Being controlled by others

Basic Desire: Protecting themselves and be in control of their life

Wings: 9-7

Growth Arrow: 2

Stress Arrow: 5

Type Eight Explained

Eights are the kind of people who are leaders. And they want to be in control rather than be controlled. They do not want to lose their power, nor do they want to be seen as vulnerable.

They are the go-getters and the can-doers. And they will likely command others to carry out their tasks if they are unable to do it themselves.

They are high-energy people but may also be prone to stress. When under pressure, they may get angry and take it out on others. This may cause those underneath the Eight to lose respect for them.

Type Eight/Wing Seven (8w7)

An 8w7 hates authority, hates rules, and hates limits. So, it's the potent mix of Eight and Seven working together. Therefore, it's rightfully deserving that they earn the title of non-conformist.

They do not care about what society wants them to do. What everyone else is doing, the 8w7 will do the exact opposite. Even if they purposely do it to anger others that expect them to follow along with something.

8w7s can make logical but fair decisions, form connections with others, be optimistic, and lead people with inspiration. They are also willing to share their thoughts and opinions with others.

But what they might not like is staying patient. And they may be overindulgent at times. And lastly, they will often have little to no sensitivity for the other person's feelings.

Type Eight/Wing Nine (8w9)

8w9s are known to be diplomatic. While they seem to be in control of the situation, they often look for solutions that can quickly end a conflict. They are able to listen to other points of view while crafting a solution that is win-win for both sides.

8w9s do not take orders, but they are also calm and more laid back compared to their 8w7 counterparts. They want autonomy and independence as well. They may have a hard time seeing different perspectives at times.

8w9s may also not be able to give attention to the needs of others and may ignore them if they seem trivial. They may not be as protective of those they care about, which may be a flaw they need to fix.

Growth Arrow: 2

Oddly enough, Eights and Twos balance each other out. While Eights are externally tough, Twos are kind and gentle. They make the perfect romantic couple and balance everything out in their relationship.

A Two will be appreciative of their partner that is an Eight. And they will go out of their way to help them while cheering them on. An Eight appreciates it when they need help with something, especially when it is something that they may not be able to deal with.

Stress Arrow: 5

Fives may be a source of stress for Eights because of the former's lack of physical presence. On top of that, Fives and Eights operate on different value systems. Eights value communication from other people who are their subordinates.

So, at some point, they must hear from a Five be it in a physical presence. Otherwise, Eights may consider a Five useless, which is something the latter fears the most.

Type Nine

The Peacemaker

Center: Head

Basic Fear: Of loss and separation

Basic Desire: Inner stability and peace

Wings: 8-1

Growth Arrow: 3

Stress Arrow: 6

Type Nine Explained

Nines are the peacemakers for a reason. They want to avoid conflict as much as possible as it will interrupt their own inner peace. But when there is conflict, they will always find a way to provide solutions.

They will not rest until both sides come to an agreement. Meanwhile, Nines are willing to listen to other people's points of view. They are not biased in the slightest, thus making them the perfect listeners and are able to understand as many points of view as possible.

Type Nine/Wing Eight (9w8)

9w8 are known as The Advisor. They encourage and support people while being assertive (especially in a professional setting). They are effective when they connect with those in leadership and will often provide them advice when it is necessary.

They are good at seeing things from numerous perspectives depending on the situation. But they struggle to balance their assertiveness with passiveness at times. As part of what Nines do, they want to avoid conflict but have a hard time doing so.

Type Nine/Wing One (9w1)

9w1s are known as The Negotiator. They want to bring peace, but they will help people find a solution to solve a problem. They can easily see many sides and arguments of a situation.

For this reason, they will help improve the lives of other people. They will help them get what they want. Their work ethic and focus are second to none.

They are motivated and open-minded, making them a tremendous asset to any team. But they may have a bad habit of being critical of themselves while overlooking their needs. When under stress, they may be aloof and unwilling to talk to people.

Growth Arrow: 3

If there is one support group that Three's need, the Nines can easily deliver. The Nines know what the Threes want, and they will work hard to help them out in any way they can. They will be able to help Threes to relax and enjoy themselves while helping them get the work done if needed.

Nines can earn their share of the credit from Threes once success is achieved. But the Nine may not care if they get credit or appreciation for their help. They just do what they can without making sure nothing is disturbing them along the way.

Stress Arrow: 6

When it comes to what's on their minds, Sixes and Nines may have a hard time expressing them. This will lead to quite an interesting standoff. Both are stubborn and quietly defensive at best.

It's like watching a tennis match where it ends in a draw. It's interesting to watch, but it can get boring fairly quickly.

Chapter 14: How to Proceed

At this point, you have been able to find out what your Enneagram type is. If you have made a guess beforehand and you were right, you can then proceed to the next steps that we will lay out for you. If you have found out about your Enneagram for the first time, you might have some mixed feelings.

You may be partly happy and anxious. You may feel shocked about yourself. Whatever your feelings, you might be thinking to yourself if your Enneagram type matches the real you. Believe it or not, it does.

What you took is an Enneagram test that is accurate. And as long as you answered truthfully, you have knowledge of your type based on the answers you have provided. So now, the question you have to ask yourself is: where do you go from here?

In this chapter, you will find out how you can proceed with your Enneagram type. This will include action steps that you need to take in order for you to grow and live your life. Needless to say, this chapter is considered your instruction manual that represents a new journey.

You're on a new journey towards growing into something better. You will grow into your role as a Type One, Eight, Nine, or whatever your personality type is. You will begin to understand why your personality type is what it is.

You will likely make changes for the better if you are somehow living an unhealthy life. There is always room for you to grow and improve. It doesn't matter how long it takes, as long as you are willing and able to grow, you will look back and see how far you have come.

And you will reap the benefits and rewards of it all. With that said, let's discuss how you can proceed with your Enneagram type:

Get to Know Your Enneagram Type Better

In the second part of Section One, there will be chapters dedicated to your Enneagram type. In this section, you will learn about the needs that your type has. For example, if you're a Type One, there will be a chapter based on the need to be perfect.

We will go into deeper detail about the healthy, average, and unhealthy traits your type has. You've already learned about the types of professions and careers that your Enneagram type may be a better fit for. This could inspire you to make some decisions that may be considered life-altering.

You will also learn more about your Enneagram type, so you know more about yourself better than others. These include knowing your key personality types, the common fears your Enneagram types have, and being aware of what motivates you or stresses you out.

We will also compare you to famous persons who share the same Enneagram type as you do. You may have in common with someone who you may have admired for a long time. Plus, you may get a better understanding of them in part (since they may behave and have the same personality traits as you do).

Make a plan to reorient your life

After discovering your Enneagram type, you might feel the need to stay the course based on the status quo. When in reality, doing so may continue to become a source of what may be your unhappiness (or that feeling that something is missing). Reorientation is basically rerouting the course of your life towards the destination of something better.

Later on, we will discuss not just reorientation, but also discuss another part of the journey that is vital for personal growth. Specifically, we will be talking about repentance. That may sound like a religious term, but to repent for your mistakes and misgivings is all part of the growing process regardless of Enneagram type.

Do away with your idealized self-image

When we get deeper into the section regarding the general practices and principles for each type, we will be discussing what is known as your idealized self-image. We will explain the definition of it and discuss which idealized self-images match with each Enneagram type.

Let's say that your idealized self-image is a version of yourself (created by you) that may serve you more harm than good. We will show you how to do away with that self-image so you can easily brace your true self over time.

Learn breathing and centering

One of the most crucial uses of the Enneagram is knowing your centers and being able to keep them aligned. One of the best ways to do this and maintain balance is by breathing. You're probably thinking to yourself: 'Breathing? Really? What about it?'

Later on, we will introduce you to a chapter that focuses on breathing exercises that will help you find your center and keep it all aligned. There are different types of breathing exercises that we will go over. And there are breathing techniques that are tailor-made for each Enneagram type.

Once you get a good idea of how they work and try them out for yourself, it will become part of your daily routine. You may feel like you won't have enough time in the day to get this done. But we will show you how, even if time isn't on your side every single day.

Understand the general principles of the Enneagram

There are six general principles of the Enneagram. In the chapter that focuses on that, we will break down every one and why it is important. You will understand that each

Enneagram type, while they differ from one another based on traits and the like, are not good or evil.

You will learn that all Enneagram types are not better than the other. But let's stop short of giving away all the details. We'll save that for the chapter itself.

Learn the practices of the Enneagram

We will talk about the practices of the Enneagram based on your personal and professional life. You will learn how to develop relationships with your friends, co-workers, and your romantic partners. You will learn about the traits of your personality type and how it fits into each type of relationship.

You will learn about how other Enneagram types handle such things like relationships, how they communicate or deal with feedback at work (among other things). Even though you are more aware of your Enneagram type, you should consider reading through the other types so you can understand the ins and outs of their traits.

That way, if you know you are working with a Five (for example), you will know how to communicate, email them, resolve conflicts, and so on. Knowing these practices will help you improve your life and strengthen your relationships.

Implement Your Personal Growth/Stress Handling Plan

Every Enneagram type has a personal growth plan (as well as their plan to handle stress). As we go through each chapter that focuses on each type, we will make suggestions and recommendations based on your personal growth.

When under stress or pressure, you will learn how you can handle them without feeling like you're lost or not knowing what to do. You will feel good knowing you have a road map towards positive growth that will serve you better in the long run.

Final Thoughts

Now that you have the instructions on what to do next, it's time to proceed with getting to know your Enneagram type better. There are parts of the book where you can skip to where it will apply to your Enneagram type.

However, we highly encourage you to get to know some of the other types as well. That way, you can understand who they are, what they have for traits, and be able to properly communicate with them in either a personal or professional setting.

Not only that, but you will also make a commitment to focus on your own personal growth so you can live a healthy life based on your Enneagram type. This is only the beginning.

So now the question is: are you ready to take on a new journey in your life?

If you answered 'yes', then what are you waiting for? Let's move on and start the journey.

Chapter 15: Vocation Triad - Identity, Purpose, and Direction

Earlier, we talked about the Gut, Head, and Heart triads. While we may revisit them later on, we will be talking about different triads. We will be talking about three different types:

- **Vocation triad - Identity, Purpose, Direction (This Chapter)**

- **Wisdom triad - Doing, Feeling, Thinking**

- **Practice triad - Past, Present, Future**

As noted, we will be talking about the vocation triad in this chapter. The Enneagram and your personality type will be leveraged in so many areas of your life. This includes your professional life and what you do in your spare time (whether it's hobbies, passion projects, and the like).

Your vocation triad is simply about what your sense of calling is in life. What is it that you were 'born to do'? Let's face it, not everyone was born to become a doctor, a lawyer, or something that you wanted to be when you grow up.

The Enneagram may be helpful in unearthing what your true talents are. If anything, those true talents may be useful in your current line of work. Otherwise, you may find yourself in a situation where what you have been doing all along may not have been your true calling.

This triad will determine your identity, your purpose, and the direction that you're going in. And we will answer three questions in relation to that. Granted, this and the chapters about the other triads may lead you to make life-altering decisions.

However, there are some personality types where you may struggle to make such decisions (like Type 6). But nevertheless, it will come to a point where you may be able to make a decision to where you can look back and say that it was the right one. One such decision could lead to a career change.

It doesn't matter if you've been at it for two years or two decades. Your true calling may still exist whether you are a certain age or not. But the question is: will you answer it?

Now, let's dive into the three questions that define the vocation triad:

Who am I? (Identity)

This three worded question is often asked by those who understand the Enneagram (and those who don't). This is a question that you ask yourself if you want to confirm your true identity of who you are. Now, you might have already answered this question in the context of who you are as an individual.

But now, we shift it to who you are in terms of what you do in a certain vocation. There are certain qualities of your Enneagram type to where you might be the perfect match for a vocation. For example, Type 8s have leadership qualities to where they can use them to run a business or a corporation.

Type Twos on the other hand may be more apt to work in the medical field given their drive to help other people. There are so many different types of vocations and fields that are fit for each Enneagram type.

Here are some additional questions that you want to ask yourself while pondering on the question of 'who am I':

- **What is the one thing that you can do a hundred times without failing?**

- **What are some special skills that you are passionate about?**

- **Can your skills be considered something that helps other people?**

- **What is your current vocation/occupation?**

- **Do your skills, beliefs, etc. match up with what you're doing right now? (If yes, explain why. If no, explain why not)**

- **If the opportunities presented themselves to where you could be able to answer your true calling, would you be able to take advantage of it?**

We can ask many questions on the topic (and you can answer them if you wish). But what is surprising is that there are a lot of people out there that are not doing something that is considered their 'true calling'. They are working jobs to where they are considered 'thankless'.

They work jobs that they know will provide them income and security. But deep down, most people feel like they can do better. But in their mind, they seem like they are trapped and can do nothing about it.

This is where the Enneagram can come into play. People can adopt the practice of being mindful of their current situation. Meanwhlle, they need to be mindful in order to harness the true power of the Enneagram.

From there, they can identify and better understand their Enneagram type. Afterward, they can determine which line of work that best fits their type. Some of them may find themselves on the right path while others may feel like they are lost (but may have an idea of where they should be going).

The Enneagram will answer the question of who you really are as a person, right down to what your true calling should be. You have the skills, the talents, and even the personality that will fit what you should be doing to make your mark on the world. Take the time to answer the questions of who you are as a person.

Why am I here? (Purpose)

This is another question that is typically followed by 'who am I'. We often ask ourselves why we are here. What purpose are we serving during our time on Earth?

The Christian faith will usually defer to the Bible and say that we are on Earth for carrying out 'God's purpose'. On another end, we often ask ourselves if we were born with an individual purpose. Are we on this planet to make a change for the better or to provide some kind of negativity that will provide balance with the positive?

There is usually a reason why you are here. But the answer to that question has a variable answer. That answer is how you live your life.

It may take years, even much of your life to figure that out. And you might even find yourself figuring that out by the ways of 'trial and error'. You may find out what's good for you personally and what isn't.

You may find out which line of work fits you best and which one isn't. It's all a part of life. We all seek to find what our real purpose is.

The answer may also depend on your personality type as well. For example, Type 4s are known for bringing beauty to the world via their creativity. And they harness the power of their emotions and express them by utilizing their artistic talents, whatever they may be.

Meanwhile, Type 5s will often find out things about the world that many people do not know about. And for this reason, they could put together all the findings and data they have discovered and publish them for all the world to see. From there, it may even stoke the flames of thought-provoking conversation.

Type 2s, being the helpers that they are, may have a purpose to instill good faith in humanity. Especially in the world where people seem to lose every bit of it day by day. For their part, they are doing everything they can to preserve and protect the good of humanity before it somehow gets snuffed out.

For every Enneagram type, there is a purpose. Whether you or any other person that has figured that out yet remains to be seen. But if you are not aware of what your true purpose is, do not despair.

You will find out soon enough. And when you do, you will feel like you are making a contribution to the world (albeit in a positive way). When you are at your healthiest both in mind and body, you will be able to recognize your purpose even if it's in the smallest of detail.

You will have an 'ah ha' moment. And you may finally realize why you are here on this Earth to begin with.

Where Am I Going? (Direction)

Not a lot of us are aware of the direction that we're actually going in. In our conscious minds we tend to think we are going in the right direction. However, the real answer may surprise us.

Think about it: in your current vocation or career, do you ask yourself whether or not you are going in the right direction? It may take some soul-searching to find the answer. And for most, when they find out that they have been going in the wrong direction the whole time, they'd be flabbergasted.

Let's say for instance that in your conscious mind, you want to become a lawyer. You want to do this because you are a big fan of legal dramas or have a deep knowledge of the law. So, you go through the motions such as schooling, internships and the like.

After a while, it may seem like that it's not what it's cracked up to be. So why stick with it? Is it the money?

Is it the hope for advancement? What could it be? There are many people that stick to jobs and careers that they are not a true fit for because of one thing or another.

They may feel like if they left now, they may lose their income and not afford the lifestyle they want. Others may stay on with the shred of hope that they may finally advance after working hard enough. But that day may never come.

Or could it be that we are fearing that we view ourselves as failures? All the time, energy, money, and everything else invested in something that may now be considered a waste. This is yet another example of where trial and error can play a huge role in discovering our true identity and purpose.

You want to do something where it can bring out the best in you both personally and professionally. When you're going in the right direction, you'll feel it. You will also feel some kind of momentum driving you to do more.

Our conscious and subconscious are two different things. The former will have us thinking we are going in the right direction (when in reality, we might not be). That may explain why many people are unhappy with their current situation as far as their jobs or careers are concerned.

The reality is they might be working against the grain and they are somehow forcing their way through. The truth is, we may have talent and potential that may go untapped for as long as we live. Isn't it about time that we unearth it along with our mindfulness?

If you are looking for a sense of direction, you may want to spend some time with yourself and be mindful of how you are feeling while you are at work. Are you feeling like you are truly going in the right direction? Are you aware of the level of happiness you have while performing the tasks of your vocation?

Vocations and Careers Based on Enneagram Types

We will now look at the careers and advice for each personality type. Before we begin, take note of your personality type. Knowing your personality type will help you determine whether or not you are on the right vocation path or not.

We will also talk about some advice we will provide about your career or your calling in general. We also will warn you that you may be tempted to make a career change at some point. We encourage you to not be spontaneous in your decisions (sorry, Type 7s... but there's a reason for this that we'll explain shortly).

With that in mind, let's take a look at some of the careers that your type may or may not be as fit for:

Type 1

As a One, you are rational. You see things in black and white. You also have integrity and virtue.

Typically, they are the kind of people who thrive on the words 'You are good at what you do'. In fact, that might be the words that everyone wants to hear regardless of their type. As far as careers and the options provided, they want to choose one based on their freedom and abilities to change things.

Specifically, they want to change the way things work. The goal here is to provide as many positive outcomes as possible. Because of your quality of being a perfectionist, you want to do something to where your attention to detail is very much appreciated.

Careers to Consider:

- **Professors:** As a Type 1, being well-organized and orderly is the norm. On top of that, they thrive on high standards. Those standards are upheld in academia. Thus, professors are among the best fit for Type Ones. Granted, there is a good amount of education that will go into being a professor. They are specialists in their field, and they teach undergraduate and graduate students to grow so they can become specialists in their own field (including those who are answering their true calling).

- **Judges:** When it comes to the law, integrity matters. And Ones are big on it. Therefore, judges should preserve that integrity at all times by making fair, objective, and ethical decisions. You may have a higher purpose for making the right call that will ensure safety and security in a society. Every decision you make is based on truth and facts.

- **Law enforcement:** Like judges, law enforcement officers place integrity at the highest level. They are also willing to uphold the law. Meanwhile, they also play the role of investigator. This will allow their attention to detail to come into play. This ability can be crucial in solving cases.

- **Environmental specialists:** This requires not just attention to detail, but also the ability to make a positive impact on the world. If there is one thing that they want to be perfect, it's the environment around them. This cannot just benefit themselves but the rest of the world (especially when negative environments can be hazardous to one's health).

- **Social workers:** For Ones, being a social worker might be a true calling of theirs. The reason being is due to their desire to create a positive impact on the world. They are realists in terms of their philosophy and therefore are able to come up with the 'next steps' people can take to better their lives.

Careers to AVOID:

- **Administrative Assistants:** In this line of work, Type Ones will feel like their perfectionist behavior is being tested constantly. This is a job where mistakes can be made, no matter how trivial they are. Type Ones will worry about making these mistakes often. Almost to the point where they overthink it and fail to focus on other tasks.

- **Retail representatives:** Flexible, even odd hours? To a Type One, that is something that may be considered a nightmare. That's because they tend to be inflexible. Not to mention, they may be intolerant of such constant change.

- **Accountants:** When it comes to being an accountant or any kind of financial field, a Type One will simply not be the best. That's because their punctuality will get in the way. On top of that, they may become 'anal-compulsive' about things.

Type 2

Selflessness is one of the most obvious traits of a Type Two. Simply put, they aim to please. As for their career choices, they can thrive in an environment where they can strive for positive change just by helping others.

Furthermore, they want their generosity to be solidified. And there are many career fields to which generosity is more than appreciated. Let's take a look at those fields:

Careers to Consider:

- **Teachers:** For many Twos, education might be one of their best career fields to aim for. Especially when they have the potential to make an impact on others. Teachers will require face-to-face interaction with many of their students and make meaningful connections in the process. Whether it's children or adults, you will leave them with things that they will learn and apply from you.

- **Doula:** Doulas provide support in various areas. Especially when mothers-to-be are in the process of giving birth to a child. However, there are different types of doulas that provide emotional support to parents who have suffered through a miscarriage and go through the grieving process. Because of their caring nature, this seems like an excellent fit for Twos.

- **Social worker:** Social workers can be Type Twos that can care for others. Those who are 2w1s will find this to be one of the best-fitting careers of their lifetime. Using their ability to care and help others, they can utilize the One wing to help other people put together a plan to live better and more enriching lives.

- **Life coach:** If you are someone with a can-do attitude and a penchant for helping others, a life coach may be someone you can become. Even better, this is one of those careers where you can work for yourself and command the rates you desire. If you are someone who isn't apt to work the 9-to-5 lifestyle, there is a way where you can work your own hours, have your ideal clients, and more. For Twos, your ability to help others can pay off in more ways than one.

Careers To AVOID:

- **Advertising:** Advertising may not be a good career for you as it might require persuading people to buy a product or a service. It may require a bit of manipulation in the process. As a Two, that isn't your cup of tea (and it touches on a negative trait that a Two may have).

- **Event planning:** Event planning may not be a good idea for Twos. They are not much of the planning type unlike Ones. Plus, they would rather be behind the scenes helping others rather than be the brains behind the operations.

Type 3

If there is one thing that defines a Type 3, it's that they are driven and goal-oriented. Their accomplishments are revered and often talked about. So how does that apply to their career choices?

Simply put, Type 3s want to be recognized for their work for years to come. Some may even want to be recognized and talked about long after they have passed away. Making a mark on the world that will last forever is what they aim for.

Careers to Consider:

- **Agents:** They are representatives to some of the best and brightest stars in the world. Whether it's acting, literature, sports, and others, Threes are the kind of people who will help others achieve their certain goals and aspirations. Their client's success is their success as well. So, there is no denying that they deserve their share of the credit.

- **Attorney:** Type 3s are driven to win. Being an attorney gives them the intellectual challenge they need. On top of that, they use their influence to ensure that their client may be not guilty or liable of such charges. They are fighters and they will do whatever it takes to win.

- **Executive:** Yes, Type 3s may make great executives along with Type 8s. When the former takes the reins of power, they may find that to be one of the pinnacles of their long resume of success. They are driven to set goals, execute the plans to achieve them, and repeat the process.

- **Journalist:** There are Type 3s who want to be remembered for that one story. They want that inside scoop of what's going on in the world around them. Journalism provides Type 3s with a certain amount of authority. At the same time, it provides them the need to feel accomplished and validated.

- **Actor:** When it comes to the arts, performance and achievement is required. This allows the Type 3 to tap into an inner energy to become the best at what they do. Whether it's on stage or the silver screen, Type 3s in this career feel that they seek that one thing: the standing ovation. Anything beyond that is a by-product of such success (awards, etc.)

Careers To AVOID:

- **Freelancing:** Type 3s want to do their own thing. Freelancing provides that. However, the reason it's not a good fit for Type 3s is due to the lack of structure involved. Achievers will want to track their success. This may frustrate them to no end if a lack of structure exists. They want to measure their success while keeping track of the goals that they have yet to accomplish.

- **E-commerce:** Type 3s want full control over their goals and how to achieve them. In an E-commerce environment, you may set goals such as how many sales you want to acquire over the period of a month. However, you may fall short of that goal. For this reason, this may cause them to have unrealistic expectations. If such expectations are not met, it will stress them out.

Type 4

Creativity is the greatest gift a Four can have. And they want to put it to good use in so many ways. Their creativity shines the brightest whenever they have the opportunity to express their true emotions.

When it comes to answering their calling, Fours want something that will allow them to leave a lasting impression. This will also give them the opportunity to share their personal insights and give them the freedom of expression.

Careers to Consider:

- **Musicians:** One of the many artful talents where emotion and creativity are mixed together, musicians can create beautiful masterpieces. Such musical talent can come naturally for those who are Fours.

- **Poets:** Think of your favorite poets for a moment. Think of that one poem that makes you love them so much. What's that one emotion that stands out? For Fours, they can showcase the emotions they feel through words that flow.

- **Painters:** Picasso is the perfect example of expressing his emotions through painting. Take a look at his works from the 'Blue Period'. You will notice a pattern of sadness and depression. Fours will draw inspiration from the greats and add their own touch to their own creations.

- **Chefs:** Food is an art. It will allow them to showcase their talents in their creations. If it tastes great, that's when their mission is accomplished. Plus, their taste buds are their guide to creating such excellent dishes on their own accord.

Careers To AVOID:

- **Servers:** If there is one job that will deprive someone of their creative skills, it's being a server. If anything, they would rather be the cook or the bartender.

- **Financial analysts:** Their individual attitude is something that will make Fours terrible financial analysts. That's because analysts work together when they are all in agreement.

- **Executive assistants:** Again, this is a role in which their individuality will make Fours less than ideal as executive assistants.

Type 5

Of course, Fives are more drawn to careers that allow them to dig for things below the surface. They'd be unhappy with any position that doesn't provide them the freedom to solve problems. They want to be viewed as capable, but should not be ashamed to ask for help if they somehow hit a snag.

Careers to Consider:

- **Law Enforcement:** Whether it's police officers or detectives, members of law enforcement are usually investigating and looking for clues. They want to know what happened, why it happened, and who is at fault. They are dedicated investigators and will stop at nothing until the case is solved.

- **Market research analysis:** Things sell. But the real questions are how, why, and what sells? This is where the market research analyst comes into play. They spend plenty of time analyzing the markets. Depending on what's being bought or sold, it's a matter of what the market wants. What's keeping them up at night? What problems are they facing? What is their age, gender, race? So many questions, but Fives love that there are more than enough for them to answer. They will be able to spot market trends and be able to provide others with other ideas of what can sell.

- **Medical scientists:** If there is one career that a Five can definitely find fulfilling, it's becoming a medical scientist. Coupling their investigative habits with a side of the Six's loyalty, they stop at nothing and work tirelessly until a cure for something horrendous as cancer or any life-threatening ailment is found. Saving lives is what they aim for. And they will make sure that such research is continued long after they have retired or passed on.

- **Construction Workers/Building Inspectors:** For Type Fives in this field, it's about making sure a plan works and meets specific requirements. Fives are also creative (thanks to the 4 wing). And it is for this reason why they will bring their creativity to light even if it means spending time finding ideas for what makes their architectural works brilliant.

Careers To AVOID:

- **Virtual Assistants:** Clients need virtual assistants that they can connect with almost daily. Fives have a desire to withdraw from others. Therefore, it would not be an ideal fit for them to work in such a career like this.

- **Small business owners:** Though they are creative and can find the right ideas, Fives may have self-doubt creeping in. Will this idea work or will it fail among some of the others they have tried? Fives almost never depend on social validation. And at the same time, they fear that their ideas may be too mainstream or played to death.

Type 6

Type 6s want to be loyal to their job or their careers. So, the key for them is to find something they know they will love and stick to it. At the same time, they want something that guarantees them security.

They want stability and safety. And they want to be in an environment where they thrive on being consistent. Even though making tough decisions is uncomfortable for them, they can learn how to make them under pressure and in the best way possible (even if they will never see themselves as authority figures).

Careers to Consider:

- **Teachers:** Sixes as teachers are those who value knowledge and helping other people. For their part, their ability in becoming loyal to their students further proves their willingness to help them strive towards being successful.

- **Caretakers:** You would think that this would be a job for Twos. That may be a possibility. However, there's a reason why it's even more fitting for Sixes. The reason being is they can be reliable and feel secure knowing they are taking care of someone who needs it. They also invest their time in improving the well-being of others.

- **Environmental specialists:** Ever loyal to the cause, this is the kind of people where people are committed to making sure the world is a better place for everyone to live in. Specifically, 6w5 will often find ways to make it all work. Using the investigative traits of a Five, environmental specialists will stick to finding the right solutions for making the planet better both inside and out.

- **Veterinarians:** Vets are loyal and caring of animals. On top of that, they are caring for the humans that love their pets. Despite their bouts of self-doubt, working with animals alleviates them of that.

- **Executive Assistants:** Those who are reliable and easy to trust will thrive well as Executive Assistants. Especially those who are among Sixes. Loyalty that exists on both sides of the life coin (personal and professional) is what Sixes are known for best.

Careers To AVOID:

- **Project Manager:** One of the reasons right off the bat, it's an authority position. Sixes don't want that. They want to be the ones that stick with authority. And for this reason, they are so great to work with (especially with others). On top of that, such a position will pressure Sixes in making crucial, if not critical decisions. And that will be a little bit too much.

- **Programmer:** This is a line of work where people work in isolation. Sixes hate working alone. They thrive on collaboration from others. If anything, a programmer would be better suited for a Five as opposed to a six.

Type 7

Sevens want to be happy and interested all the time. Yet, one of their greatest challenges is that they grow tired of something and their best solution is finding something different. As such, the same can be said regarding their careers and vocations.

They want to be completely cared for. And at the same time, they must look for something that will help them become more optimistic and fulfilled with their line of work. More importantly, Sevens are looking for maximum freedom to do whatever they want.

Careers to Consider:

- **Event Planners:** For Sevens, they don't mind something that is project-based and even has a fast pace most of the time. This is an event that involves working with various clients. This is the kind of agility that Sevens crave. Those who love a good challenge will enjoy this line of work. And if you're a Seven who loves glamour, you will consider this your lifelong dream career.

- **Fitness Instructor:** No surprise here. Whenever we think of fitness instructors, we think of them as people with boundless amounts of energy (think Richard Simmons). They have unmatched energy that will motivate people into getting into the best shape of their lives. And they know that those who follow them will get to their fitness and health goals no matter how long it takes.

- **Flight attendant:** Flight attendants go from one place to the next. Whether it's New York to Seattle on one flight or London to Paris on another, they will usually travel all over the place. As such, Sevens love the constant changes of their environment. If this isn't a job that satisfies the wanderlust of a Seven, we're not sure what is.

- **Entrepreneur:** Sevens are one of the Enneagram types where being an entrepreneur makes sense.

The truth is, they have so many flowing ideas to the point where they can try them out one by one. Whether it succeeds or fails, Sevens keep going. The thrill of being in motion and trying different things is what they do best.

- **Blogger:** Blogging can be a business venture of itself when done right. They will hustle and hustle hard to achieve success. Riding the wave of thrill while giving themselves complete flexibility is what Sevens like most. There are rewards galore for bloggers. And they come in many shapes, sizes, and monetary value. They might write about something they are passionate about or use their knowledge to teach others.

Careers To AVOID:

- **Doctors:** Those who are considered doctors are committed to a daily routine. Because of this, it will not benefit Sevens in the slightest. There are many routines and procedures that a doctor must follow. Once again, this isn't something in a Seven's wheelhouse.

- **Accountant:** It seems like an accountant may not be fitting for most Enneagram types. But not to worry, there are two other Enneagram types that we'll be going through. For accountants, they will be crunching numbers all day long. That doesn't give Sevens the freedom or the flexibility they so desire.

Type 8

Eights are confident. And they thrive in positions of authority and power. For this reason, they would be better fit for careers that are more apt to allow them to become leaders rather than followers. They have a drive and can-do attitude that may give Threes a run for their money.

They are not afraid to lead, make crucial decisions, and will never meet a challenge they can say 'no' to. Furthermore, they are the types of people who are willing to take their loyal people through the lowest of valleys and the highest of mountains.

Careers to Consider:

- **Military Personnel:** There are many Eights that are known for being courageous and putting themselves at risk to achieve a vision or goal. As such, Eights would thrive as military leaders. They are considered heroes and strive for greatness.

- **Program managers:** If there is one position of authority that an Eight would find themselves in, it's the role of program manager. They will lead the charge and oversee various teams that make it all work. Because of their can-do drive, they are better suited than anyone else.

- **Executives:** Eights are strong leaders inside and out. Their decisiveness and authoritative traits are just what they need to become excellent executives.

- **Athletes:** If there is one thing that athletes are known for, it's their high level of competitiveness. Simply put, Eights are just that. They are talented and can demonstrate leadership skills (thus making some of them captains of the team).

- **Sales Reps:** Because of their competitive nature, sales might be something in the Eight's wheelhouse. Sure, it's not considered an authority position, but it also can be because being an ethical sales rep is actually guiding the other person into making the best decision for themselves and not having it be about you. You can approach this role as being an advisor or coach for the other person to determine whether it's a good fit or not while being completely authentic about it. The more authentic you are, the better this role will play in your favor. But Eights are drawn to it because it will help them stay sharp and compete with others. For eights looking for something that's considered entry-level, a sales rep might just be the kind of job for them.

Careers To AVOID:

- **Secretary:** This is more of a subordinate role than an executive role. Eights will not thrive in roles that support leadership.

- **TV Show Co-Hosts:** Co-hosts are usually the number two. Therefore, Eights don't want to be viewed as 'second fiddles'. They want to be the star of the show. Top of the bill.

Type 9

Nines are on a mission to preserve the peace while solving problems and bringing people together. They don't take sides of the conflict. But rather they make sure that both ends get what they want at the end of the day.

Careers to Consider:

- **Social Workers:** Social Workers are among the best fits for Type 1s, Type 2s, and now Type 9s. 9w1s are looking to make sure that while there is peace in someone's life, they may also make sure that someone is following the plans as outlined by the social worker. What steps are their clients taking?

- **Yoga/Meditation Instructors:** Type Nines are known for being more in tune with their bodies and minds better than anyone. And their goal is to make sure others are doing the same. If there is someone who can help connect people to their mindfulness, it's Nines in this field.

- **Human Resource Managers:** HR managers are known for maintaining order and restoring the peace. They will step in whenever necessary should there be any disturbances in the workplace.

- **Clergy members:** Those who are religious will often find themselves in roles as members of the clergy. They are spiritual and peaceful people. And they will help those explore their religious and spiritual curiosities.

Careers To AVOID:

- **Hospital workers:** One of the biggest fears a Type 9 faces is losses. And losses in a hospital setting come In diffcrent forms. This could be the loss of patients who may not survive their illness or critical injury. This could be the loss of connection to those around them. Likewise, this also counts for those who work in a morgue.

- **Politicians:** In politics, you win some and lose some. But that doesn't stop there. There is also a clatter of noise that is constantly disturbing the peace. For this reason, it's one of the reasons why 8w9 may eschew politics altogether.

Final Thoughts

In the vocation triad, it's about finding your identity, your purpose, and the direction you are going in. This mostly pertains to the line of work you mostly fit in. At this point, you may be unhappy with your current job or career.

It might never be too late to make changes. Especially when it's a vocation that best suits your Enneagram type. Furthermore, you might have found a career that best fits your type (and if so, congratulations).

Everyone is always asking who they really are, why they are here, and what direction they are going in. The answers to these questions will usually find them one way or another. Or they may be searching for the answers themselves (but seeing the answer evade them).

The answers that pertain to the Vocation triad are like cats. When you approach them, they may run off. But if you leave them be, eventually they will come to you.

Chapter 16: Wisdom Triad: Doing, Feeling, and Thinking

Next, we'll be taking a look at the wisdom triad. In this chapter, we will be circling back to the original triad of the Enneagram (Head, Heart, and Gut). We will be talking about the intelligence that is stemmed from these three centers.

When we talk about the Wisdom triad, we will be asking ourselves questions about what we're doing, feeling, and thinking. When all three triads are aligned, we experience a full range of intelligence. We also talk about your holistic intelligence and whether or not it is fully cultivated to make a decision based on the fullness of your own wisdom.

Wisdom is defined as having experience, knowledge, and good judgment. In short, having wisdom is being wise. Digging deeper, it's about experiencing and knowing what you are thinking, feeling, or doing.

With that said, let's dive right into the Wisdom Triad and discuss the experiences and knowledge of what you might be dealing with at the moment:

What Am I Thinking (Head Center Intelligence)?

We have so many thoughts going through our head on a regular basis. It is for this reason that we are unable to access our mindfulness with ease right from the start. And it is why for this purpose we highly encourage practicing such mindful techniques like meditation on a regular basis.

When we access our mindfulness and focus on that one certain thought, we can identify what we are actually thinking. This may be a thought that will give us positive or negative feelings (which we will discuss shortly). That thought going through our heads may have been triggered by some past experiences.

Or we may be thinking about the best- or worst-case scenarios of future events. Regardless of type, all of us are thinking about positive outcomes. And we dare not think about the negative outcomes as it may cause us to feel the fears of failure and the like.

For example, Threes and Eights would be thinking about the success they want to achieve at a moment's notice. Both of them have an excellent drive to do something. And each of them has their own way of handling it.

An Eight is thinking that so long as they have control over something, they will be in good shape. A three will think that as long as whatever they accomplish yields a positive reward, they will be willing to do it. They use their heads and gather their thoughts on whether or not pulling the trigger on a certain action or idea is worth it.

215

Threes and Eights are not part of the head center. But we use them as examples of what their thoughts are most of the time. What ideas do they usually have flowing through their thought process?

Speaking of ideas, Type Sevens are not so much the thinking type. In other words, they don't spend a lot of time thinking over their decisions. They just go through with it without ever knowing what the best and worst possible outcomes may be.

Type Fives are more of the thinking type despite being in a different triad of the Enneagram. They use logic and analysis to determine their findings. And their thoughts provoke them to dig deeper. To answer the question of what Fives are thinking, two words that come to mind are 'what if'.

What if there was a way to solve a long-standing problem that the world has been facing for decades, even centuries? What if there was a solution (albeit a temporary one) to solve a certain issue that may arise after a short period of time? Fives answer these 'What If' questions with their own ideas and hypothesize both the best and worst outcomes.

Our thoughts are something we can express to others if we so choose. Type Fives tend to keep their thoughts to themselves. But they express them using certain actions.

Eights on the other hand are not afraid to tell the world what they are thinking. They don't care who agrees or disagrees. They speak their mind and move forward without looking back.

What Am I Feeling? (Heart Center Intelligence)

Next, we focus on the Heart Center and discuss what people may be feeling. This is where Types Two, Three, and Four reside. These three types share the same instinct of feeling.

How are they feeling knowing that they have reached a high point in their life based on their personality and what they have accomplished? Likewise, what are they feeling whenever they are experiencing their fears or exuding their negative traits?

Type Twos are no doubt the loving and caring type. They feel that they cannot get through the day without knowing someone important to them is OK. At times, they may feel like no one is giving them the praise that they deserve for going out of their way to help others.

Twos, Threes, and Fours take action based on their feelings. Whenever those feelings wane, they continue to do what they can in order to regain those positive feelings that they crave. Threes feel like they are riding on a wave of high momentum whenever they are recognized for their accomplishments.

They will continue to find opportunities to accomplish something with the goal of recognition in mind. They will feel that sense of accomplishment and also the feeling of being important. What they want to feel is the polar opposite of being a 'nobody'.

When Threes accomplish something without recognition, they feel angry and resentful of those who overlook them. They feel as though they are wasting their time with such tasks. Not to mention, they feel like everything they do seems to be pointless.

Fours, being highly emotional, have no problem exhibiting them through creativity. The question of how they are feeling can be expressed in such art like music, writing, or even painting. Fours are never to be underestimated when it comes to their own creativity (especially when it's a creative answer to 'how are you feeling').

Those in the heart center feel concern for their image. They want to feel like they are validated both inside and out. And they will gain any attention necessary.

Furthermore, neither one of these types want to feel any kind of shame. Especially the shame that their hard work goes unnoticed. Twos, Threes, and Fours share one commonality: recognition. Twos want to be recognized for their generosity and kindness while Threes want to be recognized for their accomplishments altogether.

Fours want to be recognized for their creativity and their ability to create beauty around them. However, of these three types, it's the Threes themselves that may have a hard time answering this question of how they are feeling.

That's because they have the habit of 'putting their feelings in a box'. Threes do not disclose their feelings. Oftentimes they will 'lie' about them (i.e. - feeling fine when deep down it's not true).

But the truth is, Threes will often express a feeling of anger by working hard. It fuels them to do better. Whether that hard work pays off or not remains to be seen.

What Am I Doing? (Gut Center Intelligence)

Eights, Nines, and Ones are part of the Gut center. They are more about the doing rather than the thinking and feeling. They want to use their instincts to make crucial decisions and actions.

Their instincts dictate on what they should and should not do. If their gut is telling them to pull the trigger, they do. If it's telling them something bad, then they will exercise some kind of caution.

The question of 'what am I doing' will allow you to be present in the moment. What exactly are you doing right now? Is there some sort of positive gain or negative loss from this specific action?

Furthermore, are you happy with what you are doing long term? These are some of the questions you're probably asking yourself. You may be getting in tune with your instincts in order to determine whether or not you're doing the right thing.

Eights, Nines, and Ones are in search of autonomy. They want full control of what they are doing most of the time. But when anger clouds their judgment, they may not be aware of what they are doing in the present moment.

Their emotions will throw their mindfulness out of sorts. And they may make decisions without thinking things through. That's why sometimes, your emotions should never govern your thought process to begin with.

The important thing that all three of these types in the Gut center must do is control their anger. If they are seeking control and autonomy, that should bleed in with how they control their emotions. Those who control their emotions will be more in control of themselves in almost every area of their life.

This will allow them to keep their gut center in line along with the rest of them. Their feelings and thoughts will also be aligned as well. Before making a decision, sometimes you should get a 'second opinion' aside from what your instincts tell you.

This means you'll want to determine what you are thinking at the moment. For example, think about your feeling of anger. Think about how it's affecting yourself and others around you.

Final Thoughts

The Wisdom triad touches on our experience and knowledge of how we are thinking, feeling, and doing. To be in the know of these things (especially in the moment) is key. Regardless of what center your personality type is a part of, it is important to keep them all aligned.

We can ask ourselves what we are thinking. But we need to know what we are feeling at the exact moment. We also need to know what we are doing that makes us think and feel that way as well.

Chapter 17: The Practice Triad - Past, Present, and Future

The last of the triads that we will be looking at is the 'Practice Triad'. For our part, we try to remember the things of the past. And we connect them to the positive or negative feelings that we receive from reliving those moments.

Meanwhile, we use the triad to experience what is happening at the moment. What are we doing right now? What is going on in our minds, bodies, and the world around us?

And finally, what are we looking forward to in the future? What are we anticipating? Is it something exciting or something that we may be afraid of?

Better yet, are we prepared for the future? We will discuss the Practice Triad and break down each part of it shortly. You will understand how this triad works and how it ties with time itself.

This triad will help you get in touch with the experiences you may have had in the past while touching on what you're doing right now in the moment. Meanwhile, you'll also be better prepared for what may be the future, no matter how bright or bleak it may be.

Let's take a look now at the Practice Triad and the three questions tied to it:

What am I remembering? (The Past)

Whenever we feel positive emotions about something, it's often linked to the good things of the past. Likewise, when we feel fear, a lack of confidence, or something similar, we can trace it back to a bad experience. We may even hold back from doing something because of the feelings traced back to bad experiences.

For example, if someone says, 'I cannot do it', it may stem from a fear developed by someone saying something negative. Such words like 'you can't do it' or 'you're going to fail' might not faze some others. But it may get into the heads of some of those who have experienced failure and the bad feelings that are anchored to it.

Regardless, it is up for every Enneagram type to ignore the bad feelings and face their fears in the attempt. Whether they fail or not, they have at least made the attempt in getting something done.

What am I experiencing? (The Present)

The present is the now. What are you experiencing at this very moment? What are the sensations and feelings?

There are so many questions that we can ask in this situation. To be present is key. Especially when you are focused on what's going on right this second.

This is also a question that applies to various situations you see yourself in on a regular basis. Let's say you have a big presentation for work today. You're a Type Three that wants to nail this presentation to win a huge client for your company.

Before the presentation, you focus on how you're feeling right now. So, you take a few deep breaths, and you access your mindfulness. You're probably feeling a little nervous or even jittery.

You're probably jittery because you feel like there is no room for error. As a Three, you might not be satisfied with coming up short on things. That may be the reason why you feel the way you do.

You might even experience uncertainty. What happens after the presentation? How well will I do?

Feeling and knowing what you are experiencing in the present will allow you to identify any potential issues you may have. And you can correct it by simply putting certain practices based on your Type to good use. If you're a Three, it is important to stay calm and know that sometimes, you cannot win them all.

As a Three who maintains a healthy lifestyle, you do the presentation anyways. But you do it without attaching yourself to a certain outcome. Even if you don't succeed in landing the client, you will at least be recognized for putting a good presentation together.

After all, you are not in control of every final decision that isn't yours. But you will be recognized for having the guts of putting something together and putting the company's best interests ahead of everything else.

To know what you are experiencing in the present, take a moment and perform the usual mindfulness exercise. Be mindful of how you're feeling, how your body is functioning at the moment, and so on.

What am I anticipating? (The Future)

When it comes to the future, some of us are uncertain about it. For others, they are hopeful about it and some are fearful of it. But what we cannot do is predict it.

The future may hold something for all Enneagram types. But it all depends on their actions and how they handle the present. Your Enneagram type does not predetermine your future.

We speak of this anticipation in the context of how we handle the future depending on the good or bad of the event. If it's something good, we are happy with it. But what if the future as we know it is anything but that?

To anticipate something that is less than good creates an opportunity. An opportunity to handle the bad news. Enneagram types such as Sixes may fear bad news as it may be a threat to their security and stability.

Not to mention, Sixes may fear being put in the position of making a decision that they are uncomfortable with. Bad

225

news will come, but it's a matter of when. It can be tomorrow, next week, a month from now, and so on.

But how you handle that bad news when the time comes is what you need to consider? Each Enneagram type will learn how to handle the negativity in life based on their personal growth plan and how they will learn from it.

The key takeaway here is to prepare for the uncertainty that is the future. You have the ability to handle it accordingly whether it's good or bad based on your type. But you want to be at peace with the fact that sooner than later, future events may throw you off course due to the impact of it.

Final Thoughts

The Practice Triad teaches us about what we remember, what we experience, and what we anticipate. It will define us regardless of Enneagram type. We experience positive or negative feelings based on our past.

Our past may also shape our Enneagram personality. While in the present, we each have our way of handling the experiences that we're feeling at the moment. Accessing mindfulness to experience and note the feelings in the present will help you make note of it all.

Lastly, the future is something that we all anticipate. It is uncertain and we cannot predict it for sure. But what we can say is that the future holds good and bad.

At the end of the day, it's all about how we handle good news or events (and the bad). The Practice Triad teaches us to prepare for the future, be in the moment, and learn from the past as to why we are experiencing good or bad feelings. But when tying it all together, it allows us to better put things into practice using the Enneagram.

Section 1/Part 2
Discovering Your Type and Its Key Features (An Overview)

In the final part of Section One, we will be taking a look at discovering your type and go in-depth to discuss its key features. You will also be delighted to hear which famous and fictional person shares your Enneagram type.

We will go over things like their key features and characteristics (and explain why they exist for such a personality type). We will also discuss how you can spot someone who may be the same type as you (or be able to determine a specific Enneagram type that is different from you).

You will learn about what will motivate you as a person while finding out what actually stresses you out. We will also discuss what will likely happen if you live a healthy, average, or even unhealthy life.

One of the key things that we must avoid for every Enneagram type is living an unhealthy life. If you may be exhibiting behaviors that are unhealthy based on your Enneagram type, it's never too late to make any changes. Every Enneagram type has its own unique needs.

For example, Type Ones have a need to be perfect. Without going into further detail, they are the kind of people that look for change and would rather live in a world where there is perfect balance. You will also find out how you can fulfill those needs specific to your Enneagram type.

This part will help you better understand who you are as a person based on your Type that you have discovered via the test. You will become fully immersed in becoming the person you want to become based on your personality.

Later in the book, we will talk about repentance and reorientation. To give you a good idea of what we mean by this, we talk about repenting for your past mistakes and misgivings while making plans to chart a new course towards a more fulfilling life.

The chapters ahead based on each personality Type are things you will expect to happen in your life. Whether you live a healthy or average life, you will do your best to experience the positives of your Type while minimizing any of the negative behaviors and traits that may arise.

You are welcome to skip to the chapter that applies to your Enneagram type. At the same time, you may be inclined to read more about the other types and how they behave. That way, you may find yourself reading a person and being able to determine where they belong on the Enneagram.

Later on, we will break down the Enneagram in relationships. We will talk briefly about how each Enneagram type can interact with the other. Though we recommend this book as something to come back to for reference, you can read through about each type once, so you get a basic idea of identifying them once you have observed and gathered some necessary evidence proving your assumption.

You may be excited, even a little nervous about how you want to live your life based on your newfound Enneagram type (or confirmation that your assumed type was the right one all along). But we are here to help you chart the course and live a positive life filled with growth and promise.

Shortly after we go through each type, we will move onto the general practices and principles based on each type. But not before we go over a few things that will help you better understand your mission to grow into the healthy person you want to become.

If you're a Type One, you can move on to the next page. Otherwise, skip to the chapter that focuses on your Enneagram type in particular.

Chapter 18: Discovering Type 1s - The Need to Be Perfect

First, we will be taking a deep dive into Type One personalities of the Enneagram. We will discuss the behaviors, needs, and what a Type One normally does in various situations. Ones strive for perfection (hence the reason why they are considered to be perfectionists).

To paraphrase an old popular TV show, they love it when a plan comes together. But when something goes wrong, they are unhappy. They try to repress their negative feelings, but it can get to the point where they may spill over.

Type Ones are punctual. They hate making mistakes. And they want to avoid them as best as they can.

For their part, planning is something that they do constantly. They want to lay out everything and make sure it all goes accordingly. They will look over the plans multiple times over, if needed.

Because of their perfectionism, they will be upset at the slightest issue. And they may be viewed as the 'bad person' in the eyes of others. Deep down, they are trying to do something good.

The last thing they ever want to be is to be seen as the villain. Although we may have covered some of the bases about Type Ones (and other Enneagram types), let's give you a refresher on the key personalities and features:

Key Personality Traits of Ones

- **Serious and straightforward, especially in conversation**

- **Considered to be hardworking and diligent**

- **Usually practical and frugal**

- **Rigid when it comes to making plans and decisions**

- **Has high internal standards**

- **Able to concentrate with intensity**

- **Have a talent for teaching or instructing others**

Famous Ones:

Martha Steward, Hillary Clinton, Mahatma Gandhi, Elizabeth Warren, Nelson Mandela, Michelle Obama, Steve Jobs, Sully Sullenberger, Mary Poppins (Mary Poppins), Steve Rogers (Captain America), Hermione Granger (Harry Potter)

The Key Personality Traits of Ones In-Depth

Ones will plan accordingly and stick with the plan. The last thing they want is change. Everything should stay the same from start to finish.

When conversing with others, they are straightforward and unafraid to say what's on their mind. They have their goals and aspirations just like everyone else. And they know that if their plans are followed right down to the letter, they are assured achievement in their goals.

Ones settle for nothing but the best. In other words, an A+ is what they shoot for. An A- may be considered a slight disappointment (while a B could infuriate them).

Because of their rigidness with plans, they are punctual. They want to be somewhere on time. Tardiness is something that they will not appreciate most of the time.

Ones will feel responsible for being the glue that holds everything together. Maintaining order and making sure things don't fall apart may be something they are more apt to doing. So long as everything is under control, Ones will not have to worry about negative feelings such as anger or resentment.

Ones consider themselves ethical people. For this reason, they often find themselves evaluating or even adjusting their moral compass. Furthermore, they are willing to go the extra mile in order to strive for that perfection they look for constantly.

For Ones, they are striving for a greater good in the world. At the same time, they want to improve the general welfare of others. However, this may not be an easy thing to do.

Specifically, this is due to their perfectionist behavior. When things don't go their way, perfectionists may try to repress their feelings in order to preserve their image. However, when they express their feelings, they may be seen as the 'bad person'.

In the eyes of others, they may be worried that someone that acts negatively may not even care about the welfare of others. And that view alone may invoke guilt in a One. They want to make things right, but when it blows up in their face, they feel the need to work harder.

Why perfection is something they want to achieve is beyond us. But we can bet that a One wants things to be perfect rather than good enough. They feel that they have achieved their life's mission if their accomplishments are seen as perfect.

What Motivates A One?

When it comes to motivation, Ones are looking for ways they can change the world. They can volunteer and help those who are among the less fortunate. They are also in search of the right solutions to problems that currently exist.

Meanwhile, these achievements will factor into their own personal growth. They want to grow into someone who can make the best change possible. They want to live in an unblemished world.

They search for peace and balance (i.e. - 1w9 or 9w1). And they will stop at nothing until such a thing is accomplished. Those who are fighting in the name of issues such as social justice are often considered Ones.

The reason for this is that they want people to be equal and be treated as such. So, when persons of color are being treated unfairly, they will make a consistent stand until such changes are made. They can be in the middle of it and find the right solutions that will provide for a greater good.

Ones sacrifice their time and energy to make changes to the world. And that is something that should be appreciated. Ones draw from some of the characteristics that Twos have (which is being loving and helping others).

It would make a lot of sense seeing that Ones are searching for peace while helping the less fortunate live their lives free of any worry or chaos. It's fitting to see that Ones will have wings such as Nines and Twos.

What Stresses A One Out?

Ones may be stressed by receiving criticism from other people. Such criticism could be considered a blemish on what they otherwise perceived as perfect. Simply put, what might be perfect in one person's view may not be the same in another's.

Because they are not flexible in terms of scheduling and planning, many people will view Ones as inflexible (and thus hard to work with). Ones simply just stick to the plan and don't want to change course even on a whim.

They are often reminded of the corruption and blemishes of the world. They view the world for example like a shirt. No matter how many times they try to iron it, there is bound to be a wrinkle or two that will recurrently appear.

As such, they may feel like they are not making the difference they thought they were. They may feel like they are wasting their time planning things. But such a thought process exists when under duress or stress.

How To Recognize A One

Recognizing personality types like Ones (whether or not you're a One yourself) might come easy. So how do you know who is a Type One on the Enneagram? What kind of actions or mannerisms can you spot from either a foot or a mile away?

If you see someone who is well-organized both inside and out, they may be considered a One right from the jump. But those are not the only traits that you need to confirm that. Ones often complement their perfectionism with being punctual.
They also have an obligation to do what is right using their perseverance and willpower. They prefer to communicate directly with others. While communicating, they are honest and intentional about what they say.

They don't care about what they wear. But they will wear something that will never go 'out of style'. When we talk about relationships a bit further, we will explain in-depth about how Ones need a relationship that will last a long time.

Ones are people who carry their perfectionism over to the jobs or careers they work for. Most of them will be teachers because of their ability to teach and instruct others. They know that they are not the only ones who should be doing their part to make the world a better place.

They pass along their knowledge and wisdom to their students. Their plan is simple, to have their students apply everything they have learned from them. Deep down, they hope that the students who are amongst the Ones will pass it on to a newer generation.

Generations exist while old ones eventually die off. And so, the cycle continues. Ones want to make sure that cycle stays in motion long after they pass on.

Ones are often involved with causes and nonprofits that are designed to help a greater good. They are more focused on helping their community whenever the opportunity presents itself. When they find a cause they are passionate about, they will do as much as they can to ensure such positive change is achieved.

They want a world that is peaceful. They want people to be treated the same. Anything that is out of order, they will iron out that wrinkle.

When it comes to performing tasks, they are careful, so they don't make mistakes. They are methodological and meticulous. And they will go above and beyond to complete the tasks before them no matter how long it takes.

Healthy Vs Unhealthy Ones

Healthy

In a healthy life, Ones will take advantage of the abundant number of situations available to them. They know that there will be chaos in life (especially when it exists beyond their own control). So, they will need to accept that as such.

One of the things that drive them is justice and fairness. They believe that nobody should be given unfair or unjust treatment. They understand and accept diversity and humanity and embrace its further progress for the better.
At the highest level, Ones tend to be wise and realistic. They are smart to take the best action necessary. They are people with strong personal convictions and can distinguish right and wrong better than anyone else.

Average

In an average life, Ones are still keen on being organized. They will still follow strict ideals and will focus on causes they care about (especially those that are considered social causes). Whether it's personal or professional in their pursuits, they will do it with vigor. They may consider themselves workaholics because of their usual idiosyncrasy of going the distance to make sure something gets done.

They fear making mistakes and may be dissatisfied with reality depending on the day. Sometimes, they feel like their responsibilities are weighing on them a lot heavier than they are supposed to. It can get to the point where they may be working harder than they need to (and feel drained of their energy afterward).

On some days, they can be judgmental and picky. And they may tend to correct people more often than not. It may get to the point where they may be badgering them to do things correctly all the time.

Some of the negative behaviors for an Average One must be kept in check. Failure to do so can lead them down an unhealthy path. To better explain what can happen, let's move on to discuss the unhealthy traits of Ones.

Unhealthy

In an unhealthy situation, Ones will end up becoming out of touch with reality. As a result, they will focus on irrelevant things. They may also develop unhealthy obsessions or compulsions.

Furthermore, they will frequently nitpick the other person be it their opinions or the way they perform certain tasks. And that can cause anger and resentment among others. They do this in order to keep their self-image in line, which unbeknownst to them is distorted (hence being out of touch with reality).

239

When they reach a very unhealthy level, they may even condemn others. They may also resort to cruel tactics in order to get rid of anyone who may be viewed as 'wrongdoers'. Mentally, Ones may be susceptible to severe bouts of depression and even nervous breakdowns.

Ones may also be likely to attempt suicide. They may also develop Obsessive-Compulsive Disorders or even Depressive personality disorders. Either way, for Ones to reach such unhealthy levels, it can be hard to imagine that when they reach the lowest of lows, it may be difficult to get them out of it.

Final Thoughts

For Type Ones, they are perfectionists who are in search of changing the world for the better. Granted, their perfectionist behavior may turn others away. But there will be those who will look beyond it and understand their true desires and their fervent passion for getting something done a certain way.

They are driven, thrive on success, and are willing to work as hard and long as possible to achieve certain results. Yes, they live by high standards. But their reasons are not malicious as some may assume.

Type Ones want reform and will make sure all of their bases are covered in the process. They will make sure things fall in place and nothing is overlooked. They are caring people for the most part (especially when they are healthy).

But when they are teetering on average and unhealthy, that's when things reach a critical point. Ones must turn the corner and live a much healthier life. Not keeping it in check may lead to a much unhealthier life to where you may fall severely depressed or have a nervous breakdown.

When we talk about the practices for each Type, we will discuss which growth practices that Ones (and others) must follow in order to live a much healthier life based on the Enneagram. To conclude, Ones are not bad people because of their perfection and aspiration for change. They are on a mission that is all-or-nothing, and they make no bones about it.

Chapter 19: Discovering Type 2 - The Need to Be Needed

For a Type 2, they are always 'on call'. They are the person who makes themselves available whenever they are needed for something. Hence, they strive to fulfill that need to be...well, needed by others.

Twos are on a mission to make the world a better place like Ones. However, they feel the need to use their generosity and loving behavior as a way to improve the world little by little. When it comes to this 'feeling-based' Enneagram type, they have a heavy focus on their relationship with others.

The need to be needed and loved drives them to make as many connections as possible with other people. Emotional connection is something they will make nine times out of ten. Even though they are focused on others, they may find it difficult to focus on themselves.

They are caring, easy to communicate with, and drawn to other people because of their warmth. They are nice and even sympathetic. They are known for giving advice, even if it's unsolicited (which may infuriate some people).

Humility is something that they hold in high esteem. They experience that without feeling the need to inflate their self-worth or ego. They feel the need to feel special and important to those around them.

Key Personality Traits of Twos

- **They are warm (which they show through their eyes and smile)**

- **Easy to approach**

- **Very kind**

- **Show no shame in volunteering or being active in a cause**

- **Caring and gentle**

- **Thrives more as a team player than an authority**

- **Very patient**

- **Very nurturing**

Famous Twos:

Mother Teresa, Jimmy Carter, Nancy Reagan, Maya Angelou, Desmond Tutu, Lewis Carrol, Hagrid (Harry Potter), Pam Beesly (The Office), Samwise Gamgee (Lord of The Rings)

The Key Personality Traits of Twos In-Depth

Simply put, Twos wear their hearts on their sleeves. They are firm believers in altruism. When there is a cause that is near and dear to them, they will waste no time becoming part of the action. They will volunteer their time and energy when necessary.

As a result of this action, they uplift others as a result. This is something they can do with little to no effort required. Their values are rooted in kindness and reciprocity, thus it plays a major role in the decisions that they make.

When it comes to spending time with their loved ones, there is no place they'd rather be. They hold their family and those close to them in their hearts and minds. To them, there is no greater feeling that they can experience than the love they give and receive from those who love them most.

Looking in-depth at 2w1s, they are looking to make the world a better place based on helping others. Meanwhile, they exhibit the traits of Ones such as being a perfectionist. They make sure that no stone goes unturned and those who are important are loved and never forgotten.

They strive to make things better and fair for everyone. Those who deserve love and appreciation get it from Twos (when no one else delivers it). Meanwhile, 2w3s are more about connecting with other people and consider their ability to do so as measures of success.

2w3s want to be recognized for their loving behavior and the impact they have made on the world. Otherwise, they may feel like their efforts have gone unnoticed and unappreciated. But nevertheless, Twos regardless of their dominant wing are on a mission to connect positively with as many people as they can.

They are supportive and encouraging of others. And they are persistent and dedicated to the tasks that they set themselves with. Furthermore, their greatest accomplishments are usually lifting up others.

If that person they uplift feels good, a Two feels good as well. But sometimes, a Two may feel like they are not doing enough. Or when they feel like they are doing the positive, they might not know that they are stepping over the line.

When faced with negativity, Twos may feel like they are unloved. At the same time, they feel alone. When in reality, they shouldn't be the centerpiece of anyone's life but their own (in an unselfish way).

Twos originate from an environment where they may have never met those emotional needs such as love. They may come from families where there may have been one immediate family member (like a mother or father) that had never provided such love and affection throughout their childhood or even beyond.

For this reason, they feel that it is their duty to provide love for those who deserve it. They repress their own desires by putting others ahead of themselves. Whether those people on the other end have grown up in the same environment or not, Twos believe that people will appreciate being loved and cared for by others.

What Motivates Twos?

Twos are motivated by the feelings of love and being welcomed by others. On top of that, they are driven to help others and accomplish the goals related to it. Because of their desire to connect with others, they find meeting and befriending others a lot easier compared to other Enneagram types.

Because of their possible upbringing where love was not as abundant, that could be considered another thing that motivates them. Whatever they haven't received as a child, they can find other ways to receive it (and spread it to others).

That desire to feel love and appreciation can be fulfilled thanks to reciprocity. Twos believe that with such kindness and love, they will likely get it in return if done right. And nothing will make them happier than that.

What Stresses Twos?

There are things that can be a source of stress for Twos. Among them is rejection. The rejection from others because of their offerings to help or even rejection from a job they want to have.

If healthy, Twos can handle rejection. But it can still sting a bit to the point where they may be in a bad mood for most of the day. They can alleviate the pain by doing what they do best: helping others.

While they are focused on other people, the needs may grow as a result. One person may need one thing, while another may need something done urgently. And it can get to the point where a Two can feel overwhelmed.

One of the things that a Two may also fear is neglect. Especially when they may have dealt with it earlier in their lifetime. Feeling abandoned or neglected will make them feel like they are back at square one.

How To Recognize A Two

Twos are easier to spot in public. Typically, the Twos are often the people who give directions or advice. To the trained eye or someone who may recognize a Two, they'll know who they are when they see them.

Their aura makes them much easier to approach. On top of that, they appear to be attuned to the needs of others. Many people who speak of these people will usually throw the words 'father' or 'mother' around or the like.

While at home or by themselves, they make it a priority to keep in touch with the people they love most. Typically, they will invite people over for a meal or just for a visit. Regardless, they want to stay connected to those who are important to them.

Healthy vs Unhealthy Twos

Healthy Twos

Twos exercise selflessness when healthy. They are also fulfilled by freely giving love that is unconditional. They are comfortable with the idea of sharing their own needs with other people. Meanwhile, they are able to balance the give and take aspect of life easily.

When they practice mindfulness, they are also understanding of the true meaning of altruism. They are much aware of their self-worth and are willing to guide others whenever the need presents themselves. They have empathy and will have an easy time making heart-to-heart connections with others.

Average Twos

If Twos are average, they are mostly assuming the roles of martyr in the relationship. Meanwhile, they are searching for any way to feel important. This feeling is often acquired when focusing on the needs of others.

When they are reminded of how grateful people are to have Twos in their lives, the latter will feel like they have fulfilled their duties. To them, this is a positive mark on their image (something they tend to care about over time). Their attending to other persons' needs is continuous.

They can even pull out the cards of flattery or compliments in order to receive acceptance and appreciation from individuals and the entire community as a whole. They will seek approval and appraisal from others. If positive, they are happy (but not so much if the result is not to their liking).

Unhealthy Twos

If unhealthy, Twos will find themselves 'drowning' in self-despair. Furthermore, they also tend to fight fire with fire (or in this case, criticism with criticism). It can also get to the point where Twos can become clingy, even overbearing.

They may even be considered intrusive in regard to the lives of others. And it may get to the point where people may block Twos out of the way (even if it's for longer periods of time). Twos could even pull out the victim card and attempt to use it to their advantage (with getting sympathy and reassurance as the main goals).

At some point, Twos may also expose a side of them that may seem like the exact opposite of who they are. They will manipulate and blame others for their pain and suffering. When faced with criticism, Twos can get stressed out to the point where they could become physically ill.

Final Thoughts

Twos are an Enneagram type that can be easy to get along with when they are healthy. If you're a Two yourself, maintaining that healthy balance will need to be a priority. Especially when you want to be surrounded by positivity and love in your life.

You can continue to do the things that motivate you such as help other people, make meaningful connections, and provide your loved ones with the love and care they richly deserve. You are well aware that such things you give can be received.

Even though you give love and care, it may never be given back to you in return from others. And that's a harsh reality that you may need to accept as you begin your growth process. Twos bring a certain balance to the Enneagram.

There are personality types that are more firm than soft. And thus, the Twos are those who bring the softness. They want to be remembered by those as the go-to person whenever they are needed for something (whether it's advice or someone who can open their home).

In a world where humanity is questioned for its behavior all the time, there is still hope that Twos can set the example of how the world should operate. A world where people can care and love one another no matter their background or walk of life.

Chapter 20: Discovering Type 3 - Need to Succeed (Performer)

Type 3s have a need to succeed. That need will grow even more when they reach adulthood. At a young age, they have already achieved success in some form. Whether it was being elected to student government or obtaining a leadership role in a sports team, there is something of that magnitude on the resume of a Type 3.

Those accomplishments were done with some work involved. However, the other half of their success is usually given credit to the peers that recognize and appreciate their accomplishments. So, they may have confidence and ambition as if they were given to them as a natural gift.

Once they reach adulthood, that's when reality kicks in. While they did put in some work and gained recognition in the process, they now realize that they must work harder than ever. Because when thrust into a new environment, they are in a new starting point (or zero).

And as the old saying goes, everyone has to start somewhere. From there, Threes will do their best to work hard and ride that wave of success and recognition. Some days they will feel like it's a pointless thing to do.

By embracing hard work, commitment, and the drive to do their best, Threes can accomplish their goals regardless of their line of work or career. Their accomplishments may be talked about well into their older years and even after they pass on.

Immortality may be what a Type 3 aims for. But that may be considered a stretch, even for a Three. But the accomplishments and accolades of one person can live on through the stories of others.

Key Personality Traits of Threes

- **A long resume of accomplishments**

- **Busy with meetings and has a full plate schedule**

- **Aware of social niceties**

- **Their appearance is refined**

- **Charismatic and easily can make first impressions**

- **Busy and usually on the move**

- **May have an interest in acting or improvising**

Famous Threes

Bill Clinton, Tony Robbins, Oprah Winfrey, Arnold Schwarzenegger, Muhammad Ali, Reese Witherspoon,

Don Draper (Mad Men), Leslie Knope (Parks and Recreation)

The Key Personality Traits of Threes In-Depth

Starting off with a story about a Three in particular, we'll talk about Bill Clinton. Whether you agree or disagree with his politics, he is considered one of the most charismatic public figures in the world. During his time as President of the United States, he had accomplished a wide variety of tasks that had benefited the country and the world.

Before Clinton graced his presence at the White House, he had already achieved plenty of accolades. In high school, he was involved in plenty of activities. It was his senior year when he accomplished many accolades, the school principal denied Clinton the opportunity to add another accomplishment to his resume: class president.

Despite that stoppage, that didn't stop Bill Clinton from achieving his goals and aspirations. Even if there is someone in the way of your hopes, dreams, and aspirations, you as a Three have an unstoppable momentum to continue on. You might have already achieved so much at a young age that you may feel like you can continue doing great things as an adult.

However, you as a Three must understand that you have to put in the work in order to achieve a new level of success and accomplishment. When you graduate from school, you technically step outside of your comfort zone. From there, it's like the difficulty of the game of life gets harder.

You start a new chapter in your life with some of what's left of your support system from school. But that isn't enough to achieve new goals and aspirations. You'll need to build a network of people who will help support your aspirations and goals.

Thankfully, you can use your charisma and ability to connect with others to lay the foundation of your next waves of success. This may seem like a trivial thing to do. But when you look back on your accomplishments, you will be proud of yourself for taking the initiative.

Threes are busy people and will always have a full plate of things going on in their schedule. Whether it's their studies, practice, or something else, Threes are always on the go. But they are not void of any social deficiencies since they will be around people almost constantly.

Aside from their accomplishments, Threes care about their outward appearance. They believe that even though they play the part of an ambitious, successful person, they must dress for the part as well. They may be snazzy dressers compared to others on the Enneagram.

Of all the types of the Enneagram, Threes have the most interesting wings (Wings 2 and 4). 3w2s are those who are outgoing, friendly, and will measure their accomplishments based on serving others. They are specialists at connecting with people and making them feel good.

For this reason, 3w2s can be great at running a business, entertaining others, or even marketing. They can be in tune with other people's emotions like nothing. And they will have no problem connecting with others.

Meanwhile, 3w4s will seek recognition in the form of their creativity. These are the types of Threes that are a bit more introverted than their 3w2 counterparts. As far as their accomplishments are concerned, they rely more on their work and creativity as opposed to making connections with other people.

Regardless, Threes are focused on their personal growth based on their accomplishments. They will connect with other people be it face-to-face or when someone is exposed to a Three's work.

What Motivates A Three?

The answer is a no-brainer. It's the recognition for all of their accomplishments. The feeling of love and being accepted by others is also another thing that will motivate Threes (especially 3w2s in particular).

Whenever there is a new goal that surfaces in their mind, Threes will waste little to no time in making sure that they accomplish it with a plan in mind. When given the opportunity to speak in a public setting or meet new people, a Three will not say no most of the time.

As long as there is an opportunity to give themselves exposure and put their names out there, a Three will jump on it without hesitation. Think about the time you had the opportunity to go on television for something you have accomplished or have taken part in.

Or better yet, think of a time when you presented something to members of the public. You showcase your accomplishment to others and people are delighted. Thinking back on it will give you the drive and confidence to get other stuff done in the future.

What Stresses A Three Out?

There are some things that can bring stress to a Three. For one, they might be stressed because they feel like they need to entertain everyone constantly. It can feel like a full-time job for them.

On top of that, they may have fears of repeatedly failing to solve a problem or even have difficulty in doing so. They hate it when they are perceived in a negative light. This perception they believe may hurt their self-image (something they pay attention to most of the time).

When it comes to their own emotions, reconciling them might be a challenge. Above all else, one of a Three's greatest fears is fading into obscurity. Even when they have found success in an earlier part of their life, to be forgotten or be a 'nobody' is nothing a Three wants to see.

Healthy vs Unhealthy Threes

Healthy

When Threes are at the highest level of health, they accept themselves for who they are. Furthermore, they are authentic and inner-directed. At times, they can be giving and modest.

They are always one for cracking jokes, especially when it's at the expense of themselves. They feel good most of the time. They have plenty of energy with a high self-esteem to match.

Threes believe in themselves more often than others. They are their own personal cheerleaders. When in the presence of others, they are charming, gracious, and good to be around.

Finally, Threes have an undying ambition to improve themselves. They may be satisfied with their current state. But they will be hungry for improvement when the time comes.

Think of it like a computer. It always has updates (be it minor or major). Threes will tend to improve themselves over time even if they are riding waves of success.

Average

An average Three will usually be concerned about how well they are performing. They worry sometimes about whether or not they are doing a good enough job. For the most part, the one thing that terrifies them is failure.

Sometimes, they may get into a habit of comparing themselves to others. They think about what they could try and do to be better than that person. That's where their competitiveness tends to ratchet up a bit.

Being competitive is the norm for Threes. However, average Threes may stomp down on the pedal from time to time. And that could also lead to them having issues about their image and how they are perceived in the eyes of others.

They may worry more about their image or the opinion of others. They may feel like they are suffering from 'imposter syndrome'. They may feel like their credibility is not what they assume.

When things start to shift towards the unhealthy side, Threes will look for attention. And at times, their ways of attracting it may borderline on overkill.

They will try to display their superiority with the intent to impress others. They can be self-promoting and behave almost to the point of narcissism. Arrogance may also be one of the Three's negative qualities if it reaches a borderline unhealthy level.

Unhealthy

As mentioned with average, a Three's competitive behavior may be taken a step up. Whereas an unhealthy Three will stop at nothing when it comes to competition. Anyone they perceive as a competition or a threat to their success, a Three will 'obliterate'.

They will exploit and be opportunistic when such conditions are present. They can even be deceptive to which their mistakes may never be exposed unless someone else says otherwise. Threes may even resort to betraying or sabotaging others in order to get ahead.

Threes will likely be jealous of others. It can also get to the point where they may display vindictive behavior. They will operate under the guise of 'if I cannot be happy, no one deserves to be happy'.

For this reason, they will develop an unhealthy obsession for destroying other people or things that may remind them of their failures. The way they will behave will be considered psychopathic. Threes are more than likely to develop Narcissistic Personality Disorder than anyone within the Enneagram.

Final Thoughts

Threes are performers, public figures, and those who want to keep a high profile. They are the most visible of any Enneagram type up to this point. Their accomplishments are always talked about and revered by many in their younger years.

They are indeed busy people with full schedules. They can handle the pressure of it all if they are healthy enough. If you're a Three, you will always find yourself hungry to achieve something and get recognized for it.

Without any goals that you aim to accomplish, you'll feel like a car without the engine. Your ambition and your goals are that engine that keep you going. The praise and admiration that you receive is the fuel that keeps you going the distance

In order for Threes to stay on top, maintaining a healthy lifestyle is important. They must adhere to practices that will ensure that they stay healthy both in the mental and physical sense. When they do, Threes will always be on top of their game when it comes to what they can achieve next.

Threes want to be in the limelight for as long as possible. Even if it means for the rest of their life.

Chapter 21: Discovering Type 4 - Need to Be Special (Romantic)

Type 4s embrace their individuality. They want to be known as the '1 of 1' rather than '1 of 100' or even '1 of 1000000'. They don't want to be the same as everyone else.

They feel the need to be special not just for their own individual identity, but also, they want to be considered a special person someone can love. They are motivated by their desires to be loved and feel special emotional connections with someone. Without it, they may seem like they have nothing to look forward to.

They fear missing out on the things that make other people happy. Specifically, they believe that feeling special makes people happy. But what makes people special in the eyes of others?

The answer to that question may vary from person to person. That person may feel special because of the love they receive from others. Or they may receive it for their praise for their creative work.

Either way, Fours are searching for some kind of connection. At the same time, they are looking for that one person that will make them special (a 'rescuer'). Fours can live a healthy life based on the Enneagram (but when it reaches unhealthy levels, that's when things can get really bad).

Key Personality Traits of Twos

- Very creative most of the time

- Passionate about self-expression

- Prominent in terms of artistic outlets

- Quirky

- Have an inner and outer presentation that is distinctive from others

- May be melancholic in expression

- Have a strong sense of identity

- May feel emptiness at times

Famous Fours

Frida Kahlo, Bob Dylan, Prince, Johnny Depp, Kurt Cobain, Stevie Nicks, Sylvia Plath, Prince Charles, Luna Lovegood (Harry Potter), Anne Shirley (Anne Of Green Gables)

The Key Personality Traits of Fours In-Depth

Taking a look at the famous Fours on the list, many of them are legendary in their own craft. That's because most of them put their emotions into their work. Taking a look at Stevie Nicks for example: when Fleetwood Mac did 'Rumors', the entire band created such excellent music that it is considered to be one of the greatest musical albums in history.

Behind the scenes, there had been emotions overflowing and tempers flaring. The band may have expressed their emotions greatly song after song. Nicks herself is known for invoking a lot of emotion in her songs.

Fours will waste little to no time at all expressing their feelings without uttering a single word. It's spoken through their work. And they will make sure that the emotion (whatever it may be) is amplified.

Fours are remembered each for their individual achievements. Kurt Cobain was remembered for his unrivaled contributions to the grunge rock genre. Sylvia Plath wrote poetry that expressed her melancholic emotions.

You may be remembered for someone who stood out among the rest in a certain way. The emotions you invoke may not matter. When people look at the work you do, there's a good chance that they'll feel it (almost to the point where it connects with them personally).

Even though Cobain, Plath, and other Fours may not be alive anymore, they achieved their goal to leave a lasting impression on the world. Their creations are still talked about even to this day. Considering they have a Three wing, they have that same aspiration for recognition and wanting to make a name for themselves.

Unlike Threes, Fours are mostly reserved or withdrawn. They can handle people in only small doses. But other than that, they may not have the same quality that Threes have in terms of connecting with people directly.

Fours can connect with others without making it a face-to-face thing. Those connections can be made in an art gallery when someone is browsing around and sees a painting that really strikes them. Or when someone listens to a song and they start to feel the emotion and relate to the musician.

Fours use their imagination and always go deep into the bag of tricks when it comes to their creativity. They instantly know the kind of emotion they want to express (while invoking a similar emotion in others). They want people to laugh, cry, smile, and so on.

What Motivates A Four?

Fours are motivated by building connections and relationships with other people. But here's where things get tricky: they tend to be withdrawn whenever they are somewhere with large groups of people present. So, they would be more comfortable with connecting with smaller groups.

They can connect with large groups of people through their work. Their work acts like a representative on behalf of a Four. That's as close as they are going to get with making their rounds with a large group.

They usually won't turn down the opportunity to meet with someone and connect with them one on one. They will usually have something interesting to say such as their past creations and the like. Otherwise, they will spend time reconnecting with themselves.

Another thing that motivates them is their desire to feel special. They want to be loved and appreciated by others. But they also want to be loved by someone who will accept them for being their own unique selves.

Another motivation may stem yet again from Threes. Fours can experience the feeling of accomplishment and recognition through their work. For this reason, they will usually use that as fuel and inspiration to do more work.

They feel that special connection with people who consider themselves fans of a Fours work. It's another one of the kinds of love that they appreciate (and makes them feel special in the process).

What Stresses A Four Out?

If there is one thing that stresses a Four out, it's their lack of creativity. When their creative juices aren't flowing, it frustrates them to no end. As mentioned, they cannot handle people in large doses.

If given the opportunity, they will find a way to escape whenever there are large groups of people in their presence. They are also no fans of meaningless conversation. Because they don't feel any kind of connection from them.

They would much rather discuss things deeply rather than make it sound casual. They search for that deep connection with other people. If there are conversations that don't produce it, it's a waste of time for Fours.

When they are in an argument, they will hate the idea of being in that argument or be interrupted for saying their piece.

How To Recognize A Four

If you see an individual who is considered off-beat, exudes a strong sense of self-identity and being unique, more than likely they are Fours. You may be listening to music or watching stand-up comedy and immediately can tell who the Fours are (assuming you can recognize them quickly).

They want to be accurate in their presentations and expose their true selves. They are open people and will make no bones about their emotions. They evaluate their decisions and determine whether or not it aligns with their personal values.

When they are out in public, they usually are in places that are not crowded. For example, they would much rather be happier shopping in thrift stores and flea markets rather than places like Wal-Mart or Target.

Healthy vs Unhealthy Fours

Healthy

When Fours are at their healthiest, their creative works can be monumental. They may have a habit of creating such works that will provoke thought and shift perspectives. Most of their ideas will be produced outside of the box.

They will be highly attuned to their emotions. Meanwhile, they may be the caterpillars that turn into butterflies. They may be dormant for a period of time only to come out swinging with very expressive creations.

And Fours are no strangers to creating beautiful things. When they do at this stage, they often will wow their audiences. And they may evoke strong emotions in them.

Average

When in a stressful situation, average Fours will take it out on their creative abilities. They may feel better connecting with like-minded people and utilize them as a source for support and inspiration.

Indeed, they seek authenticity. But they may acquire that at the expense of others (especially when it comes to their patience and their emotions). Average Fours may be self-absorbed at times.

But their individuality will allow them to maintain their own mood and inspiration. At times, they may be hypersensitive to criticism. As a result, they may be looking for praise and flattery.

Though some people do appreciate being modeled after, average Fours find it a great source of annoyance when someone tries to copy or relate to their experiences. This may be detrimental to their ability in fulfilling that desire of being loved and feeling special.

Unhealthy

Unhealthy Fours in extreme cases may lose touch with reality. And they may find themselves coping with their lives using alcohol or even hallucinogenic drugs. They will try and look for that 'missing link' in their life (even if it means hitting dead end after dead end).

In their search, they may feel like they are spinning their wheels. Meanwhile, they may exhibit self-destructive behavior and thoughts. They may feel like something about them is broken. It can also get to the point where Fours can become absolute hermits.

They will have no presence online and may never be seen by others offline. They may be seldom seen in public. Some may even wonder whether or not a Four may be alive or even dead after such time of not being seen.

Final Thoughts

Fours are their own unique person. And they want to be remembered for expressing their feelings and emotions through their art of choice. They are willing to connect with people so long as they are in small groups.

Otherwise, they can connect with people with their creations acting as some kind of buffer. They want love and appreciation just like everyone else. If and when they receive it, they will feel their healthiest and shine the brightest.

Fours must never sink into unhealthy levels as it may cause them to exhibit self-destructive behavior. It can also get to the point where they may be closed off to reality and may never emerge again (albeit for very rare occurrences). The need to feel special and loved can be fulfilled for Fours (and it can take the right kind of people to deliver it).

Chapter 22: Discovering Type 5 - The Need to Perceive (Observer)

If there is one Enneagram type that might be the most interesting or enigmatic, it's Fives. They are penchants for investigating things that happen beyond the 'surface'. The things that happen out in the open and plain sight, Fives observe that.

They have a need to perceive what is happening beyond what our eyes see. They are about knowing the 'how', 'why', and 'what' in terms of every living or working thing. If it exists, they may study it in detail.

Their attention to detail is unmistakable. It might be something that gives Ones a run for their money in that regard. Furthermore, they feel like they can help people with their investigative abilities.

However, Fives exhibit some of the traits of their Four and Six wings (which will be explained in more detail later on in the chapter). But they use them in situations where they are using their best traits, investigating, and seeking deeper knowledge of things.

Being useless is one of their chief fears. They want to be of help and want to work behind the scenes. They feel their skills of being observant are something that should not be underestimated.

Key Personality Traits of Fives

- Have in-depth knowledge on specific topics of interest

- Known for giving out insightful and thought-out responses

- Sets clear boundaries between their personal and professional lives

- Extremely independent and can withdraw themselves in social situations

- Difficult to decode

- Can be lost in thought or forgetful

Famous Fives

Albert Einstein, Jane Goodall, Stephen King, Mark Zuckerberg, Tim Burton, Steven Hawking, Belle (Beauty and the Beast), Sherlock Holmes, Dr. Gregory House (House)

The Key Personality Traits of Fives In-Depth

Fives will spend a lot of time figuring out problems that may seem difficult to solve by the average person. They will run into as many dead ends as possible, but they consider that the norm. While Thomas Edison may not have been a Five on the Enneagram, a quote of his in particular sums up a Five to an extent:

"I have not failed. I just found 10,000 ways that won't work".

Granted, this is when they are testing out different solutions. Other than that, they are just exploring the why, how, and what makes things exist or work. They dig much deeper than most people.

Since they spend time with themselves, they invest that time in whatever they can find in terms of knowledge. Like Fours, Fives can work well with small groups. So large groups may be considered a no-go.

On the other side of the Five, they have a quality that defines Sixes. That is loyalty. Fives who are loyal to solving a problem are considered troubleshooters.

They don't give up until they find a solution that actually works. Fives feel like they can serve a purpose without connecting with too many people. They may be the go-to people for their observant and investigative mannerisms.

Fives want to be helpful by providing others with ideas. Fives can create ideas for themselves. But they are faced with the issue of bringing them to light or not.
If Fives wish not to execute on their ideas, they may delegate them to someone who will (i.e. - a Seven). A Five may be the idea generator while a Seven may be the idea tester. So, to an extent, they can work in some way.

When it comes to their emotions, Fives are usually guarded. Hence, they may be hard to crack and read. For this reason, they may consider themselves enigmas (or mystery people).

They are minimalists when it comes to their workspace. But they will always keep a stockpile of things that reflect their specific interests. As such, Fives will focus on one interest as opposed to several of them.

Fives are not the 'do-it-all' types unlike Sevens. They focus on one thing and may be considered experts of such interest. They may or may not wear the 'expert' or 'guru' hate.

While they may know a lot, they may not always have the answers. But if you were to ask them a question about their interest or favorite topic, they would be happy to answer it at the snap of a finger.

Self-sufficiency is no stranger to Fives. They do crave freedoms and autonomy from the rest of the world. They will thrive in conditions where they work alone.

Fives will not work in groups. The reason being may be due to stressful situations that may exude from others working alongside a Five. Simply put, Fives do not work when there is a tense work environment.

What Motivates Fives?

The idea of discovering new things and ideas is not lost on Fives. It motivates them, even gets them out of bed on days when they want to sleep in. Because they prefer to work alone, it gives them the opportunity to reconnect with themselves.

When alone, they will find a skill or technique that they want to learn and potentially master. As long as the skill is helping not just themselves but others, they will spend as much time as they can making sure their craft is good enough. As a result, they desire to feel valued, appreciated, and able to do what is asked of them.

Once they have accomplished something, they don't care if they get the recognition or not. But they do know that their contributions are making some kind of a difference.

What Stresses Out Fives?

Like Fours, Fives cannot fathom the idea of being around large groups of people. Not to mention, they don't want to work in groups. They feel that if they do, they may feel like they have to meet the requirements of others.

Overstimulation and environments where peace and quiet are considered absent make a Five uncomfortable. They would rather work in peace (thus giving them maximum focus). Emotional situations will often be a source of stress for a Five.
They also are no fans of expressing their emotions. They are tough nuts to crack. And the last thing they want to do is crack under any kind of pressure or emotion.

You may feel the need to withdraw yourself and find a silent place to gather your thoughts and regroup. So, you rely on mindfulness exercises to identify the problem and address the issue if necessary.

How To Identify A Five

Fives will usually be more stoic than others. They may also express detachment as well. But what really makes a Five easily recognizable is their fascination for ideas that have yet to be explored.

The one thing that will excite Fives more than anything is spending hours by themselves. If they talk about it often, you know right away that they are a Five. They talk about their personal projects and the research they came up with.

Most of the time they are calm and collected. But if you bring up a subject of interest that they like, they will light up and talk about it until they are blue in the face. They may know every nook-and-cranny of an interest that not a lot of people may not know about.

They may be unaware of their hidden passions. Thus, it gives them the opportunity to explore it more.

Healthy vs Unhealthy Fives

Healthy

At their healthiest, Fives aspire to become the pioneers in their favorite interests. They express their intellectual assets in regard to it. They will educate and talk about it with others who might be interested in learning more.

When it comes to the largest and most complex issues, they use their clarity and precision to see it from various angles. They are dedicated and always curious about making changes. When it comes to bringing forth ideas of innovation and ways of thinking, Fives are confident (but keep that confidence to themselves). They believe that whatever is considered impossible may somehow become possible.

They will waste little to no time sharing their findings, predictions, and everything in between with others. They become experts and are often the go-to people in their field. When it comes to complicated things, Fives somehow make it simple.

Fives will be more apt to tackle mind-boggling topics without feeling like they are 'hurting their brains'. They are figuring out the 'how', 'what', and 'why'. And they provide the clearest insights, better than anyone else.

Average

Average Fives will exhibit some behaviors of a Four. This includes being offbeat. But most of the time, they will usually be by themselves.

Their emotions will be closed off to the world. Meanwhile, they will continue to focus on their interests while they are out of the view of the public. While in public, they may come off as aloof and distant.

Fives are considered to be 'bookworms'. They always have their noses in a book that discusses their interests. They may even have a large collection of books that they'll go through.

Their idea of fun isn't just reading. They like to play card games or even strategy games such as chess. Fives are very strategic and will usually think a few steps ahead of their opponent.

If you ever find yourself in a chess match, the length of the game will depend on your skill. If you keep making blunder after blunder, a Five could find a way to go from start to checkmate in fewer moves. But if you are equally skilled at the same as they are, it might be fun to watch as an observer.

Unhealthy

Given their desire to isolate themselves from the rest of the world, unhealthy Fives will use that to their advantage. It will get to the point where they cut themselves from their social lives. From there, they may start to develop tunnel vision.

Their views may be far-off, if not radical, from others. Their grip on reality will progressively weaken. Fives will even find themselves in contentious disputes without a clear answer.

In other words, it may be arguments with little or no substance present. For all their knowledge, this is a shocking negative trait for Fives. Fives may lose friendships for this reason and may even be taken by surprise.

However, they may rationalize that loss of friendship by saying they are better off. They think that without the company of people, things will be peaceful. This will give them the perfect reason to close themselves off from the real world.

Their power to investigate and gain knowledge will become some kind of weapon of mass destruction. To translate this, Fives may even find themselves diving into some kind of ridiculous conspiracy theories (and possibly believe them). They may cling onto them as if their lives depend on it.

At their unhealthiest, Fives may become misanthropic. They shudder at the thought or even action of interacting with people.

Final Thoughts

Fives may be the most interesting, if not enigmatic, personality type on the Enneagram. They may disconnect themselves from people or even the world itself at times. And that suits them just fine.

They will gather a wealth of knowledge and ideas. Whether they put it to good use will depend on their mood. If they feel like they can be capable and competent, they will provide whatever knowledge they can to those who need it.

They are at their happiest whenever they talk about their interests. Especially the one interest that they focus on almost to the point of obsession. You can hear them talking about their interest with passion and conviction.

On the surface, they are smart people. But at times, they can be mysterious. You cannot quite figure out how they are feeling at times.

Furthermore, they don't express their emotions in front of others. They do that whenever they isolate themselves from the world. As a Five, you may be thinking steps ahead of the rest of the world.

You may even have an 'extra pair of eyes', allowing you the ability to see things others do not. What others see in plain sight and on the surface, Fives have the power to see beyond that. The Investigator might dig as deep as they can to find the answers for themselves or others that need it.

Chapter 23: Discovering Type 6 - Need for Security (Loyal Skeptic)

There are people out there who ask for nothing more than someone who is loyal and will never forsake their friends or family. To a Six, this is something that they take seriously. They are loyal to their friends, family, causes they believe in, and so on.

However, there are times when Sixes question whether or not they are getting that loyalty in return. They may seem to question the motives of those who are treating them positively. Indeed, a Six provides security and loyalty to other people.

But they are firm believers in reciprocity. At the same time, they believe that there are people out there that won't reciprocate in the same way. As a Six, you finish what you start.

You stick with things that matter to you. You don't jump from one thing to the next quickly. Giving up is something you never even do.

If you're a Six, you might be considered one of the best people to get along with on the Enneagram. You will be admired for your tenacity and loyalty. But you may also worry about who your real friends are whenever you run into a tight spot.

You help others when they are in the same situation. You prove yourself worthy of being a real friend or family member. And you provide that person with some kind of stability (while they themselves worry about who their real friends are as well).

Meanwhile, they are the kind of people who will ride or die with those who they consider important. They will stick by the people who they respect immensely (be it an authority figure or a friend).

Key Personality Traits of Sixes

- Very good at managing their finances

- A team player

- Excellent communicators

- They are usually in a tight-knit group of friends

- Very precise and detail-oriented

- Well-liked by their peers

Famous Sixes

Mark Twain, Tom Hanks, Marilyn Monroe, Joe Biden, George H.W. Bush, Julia Roberts, Woody Allen, Ellen DeGeneres, Richard Nixon, Hamlet (Hamlet)

The Key Personality Traits of Sixes In-Depth

Despite a Sixes chief desire to be a team player rather than an authority figure, at least three of the famous Sixes listed above served as President of the United States. While they may be authority figures themselves, they may rely on their advisors frequently for advice

Sixes are separated into two different categories: phobic and counter-phobic. Up to this point, we have never separated any of the Sixes into categories that don't apply to their wings. Let's explain the difference between phobic and counter-phobic Sixes:

Phobic Sixes: One of the things a Phobic Six is known for is flying under the radar. They distance themselves from those that appear to be their sources of fear. When it comes to their vulnerabilities and weaknesses, Phobic Sixes are willing to express them. They do this in order for people to understand where they are coming from.

Counter-Phobic Sixes: Those who are considered Counter-Phobic Sixes possess an irrational fear. They may even be a little high-strung. When it comes to their self-image, they tend to be independent. They are tough on the outside, but on the inside, they face uncertainty about things.

Sixes may have grown up in situations where they had a parental figure that may have been overbearing, even overprotective. Sixes may have originated from unsafe environments or have experienced traumatic events that may be instrumental in how they see the world. They see the world as a dangerous place.

For this reason, Sixes may see non-Sixes as a threat. Especially to things such as their trust. So, they may be guarded to the max.

Sixes use their heads and therefore consider themselves to be logical. They are always strategizing and planning for the future. They may even take a page out of the Five's book and lay low while putting together a plan that they will stick with until the task is complete.

They also plan for what could be the worst. When the 'stuff hits the fan', Sixes have a plan that is set and ready to be executed when the situation warrants it. Their family is their top priority.

They will do everything in their power to protect their family and loved ones, providing them with the security they need. They want to cover their bases as much as possible. Safety and security are paramount for all, in the eyes of a Six.

You may be considered a survivalist in the view of others. Typically, those who value their life more than anything will often find ways to stay alive in the direst of situations. Sixes are the best at handling fear compared to the rest of the Enneagram.

Despite the fear of the worst, Sixes press on. Either they achieve a task, or they die trying. Thus, it's a trait that is admirable by most.

What Motivates A Six?

Sixes will want nothing more than relationships that are consistent and trustworthy. They know that such relationships are secure and are less likely to fall apart. They are often helpful and willing to assist others if and when needed.

They love spending time with their family more than others. They may have a best friend or two they may spend time with as well. When it comes to personal beliefs and values, nobody is more loyal or consistent to stick with them quite like a Six.

Sixes will most likely never change their worldview on things. It may take a lot for them to do so. But their loyalty will make them stubborn to change.

What Stresses Out A Six?

A Six will usually be concerned about security on the other end. They have provided loyalty and security to others. The question is: do they get that in return.

Sixes abhor unreliable people. And they are no fan of negativity in their environments (both at home and at work). They hate making crucial, if not critical decisions.

They feel that those decisions may be considered a bad thing. Furthermore, they may feel like they have made the wrong decision long after the fact. This is one of the reasons why they don't see themselves as authority figures in the slightest.

They always have a plan to ensure that their bases are covered. They are not perfectionists like Ones. As long as they know they have a plan in place, they will be good to go.

How To Recognize A Six

Sixes will usually blend into their social sphere without issue. They are usually those who are supportive of others and their endeavors. Most of the time, they are tolerant.

Sixes may be difficult to spot on the street. However, if you enter a professional environment like an office, you'll be able to recognize one with ease. They are the employees that stay late and work overtime.

They usually tend to be private people whenever they feel the need to keep things to themselves. Other than that, they are in search of reassurance for the actions they take. They also have an excellent skill of observing potential trouble that may be far away, but closing in.

Healthy vs Unhealthy Sixes

Healthy

While at their healthiest, Sixes are the kind of people who will trust themselves with ease. And they can trust others to an extent. They are independent but are willing to cooperate with others.

They have belief in themselves, giving them an extra boost of courage and positivity. They know the difference between authority and leadership. Thus, they would be happy to take the lead on things without wielding any kind of authoritative power.

They tend to elicit emotions that are strong. They exude a positive attitude to where people can trust them from the beginning. They have no problem bonding with others and may even make some sacrifices to push other people forward.

Sixes create what they see for themselves, stability and security. They believe that as long as they provide it, they may get it in return.

Average

Average Sixes will still focus on what they think may be stability and security. They stay organized and well-structured. However, they may seek to form alliances to ensure that their stability and security will be ever-present.

They may also look to authority on a regular basis to check on the status of their stability and security (even in the most subtle way). They are vigilant and are always on alert for potential threats to their stability.

However, they may resist growing demands being thrown their way. When stressed, they may become passive-aggressive or even evasive. They will also be indecisive and put off tasks that may be considered important.

They can be anxious regarding potential instability and danger. When faced with insecurities, a Six can become belligerent and blame others for their issues. They may even become 'guarded' towards people they are not familiar with.

Sixes can easily get defensive and reactive. This behavior may divide people and force them to choose a side. Meanwhile, Sixes are hypervigilant on who may become a potential threat.

One thing that is stunning is that Sixes become authoritative when border-lining average and unhealthy. Basically, they do something that is uncharacteristic of them.

Unhealthy

At this point, Sixes believe that their security has been compromised. This will allow them to slip into a state of panic. They may even become volatile in their behavior.

They will feel like they are defenseless. For this reason, they will seek out stronger beliefs or even a stronger authority figure to handle their problems. Meanwhile, they will berate other people and even become divisive.

Unhealthy Sixes may even develop some kind of paranoia. They will feel like someone is out to get them. They may act out irrationally at others.

Unhealthy sixes may always be searching for an escape from what they believe is their punishment. They can develop self-destructive behavior as well. It may be possible to not rule out suicide as a potential risk factor for unhealthy Sixes.

To make matters worse, Sixes may find themselves 'on the skids'. And they may rely on alcohol and drugs as possible coping mechanisms. Mental disorders such as paranoia or even Passive-Aggressive personality disorders are prominent amongst unhealthy Sixes.

Final Thoughts

Sixes are loyal at heart and in mind. But if they give stability and security to others, they will usually expect it in return. Sixes are usually on solid ground when they are healthy.

But when they are unhealthy, they will feel like they have failed themselves and those that they care about. And the way they behave will make matters worse. That is why it is paramount for Sixes (and other Enneagram types) to ensure that they instill practices that will allow them to maintain a healthy lifestyle.

Sixes are consistent and will always stick by the people who they consider most important. They are easy to get along with and they are trustworthy. They work hard and excel in situations where they would rather work behind the scenes.

While they are not authoritative, they won't mind taking a leadership role. They will use that role to encourage others to do their part. This will prove themselves to their authority figures as someone who takes the initiative and is willing to work well with others.

Whether you're a Six or not, these are the kind of people who you want in your life. Especially when you fear that you may or may not have real friends yourself. Loyalty is placed at a premium, especially in today's society.

While people may deceive and lie to other people just to get ahead, it's a sign of unhealthy behavior. A Six on the Enneagram is the antithesis of that.

Chapter 24: Discovering Type 7 - Need to Avoid Pain (Epicure)

One of the things that Sevens desire most is the need to avoid pain. To better describe this pain, it's mostly emotional and mental. If such a thing happens to a Seven, they may not be interested in doing the things that they love the most.

Sevens are enthusiastic and mostly happy. And such pain they are trying to avoid is a direct threat to their happiness and mental well-being. That's why it is important for Sevens to stay healthy or even on the 'high average' scale.

Sevens want a fulfilling, satisfying life. They know that they can achieve that with their can-do attitude. Without it, they are nothing.

Their goal is to live a good life. They don't want to be bored to death, sad, or uninspired in the slightest. So, they set out to seek multiple interests.

Unlike Fives that focus on one thing, Sevens are the kind of people that want to try anything they can (within reason). Most of the time, they never met an interest that they didn't like. One of their mottos in life is 'don't knock it until you try it'.

Key Personality Traits of Sevens

- Always on the move

- Very enthusiastic and energetic

- Have curiosity shown in their eyes

- A very wide range of interests

- Usually going back and forth between professional and personal projects

- Always upbeat

- Very optimistic

- Well-liked, even popular by others

Famous Sevens

Elton John, Russell Brand, John F. Kennedy, Steven Spielberg, Jim Carrey, Robin Williams, Elizabeth Taylor, Peter Pan ("Peter Pan"), Fred and George Weasley ("Harry Potter"), Moana ("Moana")

The Key Personality Traits of Sevens In-Depth

If there is one thing that Sevens won't say all the time, it's the word 'no'. They may say it if there are some things they don't want to try out. Another time, they will say 'no' when asked if they've had enough.

But other than that, they don't say 'no' to the opportunity of trying new things. They will have a wide variety of interests. They may want to try it all.

While they want to 'do it all', they don't aim to be the 'jack of all trades'. They just want to be good enough at doing it. Mastery is not something they want to achieve.

Sevens are versatile, curious, and willing to learn many interests. They want to be able to say 'I know how to do that. I may not be the best at it. But I am familiar with it'. They keep their minds occupied constantly.

They are always doing something fun and enjoyable for themselves. They seek stimulation that keeps them going. Even if it's something that requires trial and error, Sevens keep going.

They don't care about whether or not they are doing something right or wrong. They are having fun and enjoying themselves. When they're happy, they make those around them feel good as well.

Sevens may not know what they truly want in life. This may be one of the chief reasons why they are willing to try on so many hats. They might find one that will eventually fit.

Even in the most trivial areas of their life, a Seven is always looking for the maximum possible effort. If there are three ice cream flavors present, a Seven would want to try them all. If a Seven is traveling to another state or country, they may just stroke the curiosity flames and visit multiple states and countries in the process making it a spontaneous trip.

Yes, Sevens are spontaneous. They do things without even thinking about it. However, if their gut tells them otherwise, they won't do it.

Sevens can be highly productive in a professional setting. Some of them (particularly 7w6) may stick around at the office to snag extra hours and do it with such boundless amount of energy, they may not care what time it is when they get out.

Sevens are optimistic and upbeat. They know that tomorrow will bring them something positive. But the air of mystery of what they may be tends to excite them. They ask themselves, 'what will tomorrow be like'.

What Motivates A Seven?

There is nothing that motivates a Seven more than the thought of new ideas and experiences. They can also have a bit of a creative streak. Typically, they never run out of options and will usually choose one before moving onto another.

They love it when they meet new people. They see others as potential partners in having fun. They may enjoy and share their lives with small or large groups of people.

Sevens will often find themselves at parties, concerts, or any place where there are large groups of people. Sevens are mostly extroverted, but don't count out the possibility of an introverted Seven. Social experiences are basically the life of a Seven and they cannot live without them.

What Stresses Out A Seven?

If there is one thing that will guarantee stress for a Seven, it's boredom. The feeling that there is nothing to do will frustrate a Seven to no end. They hate it when they have to follow schedules.

When it comes to rules and limits, a Seven will not sit well with them. They like to live their life with the most maximum amounts of freedom possible. Rules and limits are non-existent in their own beliefs.

They want to do things with other people. They hate it when they have to tackle something all by themselves. Sevens will reject routines that are unnecessary and tedious.

They find that it will be pointless to do something that may be considered 'a waste of time'. They may even think that automation of such trivial things may be the best invention since sliced bread. If a lack of freedom is present, this will definitely be a problem for Sevens.

How To Recognize A Seven

Sevens may be easier to spot because of the exorbitant amount of happiness and excitement that they express. They are bright-eyed and open-minded. They will discuss not one, not two, but countless interests.

They will usually be spotted in a group of people (be it a small or large group). They are very productive and will draw other people in because of their positive aura. In a professional setting, they tend to climb the company ladder without any problems (especially 7w6s).

They tend to be the favorites among those in and outside of the office. They cannot get enough of drawing people in with the stories of what they did in Las Vegas or the new skill they've learned. If they can tell an engaging story about the interesting things in their life, they will definitely draw a crowd in.

Their enthusiasm and charisma will draw in people both extroverted and introverted. When a Seven is faced with change, they keep going like a rolling wheel. The unknown is nothing they are afraid of (another trait that a Seven borrows from Sixes).

Healthy vs Unhealthy Sevens

Healthy

At their healthiest, Sevens are grateful and appreciative for the things they have. They are also in awe of the simple things. In short, they are happy and thankful to be alive.

Of all the Enneagram types, Sevens are the most extroverted of them all. They are lively, spontaneous, and are invigorating to be around.

They are easy to approach most of the time. The more people they draw in, the better. And the more they share their experiences with others, the merrier.

Sevens will be engaged in various interests. They don't search for mastery (as mentioned earlier). They settle for 'I know how to do it'. Unlike Fives that focus on one specialized thing, Sevens are more of the generalist type.

They are usually multi-talented, prolific, and productive most of the time.

Average

An average Seven will be restless. They crave more options and choices. And they are always hungry for adventure.

However, they may lose some focus on things. But still, they place their desire for new experiences over everything else. Usually, they stay on top of the latest trends.

Healthy and high average Sevens know their limits. They will use their instincts that will allow them to say 'no' if something doesn't seem right. However, lower average Sevens will throw that ability to say 'no' out the window.

They eventually become uninhibited and will do and say what comes to mind. They will tell stories, even to the point of exaggeration. They stay in motion in an effort to stay well ahead of boredom.

Average Sevens may have ideas. But following through with said ideas will depend on the day. Some days they'll do it and other days they won't.

But when they teeter on average and are unhealthy, Sevens are a completely different animal. They take things into excess. They may even go on some kind of 'bender' or 'binge'.

They may also become materialistic and greedy. They will feel like they may not have enough. Their desire for wanting more will make them become demanding or even pushy.

They will become more unsatisfied if Sevens go unchecked. It may be at this point where they could also develop addictions while exhibiting insensitive behaviors.

Unhealthy

Unhealthy Sevens are a complete 180 of their upbeat, vivacious selves. At this point, they may have gone well into their addictions (be it drugs, alcohol, sex, or something else). The excess of it all begins to take its toll.

Unhealthy Sevens will likely engage in behavior that is considered abusive or offensive. They will act out based on impulse and do away with any opportunities that involve dealing with anxieties. Erratic behaviors and mood swings will become the norm.

It's common for unhealthy Sevens to engage in compulsive actions (to the point of 'mania'). But there will come a time when the train will come to a grinding halt. And when that does, that's when there will be a turn for the worst.

Sevens will feel like they are completely spent. They may develop claustrophobia and may even have constant spells of panic. They will also fall into deep depression and feel like they have given up on life.

Their addictions will end up becoming overdoses. Impulsive suicides may be likely for unhealthy Sevens. Mental disorders such as Histrionic and Bipolar Disorders may develop.

Final Thoughts

At their healthiest, Sevens are on top of the world and filled with life. But at their unhealthiest, it will feel like life got sucked out of them. In order to grow as a Seven, you must be able to know your limits and place boundaries on yourself.

We will discuss that in detail when we get into the practices for each Enneagram type. Sevens are the life of the party. And as a Seven, you don't want that 'party' to end due to not keeping yourself in check.

The pain you want to avoid is mostly mental. It's the kind of pain that will easily make you lose interest in the things you otherwise are enthusiastic about. To avoid it as much as possible, you must always be in motion and find ways to keep yourself busy.

Chapter 25: Discovering Type 8 - Need to Be Against (Protector)

When it comes to Eights, they have a need to go against the powers to be. They believe that they are the antithesis of what society wants, for example. They don't want to be controlled by others, but rather they are in control of themselves.

They will protect their best interests at all costs. Furthermore, they are considered one of the fiercest and direct of Enneagram types. They have an unprecedented drive that will garner respect from most but intimidate others.

Some may even be terrified of Eights. If you're an Eight, you are someone who wants to go against what the rest of the world thinks. You carve your own path and you set to it.

You protect yourself from those who may doubt you. You also protect yourself from failure whenever you decide to take on a challenge. You are independent, sharp-minded, and will stop at nothing to get the task done.

For Eights, they would rather go against authority. Speaking of that, Eights aim to become the authority (and rightfully so). And who is to say that we can blame them?

Key Personality Traits of Eights

- Self-sufficient

- Independent

- Energetic most of the time

- Usually busy

- Headstrong

- Very stubborn

- Take their ability of control seriously

- Powerful and passionate

- Determined

- Confident in their abilities to 'keep going'

Famous Eights

Winston Churchill, Kamala Harris, Martin Luther King, Jr., Ernest Hemingway, Mark Cuban, Barbara Walters, Rosanne Barr, Alec Baldwin, Alastor Moody (Harry Potter)

The Key Personality Traits of Eights In-Depth

If there is one Enneagram type that can easily rise to the challenge, Eights definitely are a great fit. They have a high amount of willpower and will feel like they are at their best when they use it. They have a high level of energy that will provide them with enough drive to get stuff done.

Eights are usually those who are aware of the challenges of building something from scratch. Whether it's a business, a city, or some kind of mission where you start from zero, Eights will boldly and bravely take on the challenge.

They know that failures and setbacks will happen at some point. But they are prepared to deal with them better than anyone else. They view them as learning lessons and opportunities to solve problems.

Eights are in a sense like Fours in terms of their individuality. The only difference is, Eights are usually more rugged than their Four counterparts. They are people who are willing to stand alone.

They do not give in to anything that involves social convention. Thus, they are good at defying fear, shame, and concern based on their actions. They may not even care about the negative opinion of others based on what they do.

Eights may be afraid of being harmed physically. But nothing terrifies them more than losing power or being controlled. If they encounter a threat trying to control them or deduct power from them, Eights will fight for it tooth and nail.

Eights can withstand physical punishment. And they may even put their health on the line if necessary. They do have a fear of being hurt emotionally.

They will use their physical strength to be protective of their families and their interests at heart. They will also do their best to keep others at an emotional distance (albeit a safe one). Outside, they are tough but inside there is vulnerability present.

Eights may feel like they are misunderstood. If they need to, they can distance themselves and give themselves enough space to regroup. They rarely talk about their negative feelings or their vulnerabilities since they know people view them as tough and impervious.

The fear of rejection also exists in Eights. They feel that such a thing may dent their ego. But through it all, their can-do attitude and their inner drive are what make an Eight stand out.

What Motivates an Eight?

The idea of taking charge and being a leader is what motivates Eights the most. They want to be an authority that is respected, saluted, and appreciated. They want to be understood by those who are their equals or subordinate to them.

They are driven to make decisions that will benefit others. They are logical and will provide practical ideas and solutions to problems. They take care of their physical self seriously, making exercise one of their routine activities.

They have energy and drive to where they can take something they want to build and make it a reality. The end game for Eights: achieve success without someone taking it away from them. The feeling of being in control is something an Eight can't live without.

What Stresses an Eight Out?

Eights cannot bear the thought of being controlled or subordinate to other people. They will not stand for it in the slightest. Meanwhile, they feel like being unimportant or insignificant may also cause them to be even more frustrated.

They also fear that their vulnerabilities and emotions may be exposed out in the open. So, they will try to keep an outer image to look like they are impervious to pain. They are unappreciative of dishonesty or blame that they are not deserving of.

The thought of feeling helpless and out of control can also bother an Eight at times. That's why they must do their best to keep in control of themselves.

How to Recognize An Eight?

If you are able to spot the leaders of a group, you can easily be able to see an Eight. These are the people that carry themselves in a way that exudes confidence and self-assurance. That also bleeds into the way they walk and talk.

If they say such things like 'luck can be created rather than exist out of thin air', that's the way an Eight thinks. They know that hard work and opportunity are the two things that make 'luck'. They are not intimated nor afraid of any confrontation.

When dealing with authority figures, it may depend on positioning. If they are an equal, then there may be mutual respect between the two due to their competence instead of things like age or status. If an Eight is subordinate to authority, they may often butt heads.

Eights are the kind of people that say 'they know what they want and know how to get it' without saying those words. They know that they have to start somewhere. But the faster they can ascend to an authority or power position, the better.

Healthy vs Unhealthy Eights

Healthy

Eights will exercise self-restraint at their healthiest. They are also merciful. They are aware that there is a higher authority and are willing to surrender themselves to it.

They are mostly courageous and unafraid to put something on the line. It will drive them to achieve what they see as the future. And they become influential to those around them.

Healthy Eights will achieve things that will make them viewed as heroes in the eyes of others. They are destined for greatness and their achievements will be talked about long after they're gone. Their high level of self-confidence and self-assuredness will make them perform at the top of their game.

They take the initiative whenever the opportunity arises. They are decisive, authoritative, and know what it takes to make things happen. They hold honor in high regard and respect those around them (even their subordinates).

They are protective of those who are important to them and even their own self-interests. They respect those around them (although that respect from an Eight is earned).

Average

High average Eights are self-sufficient and financially independent. They are prepared to take care of any important concerns or issues that they face. They are rugged in terms of their individuality.

They like to take risks, work hard, and may even eschew dealing with their emotional needs. But when it gets down to a lower level, they will begin asserting their dominance over others. They can be forceful at times.

They can be egocentric and satisfy their urges of imposing their will and vision. If it stays unchecked, Eights will soon begin to remove their view of seeing people as equal. In other words, they will look at others below them and not give them respect.

If it gets worse, Eights can become combative and increasingly intimidating to others. They will start to get more belligerent and confrontational. They will have more adversaries than friends and colleagues.

Eights will feel like their wills are constantly being tested. They are stubborn and will assume a stand that screams 'I will not stand down'. They may even resort to threats in an effort to gain respect and obedience from their subordinates.

They will treat others unjustly. And it can get to the point where subordinates may conjure up a plan to topple the authority. In short, it sets the conditions for mutiny.

Unhealthy

When Eights reach unhealthy levels, those around them will try to control and subdue them. This will further infuriate the Eight and they will defy such attempts. From there, they become more of a dictator.

They adopt the philosophy of 'might makes right'. They may even commit acts that may be considered immoral, if not criminal. They may use unprovoked violence.

As it gets worse, they may become more delusional about their ideas and their authority. They may even become a megalomaniac. They may develop thoughts that they are a 'God'.

Once it reaches dangerously unhealthy levels, Eights will destroy everything in its path without thinking twice. They could become sociopathic. They could even commit homicidal acts if they see it as fit.

Eights that are severely unhealthy may develop Antisocial Personality Disorders.

Final Thoughts

As an Eight, you feel much at peace when in control. You understand that your power must be wielded for a greater good. If it's used as a weapon of mass destruction, it can only hasten your collapse and realize your greatest fears.

That isn't to say you should be too nice. But you shouldn't be too evil either. You are assertive, so you must set the boundaries and ground rules when and where necessary.

You put your ambitions and ideas to good use. You are aware of the challenges that lie ahead. Any challenges or adversity are small compared to you (no matter how difficult things can get). You command respect through your actions rather than your words.

Eights have an opportunity to achieve something that will cement them into greatness. They may be viewed as heroes and role models to others. They take on the opportunities without fear or hesitation.

If they do great things, they acknowledge the recognition and move forward. They are forward, driven, and will not submit to any other authority other than a higher authority (such as their life's mission or even a 'higher power').

Chapter 26: Discovering Type 9 - Need to Avoid (Mediator)

Nines are the kind of people that will do everything they can to keep the peace. They need to avoid conflict rising to dangerous levels at all times. As such, they can depend on their Wings (Eights and Ones) to ensure that happens.

They know that Eights can carry out the mission while Ones will become that activist to make sure such peace is restored. The Nines might be the masterminds behind it all without assuming any kind of authority.

They want to avoid something that can disturb the balance. Because to them, balance and peace are what they consider a perfect world. Whenever needed, they can provide solutions based on everything they've gathered from every viewpoint.

Nines know what one person wants. And they also know what the other person wants as well (which may be the polar opposite of the former's wishes). They are problem solvers by nature and will stop at nothing to make sure that it is solved before moving forward.

Key Personality Traits of Nines

- Calm and collected

- Speaks in a mellow, soothing voice

- Zen-like

- Can easily diffuse conflict

- Well-liked by most

- Fluid and slow gestures

- Vast circle of friends and acquaintances

Famous Nines

Barack Obama, Queen Elizabeth II, Marie Kondo, Ronald Reagan, Ron Howard, Morgan Freeman, Abraham Lincoln, Dorothy Gale (The Wizard of Oz), Luke Skywalker (Star Wars)

The Key Personality Traits of Nines In-Depth

Nines are about making and keeping the peace. They are soft-spoken and often very calm. It's almost as if nothing can anger them.

However, Nines are the kind of people you do not want to anger. As John Dryden quotes:

"Beware of the fury of a patient man."

For the most part, Nines are often calm, collected, and coherent. When a Nine speaks, people will listen. That's because Nines speak softly but can hold someone's attention with the words they say.

For their part, they are sharp in mind and open-minded. They believe in unity over separation. They believe in relaxation over tension.

Nines each take a trait or two from all of the Enneagram. For example, they have the strength trait from the Eights, the idealist demeanor of ones, the creativity of Fours, the intelligence of Fives, and so on.

And that is why they are located at the crown of the Enneagram. They also tend to be one with something. They want to melt or blend into something.

What Motivates A Nine?

The motivations of a Nine are quite simple. For one, they want stability and consistency. Second, they can easily bring two sides together and come to some kind of agreement.

If tension was a fire, Nines are the firefighters. They will put out the flames quickly. They want to be heard speaking their every word.

They also want to feel safe and accepted by others. They may also have some motivations that stem from some of the other Enneagram types as well.

What Stresses Outs Nines?

Nines hate making difficult decisions. But they happen. Especially when it comes to providing a solution to de-escalate tension.

They may feel like their decision may benefit one party while disappointing the other. They also do not like it when they are interrupted or ignored. Their pent-up aggression will disturb their inner peace.

They also want to do their best to not disappoint those they love the most. This includes their family and close friends.

How to Recognize A Nine?

Nines are like chameleons (especially in a social setting). They will blend in with pretty much any group. And they can get along with just about anyone.

If they are soft-spoken but extroverted, odds are they are Nines. They are cooperative by nature and willing to listen to other opinions. They usually don't voice their side of the argument unless they feel it is necessary.

They don't demean someone's argument if they disagree with it. They are willing to listen to other points of view and understand why that person believes in them. If they stand in the middle of a tense situation, they will find a solution quickly without engaging in some kind of violent behavior.

Nines are easygoing. And they have a high threshold of patience. They can tolerate other people. And they have a high self-esteem that is enriched by helping others.

They live a comfortable life and may take advantage of their personal space if they feel the need to recharge their batteries. They seek deep knowledge and understanding of things. They are usually more spiritual than all the other Enneagram types.

Healthy vs Unhealthy Nines

Healthy

Nines are autonomous and fulfilled. They are present. They tend to develop profound relationships.

They can be accepting and receptive. They are mostly peaceful and emotionally stable. They usually trust most people and are at ease with themselves.

They don't believe in things like pretension. They are good-natured people most of the time. And they can be very optimistic and supporting of other people's endeavors.

They will do their best to bring peace and harmony to groups. Their communication skills are second to none. Conflict resolution is easier done than said.

Averages

To average Nines, the fear of conflict exists. They can continue to be accommodating to most. They will utilize their philosophies and default to phrases and sayings that can be used in a deflective manner.

They can be active but can disengage at their choosing. They may be inattentive when under stress. They may walk away from problems rather than solve them.

If anything, they may try to minimize the problems in front of them. They can be stubborn most of the time if they are in a state of low but average health.

Unhealthy

Unhealthy Nines will have a habit of repressing their feelings and the like. They will disassociate themselves from all conflicts. They can also pose a danger to others.

They feel depersonalized and may not even function at all. They may become catatonic and even disoriented to the things around them. They may develop multiple personalities and develop schizophrenia.

Final Thoughts

Nines may seem like a mix of some of the traits from each Enneagram type. They are peaceful and will do their best to keep the peace. Even though they are no fans of conflict, they will do the best they can to end it quickly if they are caught in the middle of it.

Nines want inner peace and will ensure that it happens. They blend in with other people without issue. They will get along with pretty much everyone.

Nines are all ears when it comes to listening to other people's viewpoints. Their skill of listening to other points of view in conflict will help them put together a solution that is a win-win for both sides rather than favor one side.

Nines will not only need to preserve the outer peace, but they must also stay in focus when it comes to their own inner peace. Otherwise, they may face issues of their own that may take a while to resolve.

Section 2/Part 1
Chapter 1: Repentance and Reorientation

Repentance - *The action of repenting; sincere regret or remorse.*

Reorientation - *The action of changing the focus or direction of something.*

Above are the definitions of repentance and reorientation. Whenever we think of the first word, the word 'sin' comes to mind. Especially when it's discussed among circles of the Christian faith.

But as we have stressed before, you don't need to be deep into the Christian faith (or even be religious) in order to truly understand the Enneagram. But repentance for any past mistakes or transgressions you may have is possible.

Once you have been able to repent, you can then take a step back and ask yourself where to go from there. That's where reorientation comes into play. The action of changing your focus or direction after repentance is usually the next step.

Now that you know your Enneagram type, you might be in a place where you fall between average or possibly unhealthy. If that's where you are, no worries. We will help you find a way to live a fulfilled, healthy life based on your Enneagram type.

There is no shame in holding yourself accountable and repenting for any misgivings you may have had. Yes, mistakes have been made. And you may feel guilty about hurting relationships based on your negative behaviors.

Using the Enneagram for repentance and reorientation is something that you must do. Consider your personality type and everything about it as your roadmap or even your instruction manual on what you need to do. Later on, we will be talking about the various practices you need to follow based on your Enneagram type.

Aside from that, you will also learn later on how to use the Enneagram to your advantage in both your personal and professional life. You will learn how to behave in a relationship with your significant other or spouse as well as how you should handle your work situation.

The Benefits of Repentance

Whether you know it or not, one of the true benefits of the Enneagram is repentance. But what are the true benefits of repenting for your transgressions and poor behavior? We will discuss that shortly.
There are many renditions of the benefits of repenting. For Christians, they have the benefit of being forgiven and developing a much closer relationship to God. They also find the benefit in being able to conquer evil and reaping such rewards.

It's important that when the time comes for repentance, it's not something you want to put off. Especially when you want to improve in various areas of your life. Let's discuss some of the benefits:

You will forgive yourself (and be forgiven by others)

The first step in forgiveness is forgiving yourself. Nobody wants to live with the constant guilt of their wrongdoings. If they do, they may not be able to live a fulfilling life.

Something will seem like it's bothering them all the time. It will block their thought process and interrupt something that they're doing. It will make us lose focus on the more important things.

The key here in self-forgiveness is acknowledging the mistake and moving forward. Take it as a learning lesson rather than something you can dwell on. After you are able to forgive yourself, next is receiving forgiveness from others.

Understandably, this will be a difficult task. One of the reasons is some people will be more forgiving than others. Some people may hold on to grudges for a long time.

They may not be ready to forgive just yet. Or they may not want to forgive at all. Regardless, this is something you shouldn't take personally.

The conversations you will have with the people you may have hurt in the past will be difficult. But in the end, it will be worth it. You will sit down with a person and admit the mistake that you have made.

Make a pledge to them that you will do better. Let them know that you are willing to fix the relationship and reverse any damage that may be caused as a result. Furthermore, you'll want to understand that not everyone has the same Enneagram type as you.

You may be a Seven and one of your friends is a Five. You may be an Eight, but your previous significant other was a Two. Depending on the Enneagram type, forgiveness can be processed in different ways.

There are times when people ask for forgiveness during a time when someone may be dying. Someone may be close to death and ask for forgiveness before passing on. Likewise, there may be someone who is asking for forgiveness or may be forgiving someone who may be dying.

Either way, the best time to forgive is as soon as possible. Don't wait for a situation like someone on the verge of death. The sooner you can forgive or ask for forgiveness, the better focused you will be on building a much healthier life both mentally and spiritually.

Reminding yourself of your mistakes

Although we should not dwell on our mistakes. We must remember and remind ourselves of them and how we can learn from them. We think back and remember the shame and the guilt we felt at the initial moment.

To acknowledge the mistake and what you've learned from it are two things you must do. After that, you put it back 'in the box' and put it back on the 'shelf'. Repenting on a regular basis will help you stay in the know while allowing it to serve as a reminder of how far you are coming along with the improvement process.

When you answer to God or a 'higher power', you may think to yourself that you'll feel fine without them. However, without relying on a higher power, you'll feel like you're nothing. This higher power is the one thing that is holding you together.

It's also important to receive mercy. Mercy is way better than receiving a punishment that may be considered 'deserving' or receiving blessings that you may not deserve.

You are at peace with yourself

There is no greater feeling in the world than being at peace with yourself. It's that feeling that you will be OK. You feel that you are in control of things and nothing can stop you at this point.

Even though you are at peace with yourself, it is important to keep sharp of anything that may cause you to fall through the cracks. It's important to focus on the things based on your Enneagram type such as the things that motivate you.

Sure, there will be times where things may stress you out. But knowing you, you'll always find a way to handle that stress and keep it at bay. There is nothing wrong with accessing your mindfulness and identifying what is bothering you.

Take a page out of the Nine's book: keep the peace. In this context, repentance will allow you to discover a newfound peace within yourself. You have forgiven yourself for it (and have been forgiven by others). Your inner and outer peace may be disturbed or even interrupted.

But you can find a way to control it should it arise. All it takes is a few minutes out of your day to keep yourself in check. After that, you can get on with the day knowing you can tackle it despite the craziness.

You can easily conquer your negative traits

Arrogance, the feeling of being unloved or unwanted, and everything in between. There may be negative traits that are common among Enneagram types. With repentance, you have an understanding and ability to recognize what they are.

From there, you can identify any negative energy coming from a mile away. Take a moment to remind yourself that regular repentance is normal. You can conquer your negative traits by going in different directions (i.e. - not acting out on them).

Especially when you have worked hard to improve yourself and the relationships you have with other people. When you act on them, you don't live up to your end of the bargain. Especially when you made a pledge to do so.

Don't be the person that breaks their promise. Be the person who keeps the negative traits at bay.

Reaping the rewards of repentance

The ability for repenting is rewarding enough. But there are more rewards that you can reap from it. They come in the form of things like better relationships, an improved attitude, even a new lease on life.

You may have taken a few good risks to make some monumental changes in your life like a career change. You took on a few challenges and decided that it was for the best. And the reward for making such decisions is the feeling of accomplishment and knowing that you've done the right thing for yourself.

Reorientation

The ability to change direction is easy. Jimmy Dean said the following:

"I cannot change the direction of the wind, but I can adjust my sails and always reach my destination."

This couldn't be said better ourselves. The key to reorientation is knowing your destination and changing the course to get where you need to be. It is also important to reorient ourselves from any actions that may be considered negative and travel towards the positive.

Circling back to the chapter on virtues and passions, there are various Enneagram types that have virtues and passions. Passions are considered negative, making virtues positive.

Let's revisit them based on each Enneagram type:

Type One: Serenity - Anger

Type Two: Humility - Pride

Type Three: Veracity - Vanity

Type Four: Equanimity - Envy

Type Five: Non-attachment - Withdrawal

Type Six: Courage - Anxiety

Type Seven: Constancy - Gluttony

Type Eight: Innocence - Lust

Type Nine: Right Action - Self-forgetting

Considering now that you have an understanding about each Enneagram type, it starts to make sense. For example, Type Threes may have that negativity of focusing on their image (to the point where they may be seen as vain). Meanwhile, they want to steer clear from that and focus more on their voracious appetite for being recognized.

For another example, let's take a look at Sevens. Being the enthusiasts that they are, they may risk becoming gluttonous and wanting more of what they crave. However, they want to focus on being constantly in motion while knowing their limits.

Lastly, it comes as no surprise that courage is listed amongst Sixes. They fear nothing in terms of what they set out to do. But they may feel anxiety because of the potential of not getting the security and assurance they want in return for giving it to others.

The point of this is that there is a positive thing you can do and there's something negative. It's better to always direct yourself to the positive. It may be difficult to stay that course, but it's possible to make it easier on yourself.

It's kind of like a good habit. It's hard to stick with it compared to bad habits, which are easy to form and hard to kick. The important skill you want to teach yourself is self-restraint. Regardless of your Enneagram type, it's all part of knowing what you are doing in the moment (i.e. - being mindful of your actions).

Self-transformation is the name of the game. And the Enneagram will help you transform into something better. A year from now, you may feel like you don't recognize yourself (but you will feel like you've been born again).

Final Thoughts

The first couple of steps after learning about your Enneagram type are repenting and reorienting. Repenting may be the hardest part as it may cause you to confront some of your worst mistakes. The pain and the regret will come back, and you may feel the emotion from it.

It is important to forgive yourself and receive forgiveness from others. Inner peace and stability will be rewarding once you are able to repent. From there, you can reorient yourself and change direction in your life.

It is important to practice the virtues based on your Enneagram type rather than your passions. You must be mindful of knowing what you are being drawn towards. If you are being drawn towards your 'passions', remind yourself about the consequences that you have experienced by way of repenting regularly.

Chapter 2: Idealized Self-Image and Guilt Feelings

For every type, there is an ideal image that someone must adopt for themselves. And it should be a positive one rather than negative. We take pride in who we are as individuals.

We do care about our appearance and our image to an extent. Some others may take it way too seriously. We try our best to look good in front of others.

Some may use their self-image as a tool to gain approval from others. They seek validation or otherwise suffer with the feelings of being unimportant and the like. The truth is, seeking such validation is not something we should worry about.

Having a positive self-image is one thing to improve in your area of life. Meanwhile, we also deal with feelings of guilt. The guilt stemming from the transgressions that we have made in the past.

The poor actions we have made, and our self-image go hand in hand. We may be viewed negatively in the eyes of others. But how can we make a 180 degree turn to ensure that it never happens?

The Enneagram will help us grow in so many ways. We will talk about how the Enneagram can improve your self-image and what you can create based on your Type. We will also talk about how you can deal with guilty feelings.

Once more, we take an important step in improving your life based on the Enneagram. But we are not out of the woods yet. With that said, let's get started.

Idealized Self-Image Explained

To understand our self-image based on our Enneagram type, let's do a little exercise. Imagine yourself in your younger years. If you are in your 30s, 40s, 50s and beyond, think back to your late teens or early 20s.

If you somehow come across this and you're still young, imagine an identical version of yourself. Let's say that you get very frustrated after missing something that seemed like an obvious opportunity. Just looking at that younger or identical version of yourself, you can tell that they didn't want to miss that 'chance of a lifetime'.

The anger that is expressed stems from relying on unrealistic expectations and the like. An idealized self-image is someone who might consider themselves much greater than their current self. For example, a young basketball player may have an ideal self-image that he is a young professional ballplayer.

For his self-image, a professional ballplayer should be making fewer mistakes. He wants everything to be perfect. But make no mistake, even the best in their profession make mistakes and the like.

He believes that he is missing opportunities to compete at the next level. Soothing him may seem pointless because we might not understand how talented he is on the inside. Those who have an idealized self-image will often defend it to the death using emotions such as anger.

The truth is that we all have self-idealized images of ourselves. And it also provides us with a visual definition of our Enneagram types. What exactly are the idealized self-images based on yours?

For example, let's take a look at Eights. Eights have an idealized self-image that they are on top of the world. They are in control and have many people under their command.

However, if a sliver of their vulnerability is showing, this will anger the Eight. They want to be viewed as someone that is impervious to pain. They want to be seen as steel rather than human.

Twos have an idealized self-image that stems from pride. They see themselves as too proud to have any needs due to their ability to give to others. They feel like their needs are minuscule compared to the rest of the world.

But Twos should focus on themselves to an extent. They have their needs to tend to. Therefore, self-focus is important when they are not out and about helping others.

Threes have an idealized self-image of being recognized on the street. They are the talk of the world. People cannot shut up about them.

They want to live in a world where their accomplishments are something of 'biblical proportions'. However, if they accomplish something and no one seems to take notice, Threes may reach an immense level of frustration.

Of these examples above, you get the idea. Having an idealized self-image may be a person who looks like you but has already achieved the aspirations and wants that you're going after. But that image can't become reality unless you work on yourself to make it happen.

Do not put unrealistic expectations on yourself. It's important to know your limits as you are growing into something better. Always adjust the bar to a new height once it is necessary to do so.

Your Idealized Self-Image and Reality

An idealized self-image is created when you repress specific parts of your personality. It is important to not focus on the things that would contradict our true self-image. You also want to prepare for those who may spot a flaw and let you know about it.

For example, someone may tell a Three about a failure that the latter suffered. A Three may not express their emotions to that person (but deep down inside, they feel like curling up in a ball). Someone may try to convince a Four how fortunate they should be and get anger from the latter in return.

Let's admit it: there is a part of us that will fight for our idealized self-image. However, they tend to be less healthy compared to those who are. Healthy people are more in tune with realizing that they know that their idealized self-image is an exaggerated version of themselves.

Those who are healthy are less defensive about their idealized self-image. In fact, they might even tear it apart themselves because they realize how foolish it might be to thrust very high expectations.

We create this idealized self-image based on what may be considered as 'unused parts'. We may often mistake acknowledged potential as talent that is already developed. We also create this self-image based on what we consider our faults.

Some may negatively perceive us in some ways. For example, if we are trying to be honest, someone may assume that we are displaying hostility. Even people of certain Enneagram types will see some kind of negativity and use it to their advantage.

For example, Fives may be stingy in the eyes of others. But to the Fives themselves, they are careful with what they have in terms of resources. As mentioned before, Fives are smart with their money.

Sixes may have a slight paranoia about instability that they develop some kind of ability to read others. If they pick up on something that they don't like, they may pay less attention to it (or even not associate themselves with it). When Sevens have a good time, others may view them as 'wild' or chaotic.

Our idealized self-image may also give us clues on how to figure out our own style. We also need to acknowledge the faults that we don't commit. Rather than worry about our idealized self-image, we must be in touch with ourselves to develop our real identity based on our Enneagram type.

What we do based on our Enneagram type may be easily misunderstood by others. For our part, we must not let that get the best of us. Furthermore, we shouldn't have to explain or justify ourselves to others if we don't have to.

The Feelings of Guilt

When it comes to defending our idealized self-image, we seem to behave in a certain way that may hurt others. We may feel guilty potentially damaging relationships because of our defensive behavior. There is also that feeling of guilt that we focus more on our idealized self-image as opposed to our true identity.

We feel guilty for missing out on the opportunities to improve ourselves. Acknowledging the guilt that you feel is the first step. The next step is getting rid of that guilt.

We make mistakes such as having high expectations of ourselves. We must know our limits to who we are. There are things we can do and things we can't (be it due to physical abilities or otherwise).

As for which types are feeling the guiltiest, what are they? Type Fours may feel guilty for being too sensitive. Twos may feel guilty for being intrusive or overbearing.

No one knows for sure which type may be connected to natural feelings of guilt. But it's safe to say that everyone will feel it to an extent regardless if you are a One or a Nine. Guilt is something that you should let go of as it is one of the steps towards healing and rebuilding yourself.

Final Thoughts

Having an idealized self-image is defined as having an 'imaginary' version of yourself. It's held up by the unstable ground known as your unrealistically high expectations. There are those who will get defensive when it comes to their idealized self-image.

They hate it when people point out a flaw or even bring up something that might be considered bothersome to their psyche. Their idealized self-image is designed to pull them away from reality (when they should be more in tune with it).

This is why it is key to focus on being healthier. When you are healthy, the less likely you are to focus or even defend your idealized self-image. You will know your limits and even be aware of your limits and abilities.

You may feel guilty for focusing on your idealized self-image as opposed to your true self. But you must acknowledge it and move forward. Doing so is all part of the growth process based on the Enneagram.

Chapter 3: Breathing and Centering

For each Enneagram type, it's about putting things into practice. Two of the things we will be talking about are breathing and centering. There are different types of breathing and centering exercises that each Enneagram type will have.

We will unveil what you need to do based on your type in this chapter. When it comes to our breathing, it is key for us to pay attention to it. This is one of the most basic practices when we focus on growing ourselves both personally and professionally.

If you are aware of your breath and the techniques that you use, you will see shifts in your various experiences. This includes physical, emotional, and internal experiences. We have a habit of holding tension in our body, even for lengthy periods of time.

While under pressure or dealing with conflict, we may be holding our breath and tension at the same time. This will create a restriction of inner space. We need this inner space in order to keep our personal emotions and reactivity in check.

With plentiful amounts of space, you will be able to center yourself in even the most stressful situations. It will be as if nothing will get the best of you. You will learn to be calm under pressure regardless of your Enneagram type and how you handle your emotions.

This is a chapter that we highly recommend that you read through. The breathing practices will be all part of our self-growth routine. Let's keep going and explain the importance of breathing:

The Importance of Breathing

Breathing is something that helps us clear our heads and handle stress and pressure. But it can also do something more. For one, deep breaths allow you to experience any emotions or physical sensations. Holding that breath will cause those feelings to diminish.

The less we breathe, the less we feel. And this can put a good amount of stress on our bodies. This can even affect our overall health (especially in the long term).

If we are overcome by negative feelings or reactions (stemmed by events or other people), breathing consciously allows us to calm down. It also provides us with plenty of flexibility in how we respond to such negative situations. Breathing also allows us to focus on ourselves from the inside.

When we practice breathing, we begin to understand why we must establish inner and outer boundaries with ourselves. We also learn the difference between what's inside and what's outside of us. Breathing mixed with being self-aware of ourselves is something that can be done anyplace, any time.

Basic breathing practice

This may sound like the simplest breathing advice ever given. The basic way to breathe in meditation is just by following your breath. As you do this, you pay attention to the sensations while you inhale and exhale.

This will allow you to get in tune with what's going on internally. You will start to relax or even quiet down. If there are some thoughts running through your head, don't be laser-focused on them. While they do, all you have to do is acknowledge that they are there and stay focused on your breathing.

As we breathe, we are opening up spaces that will allow us to reflect on ourselves. We can also use it to observe our habits and activities based on our types. This includes what we are feeling, thinking, and what state our body is currently in.

While performing this basic practice, it allows us to become more present and aware of what's going on around us. This is perfect for those who want to build rapport and communicate effectively. This will also allow us to improve on our emotional intelligence and our empathy.

Active Practice

Another breathing practice that we'll be looking at is known as 'active' breathing. This practice will allow us to use our breath for the purpose of mobilizing our energy. This will best serve us whenever we want to relax and conserve our energy.

There are four different practices for active breathing. Some of them may be based on your personality type. Keep in mind, each Enneagram type has its own breathing pattern.

Before we unveil them, let's take a look at the following practices for active breathing:

Clearing Breath: This is a practice that may be useful if you find yourself in a stressful situation. Especially if you have a habit of holding your breath and building up tension at the same time. The way this works is simple: just take a deep breath. As you do this, make sure that you are expanding both your belly and your chest. As you exhale, make it similar to a sigh of relief or some kind of 'woosh' like breathing. If you are doing this while in the presence of others, people may give you strange looks. If someone asks if something is wrong, let them know that you're good and move on.

Energizing Breath: If you need to be more energetic (especially on a busy day), take a few big breaths into your chest. As you extend the inhale, be sure to stretch the rib cage and the diaphragm. While you exhale, be sure that you relax. Refrain from using your neck or shoulders for assistance.

Relaxing Breath: Here, you will need to take big, but slow breaths. These breaths should travel down your belly. This will allow you to send energy down your legs and your feet. Start with 5 breaths and work your way up to 10 breaths when comfortable.

Counter Anxiety Breath: Anxiety may creep up on you. Especially in the worst times. For this reason, you want to have this active breath practice on hand. If belly breathing doesn't seem to get the job done, try taking a deep breath into your solar plexus. While inhaling, you want to stretch your diaphragm. Rather than exhale at the top of your breath, hold it back against your lips and exhale slowly. Think of it like slowly letting out the air of a balloon. Relax your chest and diaphragm while exhaling. The exhale should be at least five times longer than the inhale. For best results, count slowly.

Breathing Practices Based on Enneagram Type

As mentioned, there are breathing practices specifically based on your Enneagram type. If you know your Enneagram type, find it and read carefully what you need to do. Here are the following breathing techniques:

Type One

Type Ones are the kind of people who want to have a good sense of 'knowing'. The problem is, most of them are not always consciously aware. For this reason, they develop the bad habit of creating physical tension while trying to focus on making sure things are done correctly.

When breathing, your priority is to focus on physical relaxation. Use a breathing technique that will allow you to relax the diaphragm. Therefore, the Relaxing breath is your go-to option here for obvious reasons. Alternatively, you can use a different variation that will allow you to stretch your diaphragm and rib cage while breathing in slowly.

While exhaling, be sure to let go of any tension as much as possible. If needed, spread energy and sensation throughout your body. Or continue to slowly breathe while switching to your belly.

Refrain from using your chest. If there is anxiety still present after using these techniques, use the counter-anxiety breath as a last resort. This one will likely guarantee to get rid of any anxiety you may have.

Type Two

As a Two, you are someone who relies on your feelings. At the same time, you may have a large amount of empathy inside of you. However, this might be an issue if you are dealing with someone who may have the same emotional state as you.

If you're a Two, you may be breathing with your chest instead of your belly. You may hold your breath in anticipation of something positive. As a Two, you must focus on your personal needs and feelings.

You should also focus on the sensations of your breath as well. While breathing or meditating, you may feel something provoke your thought process. It may be your inner voice saying that you are being selfish.

Ignore that 'voice' and stay focused. Focus on bringing attention to the physical sensations that you bring to your body. Focus more on yourself than others during your breathing exercise.

As for the exercise itself, take slow, full breaths into your belly. Refrain from using your chest. Connect yourself with the ground and transfer your energy to the legs and feet. This sounds similar to the Relaxing Breath technique listed above.

Should you feel overwhelmed, shift your attention towards your physical environment. What are the things you notice? Also, take a moment to move around, but don't move too much.

If you are in the presence of others, be sure to focus on the physical sensations and the breath itself.

Type Three

Threes want to meet people's expectations and achieve success. For this reason, they exude high amounts of energy. They use it to their advantage because they are constantly on the move.

They are mostly assertive but can be impatient at times. Because of this, they can begin to build tension and pressure in their chest (especially around the area of their heart). This may be an issue for them health-wise (including the possibility of suffering a heart attack later on down the road).

Threes may be on the go, but it never hurts for them to slow down for a bit. Especially when they must focus their attention on what's going on internally. They should connect to their deeper selves and their true priorities.

Threes should spend a few moments taking slow deep breaths. While doing so, they should consider following the sensation of their breath. Deep breaths should be going into their belly.

They must distribute their energy throughout their entire body. As you exhale, relax and just let go for a moment. This will allow you to create a lot of open space that is reserved for your emotional intelligence.

Type Four

Type Fours have intense emotions. That's no secret. Because of this, they go through a large amount of ups and downs.

They have a habit of searching for recognition while shifting to going deep into their inner world to acquire personal authenticity. They will switch back and forth between the two regularly. They have aspirations of connecting with other people on a personal and meaningful level.

When things don't go their way, they will mostly feel disappointed and find withdrawal to be the best course of action. If excited or anxious, they will tend to spill those emotions. Fours should consider establishing a balance between their emotions and relationships.

As they focus on their breath and physical sensation, they need to make sure they are grounded and connected to their instincts. While performing creative activities and staying grounded, they will channel their emotional energy.

Fours should focus on normally breathing in and breathing out. Take slow, deep breaths and let go of any tension being built up in your chest. Hold back your diaphragm while exhaling.

You may also have to switch up your breathing depending on which wing is strongest. If you are a Three wing, use that breathing technique as mentioned. If you have a strong Five wing, practice breathing into your chest and belly while building up energy.

Regardless of which wing is dominant, the goal here is to make sure that your breathing is calm and steady. If you must, use the counter-anxiety breath technique.

Type Five

Type Fives are often using their brains to think deeper than the average person. At the same time, they are doing so while searching for knowledge and gaining their expertise. They also prefer to be in the company of themselves while doing this.

Fives may be detached most of the time and may be considered lacking in the warmth and rapport areas. They will rely on their mental center of intelligence over the other centers more often than not. As a five, greater contact with both your body and emotions is what you need to do.

You may be finding yourself in the position where you want to avoid expressing your feelings. So, you're likely holding your breath as a result. Thus, it cuts off any sensations that you may feel as you inhale and exhale.

You're probably doing this as a defensive strategy. But the reality here is that you are constricting any vitality that may be running through you. You'll also find yourself staying in your head.

You'll want to access energy based on your instinct while increasing your capacity that can be filled with sensations and overall pleasure. If you do this, you will be able to tolerate connecting with other people and the environment that you're in.

As you do breathing exercises, you want to focus on expanding the diaphragm while deepening your breaths. As you start out, you may feel a little uncomfortable. That's why it is important to take it one breath at a time.

When you do this, it will help you build up tolerance for increased sensation. From there, you'll be able to work on increasing your vitality capacity. When you breathe into your belly, you will become more grounded.

You can also breathe into your chest, allowing you to open up plenty of space that will be great for those who may be lacking in emotion and empathy. This will allow you to develop a stronger connection with your head and your heart (not to mention your gut center).

Type Six

Like Fives, Sixes use their mental centers to their advantage. They do this as a way to keep an eye on problems that may approach from a distance. They might as well be just as observant as Fives when they see certain issues before they even become a greater problem.

They are usually on alert for threats that they believe are a threat to their stability and security. Sixes are often cautious and usually hold back whenever they are faced with a crucial decision. They will usually take a position based on their intellectual or physical strength and dive into whatever action they find themselves in.

Sixes will need to develop safety and security in themselves. They should come to the realization that not everyone they meet and know will provide it for them. Sixes must go from being fearful to having the courage to get through everything.

When Sixes practice their breathing, they should take slow but deep breaths. While they do this, they need to stretch the muscle of their diaphragm. When they exhale, they should do so with as much force as possible.

They should breathe into their belly as a way to quell any anxiety they may have. At the same time, they should let the pleasurable sensations that exist with these breaths take over. You may find yourself overthinking things and holding your breath.

If this happens, practice steady breathing for a few minutes. This will allow you to calm your brain and allow you to think more rationally. You want to be mentally sharp while lessening the fear of instability and insecurity.

Type Seven

Sevens are looking to have fun and go on plenty of adventures. They even want to be a little creative in what they want to do. Sevens can mentally handle a lot of information and stimuli.

They consider themselves multi-taskers rather than people who focus on one thing at a time. They live by the personal philosophy that there are no rules and no limits. If anything, they should focus on breathing exercises that will help them become more self-aware of what's around them and what's going on.

It's okay to get lost in the moment. But it's also another thing to know what you're doing. But don't let that spoil the fun.

For Sevens, breathing into your belly will be important. You will want to pay attention to the sensations located in the lower body. Also, focus on your feet as they touch the ground.

During these breathing exercises, imagine yourself as a plant. Your feet are considered the roots and you are planted into the ground. Once you feel like you are 'leaving your body', drop back down so you can feel the breath in your belly and the sensations in your feet.

Pay close attention to your breath so you can slow down and be in the moment. This will come in handy whether you are at work, at home, or anywhere else.

Type Eight

By nature, Eights are naturally assertive. And they are very good at accessing their instinctual energy. They are driven and highly confident in themselves.

However, when they feel angry, that emotion might be within an arm's reach. They do their best to distance themselves from vulnerable feelings. When under pressure, Eights are hardened like steel.

If they mix high energy and enthusiasm, Eights risk overexerting themselves. And that can get to be a little too much. That is why breathing exercises are so vital, especially for Eights.

You must relax and soften your strength so you can be more in tune with your feelings. As you allow yourself to open your heart center, you will increase your capacity for empathy and emotional receptivity. This will allow you to have a better time building relationships with those who are considered equals or even subordinates.

While you practice breathing, refrain from using your chest. The last thing you want to do is 'power up'. So, what you'll need to do is breathe into your belly, allowing yourself to calm down.

If you are angry, take 10 slow breaths. Whoever came up with the old 'count to ten when you're angry' idea obviously was onto something. Before you react to something that may be considered bad or not-so-good news, practice where you're following your breath 'down and in'.

This will allow you more flexibility. And it will allow you to relax, even in out-of-control moments.

Type Nine

Nines may lose touch with their bodies at times. But they are more in tune with their intuition than anyone else. They may focus on their gut, but they need to pay more attention to it.

They must stay comfortable most of the time. So, it would be ideal for them to practice breathing exercises that will help them stay focused and maintain their inner peace. Nines are people who know what they want, and they know how to get it.

They may be uncomfortable with breathing practices at first. But they will get the hang of it sooner or later. Most of the time, they need to focus on conscious breathing practices. This is especially when they need to get in touch with their bodies, feelings, and intuition. While they are breathing, they will be in touch with themselves internally. You should focus on breathing into your chest so you can build more physical energy and vitality.

Final Thoughts

Breathing regularly (especially when practicing) will allow you to increase your capacity in many areas. You will become more in tune with yourself emotionally and physically. These breathing exercises may be uncomfortable to do from the start.

But when you start doing them regularly, you will feel a lot better after each practice period. You will find yourself more in tune and aware of yourself. For every Enneagram type, there is a unique breathing pattern that needs to be followed.

However, if there are some breathing practices that are not working in your favor, you can always fall back on some of the active breathing practices. If the anxiety isn't coming down after regular breathing, then you can rely on the anti-anxiety breathing patterns as a last resort.

Regular breathing practices are all part of the growth and living process when you rely on the Enneagram. No matter your type, make yourself time to perform the breathing exercises as listed above (even the practices based on your own type).

Chapter 4: The Principles of The Enneagram

The next big part of the Enneagram that you must understand are the principles. We will be taking a look at six of them and discussing each of them in detail. At this point, you already have the various breathing exercises (including the exercises that are based on each Enneagram type).

The Enneagram is something that we should live by. But we should also understand what the Enneagram is and what it stands for. Yes, it can change you for the better, but it does not define whether or not you are good or evil.

You may have had some assumptions about the Enneagram and what it can do for you. Once you learn these six principles of the Enneagram, you can get a good idea of how to actually use it. With that in mind, let's dive right in:

The Six Principles

1. Your personality does not change from one type to another

To kick-off, we begin with the first and most important principle of the Enneagram. Your personality based on your

Enneagram type is something that you will have for as long as you live. In other words, you cannot be a Type 8 and then turn around and change into someone who is a Type 2.

Likewise, you cannot become a Type 7 and change yourself into a Type 5. There are qualities and traits that are further embedded into your mind and soul that will define your Enneagram type. You can make as many external changes as you want (but internally, you will be more of the same).

When you discover your Enneagram type, you will need to work with what you've got in order to become a healthier version of yourself. Working on yourself to accommodate your Enneagram type is what we aim for. Your personality is your personality no matter how hard you try to change yourself.

Simply put, you don't 'change' yourself. You 'improve'. There is a difference between change and improvement.

2. Each type is universal and can be applied to all genders

Every Enneagram type will carry no favor to one gender. Not every Two is female and not every Eight is male. All genders can apply to any of the nine types of the Enneagram.

You may be thinking to yourself if you are feeling like you are acting more feminine because you are loving and supportive as a Two who is male. That is far from the truth.

Or you may feel like you are being overtly masculine as a female who is an Eight, but you are someone who likes to take charge and lead. Your personality does not define your gender (and vice-versa). Our Enneagram type defines us in our own unique way.

3. Each type cannot be applied to someone forever, as human nature fluctuates

To better explain this, human nature can fluctuate between two levels, healthy and unhealthy. You may do your best to keep yourself at a healthy level. However, if you don't keep yourself in check because of the way human nature fluctuates, you may fall into unhealthy levels that will allow you to access your negative feelings and traits.

The description of each type may change over time. But it may not change your Enneagram type in the slightest. But you may experience typical negative behaviors displayed by unhealthy versions of your type.

That is why it is important to keep yourself at healthy levels. If you see the slightest hint of any unhealthy traits, you may want to keep them in check and keep away from them. You can improve in many areas of your life, even if you somehow find yourself in a not-so-great situation that causes you to reach unhealthy levels.

4. The numbers are considered neutral, but they represent each type

When we talk about Ones, Twos, or Fives, we're not just talking about specific Enneagram types. These numbers are simply...well, numbers. They are considered neutral and do not represent a scale of good or bad, best or worse, and so on.

These types typically will need a name in order to distinguish themselves from one type to the next. Yes, there are different types. So, naming them with the use of numbers will allow us to easily identify them.

5. The order of 1 to 9 does not represent good or bad

Tying to the point of the fourth principle, the numbers of one to nine do not represent good or bad. For example, one being good and nine being bad. The numbers are there as labels to distinguish one type from another.

Furthermore, neither Enneagram type is considered to be nicer (or evil) compared to the others. So, don't think for a moment that Type 2s are nice while Type 8s are evil. Having said this, let's take a closer look at the final principle.

6. No type is better or worse than the other, they all have advantages and disadvantages

Each Enneagram type has its own advantages and disadvantages. A Three should be considered in no way better than say a One. Even though they may have accomplished more than them, it doesn't make a difference in the eyes of the Enneagram.

Threes will be easier to connect, driven to achieve certain goals, and want to gain recognition for those accomplishments. However, they have the disadvantage of having a competitive drive that can get the best of them if they are not careful. On the other hand, Ones are looking to make changes in the ways that they see fit.

But one glaring disadvantage that they have is their strive for perfection may anger them at times. When something they thought looks great sports a blemish, they will feel disappointed and feel like they can do nothing right. Each personality type can live a healthy life and be aware of the advantages and disadvantages of their personality.

Despite the One being a perfectionist, they need to come to the conclusion that nobody is perfect. Especially when it's defined by their own Enneagram type.

Final Thoughts

Now that you know these six principles, you can see that the Enneagram doesn't define who is better or worse in terms of their personality. It doesn't label who is good and who is evil. And it shows that you have a unique personality that cannot be changed no matter how hard you try.

You should also understand that because of human nature, personality types (be it your own or others) may have their health levels fluctuate. Some Sevens can be healthier than others. Some Sevens may also feel like there is no point in living their life anymore for some reason.

This is why it is so important to try your best to be your healthiest. Keep in mind that just because you are a Type One, it doesn't make you nicer or eviler than a Type Two. And a Nine isn't superior to all other Enneagram types because it is the highest number.

The numbers exist as labels. It's used to distinguish one type from the other. Follow these principles and you will be able to get a better look at the Enneagram and how it works.

Chapter 5: The Elements of The Universal Growth Process

For the next two chapters, we will delve into the growth process using the Enneagram. In the first of these two chapters, we will talk about what is known as the universal growth process. There are three different developmental elements that encompass universal growth -- personal, professional, and spiritual.

Growing into a much-improved version of ourselves will take time and effort. We are looking to cultivate ourselves into much healthier versions of our Enneagram type. We won't strive to be perfect or flawless by any stretch of the imagination.

But we are trying to be our best without slipping into an unhealthy lifestyle that may be rife with destructive behavior towards others and ourselves. You can grow with the Enneagram in ways where it can improve your personal and professional relationships. Furthermore, you can also improve on being more spiritual.

In this chapter, you will learn the definition of the universal growth process (all while understanding the elements in more depth). This includes the '5 A's' that make up this process in particular. With that said, let's not waste any more time and dive in:

The Universal Growth Process Defined

The Universal Growth Process is a process that is based on three major areas of your life: personal, professional, and spiritual. You can grow as a person to where you become a better friend or partner. You can grow into being that model employee or later employer.

And you can also grow into someone more spiritual and more in touch with yourself. There is always room for improvement no matter where you are in life. If you're in an area where it is considered unhealthy, you have no place to go but up (if you so choose).

The Five A's of Universal Growth

There are 'Five A's' of universal growth. We will be taking a look at them and explaining why they are a part of this group that pertains to the growth process. This is a practical and powerful way to develop yourself in the personal sense.

Once you have a deep understanding of each of these Five A's, you will be able to know the ins and outs of universal growth. You will see the results through your cultivation in many areas of your life. The Five A's are as follows: Awareness, Acceptance, Appreciation, Action, and Adherence.

Let's go further in-depth with each one:

Awareness

The first A is 'awareness'. This is the practice of being able to increase our receptivity and be able to ground ourselves while being present in the moment. This is the most crucial of the A's.

Without awareness, we would have no clue about where we are, how we are feeling, or what we're doing. We wouldn't be able to make conscious or even thoughtful choices that will either better or make our lives worse. Living without awareness is like flying a plane into dense fog at night without knowing where we are.

To access and even sharpen our awareness, the key is to use the breathing exercises of the previous chapter. Making sure that you are centered will also open up and increase your overall awareness. Ongoing practice is what keeps your awareness alive.

While practicing awareness, you are able to increase your self-observation as well as your grounded presence and your receptivity. You can grasp onto actual core beliefs while letting go of other beliefs that are considered irrelevant. From there, we are able to increase our understanding, flexibility, and adaptability.

As our awareness heightens, so does our ability to change, grow, and develop. We are able to witness what we see while we're in the moment. Any breathing practice, whether it's based on your Enneagram type or a simple five-minute session will develop and heighten your overall awareness.

Basic breathing practice for beginners

If you have yet to start the breathing and centering practices, refer back to that previous chapter. If you are a complete beginner and have never done breathing exercises before, you can start with a simple breathing exercise. For beginners, a simple five minutes is a good starting point.

Here's what you need to do:

- Find a chair to sit in or sit on the floor in the lotus position. If sitting in a chair, make sure that your feet are touching the floor

- Close your eyes and remove any attention you are placing on any external stimuli that you may be focusing on

- As you sit in your desired position, make sure you relax. Start breathing and begin to follow your breath. When you breathe, you will notice your body starting to soften. Be sure that you are aware of this rather than be distracted by external stimuli or even thoughts running through your head

- Continue to follow your breath. Allow it to get deeper and deeper. Meanwhile, allow it to disappear just below the area of your body where the gravitational center is located

- If you notice your attention starting to focus on a thought, sensation, or feeling, just acknowledge it

357

and divert your attention back to the breath. Continue to follow that breath

- After that five-minute session (or however long you set it for), slowly shift your attention back to the world around you. Focus on you sitting in the chair, the sounds that exist around you, and slowly open your eyes.

After a while, you may feel like five minutes may be a little too short for time. You can increase your time by five minutes. So, after doing five-minute sessions, you can up it to ten minutes.

Then you can up it to 15 minutes and then go up to 20 minutes when you are comfortable. But what if five minutes is a little too long for you? Not to worry, we have an idea that can allow you to start.

You can start with sessions that last two minutes. You can take two minutes out of your day to do a simple breathing exercise that will allow you to be aware of what's going on and quickly center yourself. Alternatively, you can also do short periods that are spread throughout the day (at least two to four to be specific).

These breathing practices can be done solo or with a group of people. And remember, there is no such thing as bad practice. You may struggle at first, but you will get the hang of it over time.

Acceptance

The next stage is acceptance. With awareness comes accepting what is occurring in the moment. In order to increase that acceptance, you want to have a positive attitude (especially one that is caring).

With acceptance, you will be able to be friendly towards your reactivity. At the same time, it will allow you to easily work with your judgment that pertains to yourself and other people (along with the feelings and sensations associated with it). You may ask yourself the following questions based on specific feelings.

Are you feeling angry, sad, jealous, happy? It's important to answer this question with as much honesty as possible. If we become judgmental, it's become defensive and even rationalizes what we are doing or how we are feeling.

Judging ourselves and others usually come naturally. We feel the need to justify and defend our judgments. Instead, we must be present with a state of curiosity.

If we cannot have acceptance, then awareness will create an endless cycle of suffering that we will never get out of. It is best for us to open our hearts and accept the things that we are aware of at the moment. You can work on yourself from where you currently are and travel on a journey towards wholeness.

If anything, acceptance should not be confused for many things. It shouldn't be confused for permission, agreement, condoning, or resignation. Acceptance is defined as taking a stand.

It's a stand from being non-judgmental. It's a stand from receptivity. You can use this for the purpose of making changes and finding positive resolutions. Everyone regardless of their Enneagram type has to start somewhere (and it's likely a different place from where you are).

But the journey that we go on is usually the same. It is the journey towards personal, professional, and spiritual growth. Some may get to their destination quicker or slower than others (and that's OK).

The Superego or critical mind

As mentioned, understanding acceptance is knowing that it doesn't mean condoning, agreeing, and so on. This requires an even deeper understanding of something known as the superego or the critical mind. This will allow you the ability to develop a healthy conscience.

Or it can also develop a barrier that may separate you from true acceptance. The superego is defined as a structure that includes ideals and standards that are considered acceptable and reasonable. It is developed through internalizing and identifying the values, rules, and beliefs of culture and authority figures such as your parents or guardians.

It is important to have positive functions that will support your personality structure and provide you with guidance for a healthy life. However, the superego can prevent that from happening since it acts like a barrier. It will stand against anything that represents the expansion of awareness and growth.

One of the greatest characteristics of the superego is that it is grounded in the past. Its job is to preserve what is considered as the 'status quo'. It also creates things such as conditional love and constantly rejects ideas that are considered new.

It can also create aggressiveness or even anger while creating distress and suffering. A negative superego can and will hinder your growth process. But there is a way to work on it.

Working with a negative superego

A negative superego has various elements. These include but are not limited to anger, tension, defensiveness, complaint, reactive action, and criticism. To recognize this superego's existence, you must develop awareness to know that it's just there.

The way to work on this negative superego is treating it like a beast. You have to 'starve the beast'. You should not feed it.

To kill the beast is to starve it or pay no attention to it. And the best way to go about doing this is by doing our regular breathing exercises and disengaging the superego. Reminding yourself that you want to be aware while being good to yourself (even in the moment) is the best route to take.

Keep in mind that when doing this, this isn't condoning or agreeing with the behavior. You are taking care of the problem by acknowledging it and doing something about it to where your negative superego is shrinking.

Appreciation

The third A is appreciation. We take notice of what we are grateful for in our lives (especially with an open heart). We focus on the positives whether they are unique or ordinary.

We allow ourselves to be in a natural flow where we are able to give and receive. When we do this regularly, we start to feel the flow of good feelings. When we open our hearts, we want to feel good all the time (which is key to living a healthy life).

Action

We will be taking a look at three non-linear steps that involve this 'A' in particular. Taking action in this context is defined as conscious conduct. In other words, you will learn to rid your life of old habits or least stimulating activities of discernment.

Let's take a look at the first step:

1. **Pause:** This starts after you notice your reactivity. You pause, collect and contain your energy. Pausing will allow you to delay the response and

allow you to recover. At the same time, it increases the capacity of 'knowings'. This requires using your awareness and non-judgmental acceptance. Furthermore, it will allow you to pick up more on your reactions and distress. You can pause this by using the breathing and centering exercises described in the previous chapter (or the basic breathing practice from earlier).

You will be able to collect your energy and draw it back to your gravitational center with the help of deep breaths. This will allow you to be aware of the negative feelings so you can get rid of them just by 'accepting' them. Moving on from them and not letting them get the best of you is the key here.

Practicing containment will allow us to hold our center and ground us with what is going on.

2. **Inquiry:** The question here is what is driving our reactivity? To know this, you want to practice what is known as gentle inquiry. This will allow you to discover, discern, and work with the issues that arise and trigger that reactivity. This could be anger, distress, or the like. It is important for you to adopt a stance that is made of genuine curiosity so you can learn the truth about this reactivity. This inquiry is about considering our usual reactivity and the responses are 'automatic'.

The responses will allow us to develop further and make changes due to the following: One, it allows us to identify old core beliefs and discover the associations and feelings tied to them. Each Enneagram type has its unique old core beliefs. For example, Ones have the old belief in wanting to always be right or good and never being wrong. We must also dig deeper with personal stories or wounds that are connected to this old core belief. These are known as the root origins as it writes the personal story of our lives.

3. **Action of Conscious Conduct:** What you may need is an 'inner coach'. There is no one better fitting and capable to do the job than yourself. To do this, you want to be thoughtful, supportive, and non-judgmental. You want to encourage yourself. You want to be accepting, take conscious outer action, and combine both acceptance and outer action. To release yourself into acceptance, you want to stay with the experience and relax into the inner knowing. You will also realize that your old habits and reactions are no longer valid. It will be easy for you to let go and be more aware. We experience our essential qualities that we must be more receptive to. Keep in mind that these qualities don't come and go, but rather our ability of being in touch with them do.

Adherence

This is the final "A" that we must use for daily practice. Adherence is defined as the recognition of the reality that allows you to learn new things. This is done by combining observation, experience, and practice.

Without any of these elements in the combination, nothing happens. What we look for is intention. This is the key that will allow us to acquire adherence. This will allow us to find pleasure and relief from any pain while acquiring a greater freedom from them.

Adherence is like feeding ourselves daily. When we're hungry, we eat. If we don't eat, we starve.

The truth is, we must care for ourselves spiritually and emotionally on a daily basis. We must have that intention of doing so. We also face the prospect of getting into situations where reactivity and challenge will exist.

These situations present the perfect opportunity to work on our own self-development. We come to the realization that we can use our type-based gifts and strengths while identifying the things that upset us or challenge our daily lives.

Using This Process in Our Personal and Professional Relationships

This growth process is indeed universal (hence the name). Performing the practices based on the five A's of Universal Growth does apply to our personal and professional relationships. The things that stress us out and give us great pain can exist anywhere.

So, it is important for us to be sure that we put things into practice on a regular basis. Especially when we are in times of stress. It is also important for each type to shed their own old core beliefs (which we will cover briefly).

In personal relationships, you will do your best to ensure that you will do your part to improve on them. In professional relationships, the same concept applies whether you are an authority figure or a subordinate.

Old Core Beliefs Based on Types

Our core beliefs are built on the three basic needs of love, worth, and security. However, our old core beliefs may disrupt these needs. For each type, we must identify these and shed them.

Let's take on each old core belief based on type:

Type One: Their old core belief is the wanting of being right all the time and avoiding being wrong.

Type Two: To give all the time and not be rendered useless.

Type Three: Being successful and not being unable to do it completely.

Type Four: Feeling special or complete and not feeling deficient.

Type Five: The need to be self-sufficient and not feeling depleted.

Type Six: Being certain or sustaining and not feeling dependent or helpless.

Type Seven: Keeping life open and free of boundaries instead of feeling limited.

Type Eight: Being powerful and strong without feeling powerless at all.

Type Nine: Seeking significance without feeling dismissed.

Final Thoughts

Developing ourselves based on the universal growth process is essential. It starts by knowing and understanding the Five A's of Universal Growth. Acceptance is the first and foremost step.

Without acceptance, you may not be able to rely on the rest of the A's to grow. You may not acquire appreciation, take action, and gain adherence. Being aware of how you feel, what's going on around you, and where you are in life is essential to growth.

The Universal Growth Process also allows you to identify and get rid of the old core beliefs that may be a source of distress, anger, and frustration. You want to replace those beliefs with the idea that while you are able to contribute to things that will yield positive results, there will always be the negatives that will attempt to throw you off.

But it takes regular practice to ensure that you are in the moment and accept that not everything will be perfect. Using this growth process will help you improve considerably in a personal, professional, and spiritual sense.

Chapter 6: Growing with The Enneagram

The Enneagram is essential for growth. You can grow spiritually, personally, and professionally using the practices based on your type. Later on, we will discuss the specific practices tailored to your type, so you know what to do in certain situations.

Being able to grow and improve yourself for the better will be a greater accomplishment. If you are a type Three that thrives on them, you may find this to be one of your greatest accomplishments yet. The recognition for it is when people around you will notice that you have grown and how far you've come from start to finish.

Speaking of practices, this chapter will introduce you to the personal growth practices that you must use based on your personality type. We will revisit these again later on. But until then, we will do our best to give you an overview of what you should do in order to grow, whether you are a Type One or a Type Nine.

We will also focus on how you can grow in a professional setting. Each Enneagram type has something for everyone when it comes to their professional life. Some Enneagram types are more drawn towards authority while others are more drawn towards being a subordinate.

Likewise, there are Enneagram types where people can work with groups while others tend to work alone. The more you follow these practices, the better. Now, let's begin with the Five Steps for Growth

The Five Steps for Enneagram Growth

Before we unveil the growth practices based on type, we will go over the five basic steps that you will need to follow for using the Enneagram for such a purpose. This will allow you to know where to go when it comes to achieving growth and eventually total freedom. Let's begin with the first step:

1. Make peace with your Enneagram type

When first discovered, there are those who are resistant to their Enneagram type. They may deny this by saying 'I am not this person' or 'I am nowhere near this' (or the like). As mentioned in an earlier chapter, you cannot change your personality or Enneagram type.

So, the best thing you can do at this point is make peace with it. There is no shame for who you are. The Enneagram is as accurate as possible.
As one of the principles states, there is no right or wrong as far as personality types are concerned. You are unique in image and character. You have strengths, weaknesses, advantages, and disadvantages.

You are you for a reason. And if you are a believer in God, you will say that he made you for a reason. And he put you on Earth for some kind of purpose.

2. Identify the areas where you wish to grow

After accepting and making peace with your Enneagram type, you have cleared a great hurdle. At this point, you will need to find areas where you want to grow. You can identify this by taking a look at the issues that you may be facing right now.

This includes thought patterns that are considered negative. It may be a bad relationship that you're in, or a destructive behavior that you're doing and not knowing that you are doing harm rather than good. You know that you want the exact opposite of the negative things you are experiencing at the moment.

Once you are able to identify the area of growth, you want to remind yourself that there are two ways to use the Enneagram. There is a right way and there's a wrong way. You do not want to use it as some kind of weapon that will be used to attack others and justify your negative behavior.

Also, it should be used to shield ourselves from negative criticism and the like. The Enneagram is used as a navigational tool. It's a map or a GPS that will take us from Point A to Point B.

We must navigate through obstacles and everything else to ensure that we live our healthiest lives. Likewise, we must use it in order to stay the course and never stray off of it.

3. Surrender to your journey

Your journey towards a healthier life is your mission. You should surrender yourself to it. You must not surrender yourself to the things that are considered a source of stress, anger, and the like. If you are spiritual or religious, you can surrender your journey to God or that 'higher power'.

Surrendering to your journey will make putting the pieces of your growth strategy together a lot easier. Surrender your old core beliefs and accept the new beliefs that make you healthy. Surrender your unhealthy behaviors and exchange them for new ones.

Accept the fact that this journey will not be easy. There will be potholes, setbacks, and everything in between. But you have the Enneagram to rely on to get you through it all.

4. Putting knowledge into practice

You can talk the talk. But the question is: can you walk the walk? Taking this important step will answer that question.

The Enneagram is something that will allow us to keep us on the path when we are en route to better growth. While we mentioned it as a navigation device, it also works as something else. Imagine driving down a highway in the middle of the night.

You fall asleep for a bit and veer a bit off the road. Suddenly, you are awake after hearing a rumbling noise. The Enneagram is that rumble strip that keeps you on the road instead of off course.

That veering off is paying attention to your old core beliefs that you are moving towards after separating yourself from them. The Enneagram will gently pull you back. It's a way to remind you to not go back to the way things were.

Once you know what you know, putting it into practice might be difficult. But don't let that discourage you in the slightest. The more you put things into practice, the better off you will be.

5. Application of the Enneagram by way of grace

Giving yourself grace is the best thing to do if you hit those potholes or veer off course. By doing this, you can easily apply the Enneagram in both a personal and professional setting. Being gentle with yourself is a lot better than being rigid.

Growing into an optimal version of yourself will give you an easier time to be graceful with yourself. It also gives you the will to press on no matter how many times you reach a dead end. Even if you've reached your ideal self, there is always room for improvement no matter how large or trivial it may be.

How to Speed Up Your Personal Growth Development Based on Type

Every Enneagram faces their unique challenges. And they have their own coping mechanisms. However, we want to grow at a personal level even for a short period of time.

Our personal development will rely on solutions rather than exacerbate the problems we face. We must also avoid those problems altogether. Let's take a look at how you can speed up your personal growth based on your Enneagram type:

Type One

If there is one type that is 'best friends' with their inner critic, it's Type Ones. That inner critic has a loud voice that would often measure the actions against their ideals. This is something that repeats itself over and over again.

Ones believe that they should satisfy their inner critic. They believe it can lead them to self-actualizing themselves. However, this achieves the exact opposite.

In order for Type Ones to grow personally, they need to come to peace with the fact that trying to perfect themselves is a waste of time. Instead, they need to accept their core nature. Furthermore, you need to silence that inner critic by setting yourself free from such judgment.

You can allow other people to silence their inner critics as well while providing the world with more compassion and grace. You are on the mission to make the world better. And what a great starting point than providing it with compassion, grace, and all kinds of positivity?

With that said, Ones should enjoy their freedom that exists beyond judgment.

Type Two

Type Twos are people pleasers. Doing this may be very hard to resist. They feel good knowing that they can help others.

But, for a Two to develop at a personal level, they want to practice radical authenticity. By doing this, you as a Two will need to think less about the needs of others (to an extent). It may sound like what you're doing is selfish, but it really isn't.

You want to be confident enough to express yourself. Even if you have to set that example, so be it. This is where focusing on yourself as opposed to others in one area comes into play.

So be authentic when you want to set a good example for others to follow.

Type Three

Threes are shapeshifters by nature. If they fill a role, it's one that receives the most reverence. Hustling hard may be the modus operandi of the Three. But it's usually the complete opposite at times.

A personal development step for Threes to take is focusing less on the illusion that you want to create for yourself. Instead, you want to make peace with the realities of what you are capable of and what you can bring to the table.

Authenticity is important here. And you want to make peace with the hard truths. You can lead with a purpose, understand the hard truths, and let people know about them so they understand.

A true mark of a leader is being transparent and being truthful with others. You will gain acceptance of these hard truths and be able to accomplish what you can while feeling happy.

Type Four

Fours are acutely aware of the things that are considered lacking in the world. But they should use this as a tool for their own personal development. Therefore, a Type Four would need to embody those things they see as lacking.

This will depend on what you might be craving as a child. It could be leadership that is considered just and compassionate. However, that leader that displays these qualities should be you as an adult.

The key takeaway is to become the person you needed early in your life. If you cannot get what you want, become that. It's the equivalent of wanting something you cannot find, so you make it based on your own ideas and needs.

Type Five

Fives are often looking for new ideas and facts. So, it might make sense for them to find ways to improve themselves for personal growth. They have a penchant for learning, thus it could be easier for them to find a way to expand their awareness.

They are looking for a willingness to act on their own understanding of things. That's why it is important for them to use the complex part of it to whittle down which changes will need to be made. From there, they will need to prioritize it from what needs urgent attention down to those that can be solved but are not as urgent.

Instead of relying on more research, you can make the changes yourself. You have the gift of capability and competence. Why rely on others to carry out those changes when you can do it yourself?

If nobody is making changes, it's up to you to do it yourself. After all, you tend to work alone. Therefore, it allows you to better focus on the mission you set out to do.

Type Six

Reliability and trustworthiness are what the Six wants. They may have an obsession with it. Because of this, their path towards personal growth may lead them to take detours that are supposed to lead to their pursuit of truth.

In other words, Sixes may be more apt to take side roads rather than staying on the main one that leads to personal growth. For this reason, there need to be roadblocks for those side roads. And it must be the Six's responsibility to set them up.

Therefore, a Six must focus less on their insecurities. Instead, they should reinvest their attention and energy on intellectual gaps that are creating division in the world. You have the ability to discern and discover things.

Use those abilities to identify what is trustworthy in a world that direly needs such a trait. This will be something that will allow you to grow not just personally, but intellectually as well.

For Sixes, finding the answers that will bridge the world together is what they should do. And they should stick to their pursuit.

Type Seven

Sevens are firm believers in being limitless. It can get to the point where they may neglect their own personal and intellectual development. They never say no to new challenges, so they may want to be willing to develop better growth in these areas.

Sevens should find that internal knowledge that will open the gateways towards more external freedom. Because of this, they will have a deeper understanding coupled with many opportunities to share their experiences with others. They also use this to teach and connect with others that are pursuing various interests.

If there are people who are interested in the things you care about, this is your time to shine. You will give yourself more opportunities to connect with others while experiencing maximum freedom. Your curiosity is your ticket to freedom, so don't waste it.

Type Eight

Eights are strong-willed. They know what they want, and they can easily get it. They exude that attitude every single time.

Granted, they struggle with will most of the time. Eights can easily tackle obstacles, but it seems counterintuitive to them as far as their personal growth is concerned. So, what will it take for an Eight to be more focused?

An Eight's path towards self-development boils down to making an impact on others. It should not only matter to them, but also to the people around them. Eights are contributors to causes that are looking for someone strong enough to push it through.

Hold yourself accountable. At the same time, watch your growth materialize into something greater.

Type Nine

Type Nines see the ways that the world is being torn and busted apart. However, they are unfamiliar with the impact being made due to it. They should stand out in multiple ways.

Therefore, they want to hustle for wholeness in the world. Their natural understanding of the issues surrounding the world will lead to the solutions. You have a set of eyes that allows you to see things beyond what everyone else sees.

From there, you can find the solutions that will solve these problems as a whole rather than partially.

Final Thoughts

Growth with the Enneagram is possible. Especially when you are focused on personal growth. Before you start your journey, you need to understand the five major steps we have outlined.

The Enneagram is a tool that should not be taken for granted. And it certainly shouldn't be used for something that would be considered 'improper use'. This is your map towards better growth.

And your growth goals are based on your Enneagram type. Realize what you need to do in order to grow based on your type and you will be able to fulfill your mission with ease. And finally, be sure to stay on the main path rather than veer off course and end up in a ditch of despair and unhealthiness.

Chapter 7: The End of Determinism

Determinism: *The doctrine that all events, including human action, are determined by causes external to the will. Some philosophers have taken determinism to imply that individual human beings have no free will and cannot be held morally responsible for their own actions.*

Above is the definition for the word determinism. Are we to believe that people may not have free will and not be held responsible for their actions? Maybe.

But when you think about it, determinism may seem like a glorified term for making excuses for ourselves. We also may be more apt to blame others for our own actions even if it isn't their fault. You may or may not have done this in the past, but it is time to put an end to this practice.

In this chapter, we will talk about determinism and how we should end such practice. We will explain what it is and how it differs from free will. We will also discuss how it all ties into the Enneagram.

Now, let's discuss determinism and the types that exist:

External vs Internal Determinism

There are two kinds of determinism: external and internal. What makes them different between the two? Let's discuss:

External Determinism

External determinism is also known as environmental determinism. What this is defined as is the cause of behaviors outside one individual person. Specifically, these causes include influence from parents, educators, the media, and so on.

In other words, someone can develop certain habits and behaviors based on what they have learned from these external influences. And it could also determine some personality types at a young age. For example, Twos may have grown up without receiving a lot of love from their parents.

For this reason, they will reach deep down inside them and be able to love and give to others. They make it their mission to make sure people feel appreciated, even if they don't get it from those who are supposed to do so by default (like family). So, Twos will feel like they are on a mission to right the wrongs that they have suffered themselves.

Another example of external determinism, we'll be looking at Ones. Their mission is to make the world a better place. But they want it to be perfect to the point where it can be portrayed in the media or some other medium to let the world know about it.

They watch the news and everything they see is bad. To this end, they are angry. And they want change.

This anger drives them to become active in creating some kind of change or reform. And they will stop at nothing to make sure that they and others who join their cause get it right. What they see as negative, they want to turn into a positive.

These are just examples of Enneagram types that are going by the opposite of how those external influences operate. Twos don't get love, but they give it to others. Ones see the wrongs in the world but want to make it right.

But what about Enneagram types that run concurrently with such sentiments? Let's take a look at Type Threes. Threes may come from families where their parents want to see them succeed.

The parents of Threes may be Threes themselves (or something different). They want their children to succeed in some way they see as fit. They have specific measurements of success depending on their philosophy and culture.

For this reason, the younger Threes may feel family pressure to live up to their family name by achieving success in what they believe is their own right. So, the question that has to be asked is: is a Three's success their own or is it the success of their parents who may live vicariously through their lives?

That's a thought-provoking question for the ages. But this is one example of which an Enneagram type may do something similar to what the external influences expect them to do. While most Enneagram types may develop their personalities based on the opposite of what these influences do to people.

Internal Determinism

Internal determinism is adopted based on a biological perspective. What can be created based on this? Personality traits such as being an extrovert or even neurotic may exist through internal determinism.

These traits may be triggered by processes that are neurological or even hormonal. Some may view this as us being biological machines. We may even link internal determinism to how we behave ourselves based on childhood events or even unconscious motivation.

Free Will

Free will allows us to make the choices we want. It allows us to take the actions we want to take. It is free will that will allow us to make a choice of whether or not we do something wrong or right.

The actions we choose based on free will are not chosen at random. We think the decision through with consciousness. Furthermore, we are aware that whatever action we take, we are responsible for them.

There is an argument that because of free will, not every behavior will be determined. We base things on personal agency (or the exercise of free will). Personal agency is the choices we make, the paths we travel, and what we face as rewards or consequences.

As with any Enneagram type, you have a choice to do what you believe is the best course of action. Sometimes, the choice is a no-brainer because it fits your personality type. For example, a Five may choose to interact with some people, but feels that it may be better not to.

Or if a Seven, with an abundance of options, wants to choose to do something that is 'spur of the moment', they'll do it. Sevens are probably the most advantageous when it comes to free will. That's because they are firm believers in living life without boundaries or rules.

Determinism, Free Will, and the Enneagram

Before going any further, let us circle back to one of the principles of the Enneagram. There is no type that is considered good or evil. Especially when they are compared to each other.

In other words, no matter what Enneagram type you are, there are things for certain: one, you are always responsible for your actions, no matter how trivial they are. Two, you have free will that you can exercise if you so choose.

For example, you have a choice to improve and grow based on the Enneagram. Or you may choose not to improve and grow at all. But given the benefits that outweigh the liabilities, the choice is a no-brainer.

The truth is, each Enneagram type needs to get rid of determinism since it may promote unhealthy traits. They should not be in the position to blame others for their mistakes or even their personality as a whole. They must make choices that will help them stay on the path of growth.

What the Enneagram tells us is that most of us are not acting out of free will. This is a surprising discovery. Instead, we may have spent time defending and justifying our actions based on our sense of self.

We feel like we need to defend, explain, and justify why we do things. This is a complete waste of time, especially when you want to focus on improving yourself in areas of your life. We must not live with a limited sense of self.

The Enneagram will allow us to find the areas where we are stuck, and we can choose to 'unstuck' ourselves. Therefore, we must free ourselves from the things that stunt us from achieving our full potential.

It's true that the ups and downs of everyday life veer us off course. But the truth is, as long as we are grounded, we are able to face adversity every single day. And we can act on our own free will accordingly.

Final Thoughts

Determinism and free will are two different things. But most importantly, we must hold ourselves accountable for our own actions. Regardless of Enneagram type, deferring blame to others as opposed to yourself is often seen as unhealthy.

Free will should be used for a greater good as opposed to a weapon of mass destruction. Free will is just as powerful as the Enneagram itself. You choose to chart the course of your life and carry out the plan.

You choose to make the decisions and the way you react based on good or bad situations. Your personality may be developed by external or internal determinism. It may also stem from both.

Either way, you must come to the realization that you have the freedom of choice when it comes to the way you act, the things you do, and how you can use the Enneagram based on your personality type.

Chapter 8: The Enneagram in Practice

There are different practices of the Enneagram each based on type. In the following chapters after this, we will provide you with the practices you must follow based on your Enneagram type and how to follow them.

This chapter is an overview of how they will work to your advantage. Now that you have an understanding of how to use the Enneagram (along with the ability to access your mindfulness at any given time), we will unveil how exactly you can use it as a guide to live a healthy life.

We will be focusing on how you can practice the Enneagram at work, with your romantic relationships, in ways that it will improve your life while strengthening both personal and professional relationships. As one of the principles states, it's more of a GPS to guide you through a healthier life.

As you put things into practice with the Enneagram, you will start to notice some shifts in your life. To be more specific, they are shifts and changes for the better. Your path towards a healthier life will start to take shape (especially when you begin implementing personal growth practices that we'll outline in each chapter).

The personal growth practices not only apply to how you handle things and yourself at home, but it also applies to the workplace as well. We encourage you to read your personal growth tips carefully once you reach the chapter that pertains to your Enneagram type.

We highly suggest that you do not skip this chapter as it provides you with an overview of what is to come in the final nine chapters of this book. With that said, let's begin:

The Enneagram at Work

As we break down each chapter, we will discuss how you can use the Enneagram at work. This includes the practices and preferences that apply for every Enneagram type. We will break down how each type prefers and performs in a certain way based on various tasks.

For example, you will learn how a One communicates via email (while knowing how they want a specific email set up). You will learn how to give feedback as a Two while you learn how you want to receive it yourself even from non-Twos. You will also learn how each Enneagram type resolves conflicts in the workplace.

If you are an employer, you will be able to match an employee based on their Enneagram type (if you so choose to observe and assume what their type is). From there, you can make notes on who may be the Ones, Twos, Threes, and so on. If you are an Eight that plans on running a business and overseeing employees, you may want to get a good idea of how each Enneagram type works in a professional setting.

You'll be able to determine which ones tend to work alone and which ones are more comfortable working with others.

This will make it easier for you to assign group projects, if necessary. In a professional workplace, you may have a way of getting things done and your preference as far as working with others.

However, with the growth practices based on the Enneagram, it may include steps that are designed to get you out of your comfort zone. It may be uncomfortable at first. But you may find yourself in a better position than you currently are now once you start to notice your growth and progress.

Enneagram in Relationships

If there is one thing that we want for every Enneagram type, it's a healthy relationship with the ones we love. Not every couple is a pair of Eights or Twos. Some couples have one that is an Eight while the other can be a Two.

While there may be opposites between two Enneagram types, there may be something that attracts them to one another. And that's something to keep in mind if you are one Enneagram type and your partner is the other. But it's always best to find ways to keep the relationship alive if you both can.

We will discuss how each Enneagram handles relationships and what they want out of them. We will also discuss what issues can occur based on one Enneagram type. What are the negatives that a Three can have in their relationship (for example)?

If you can handle the negatives and learn how to weather a storm with your significant other, the two of you can grow together.

Using The Enneagram to Improve Your Life

The Enneagram can be useful in improving your life. With your Enneagram type, you will be able to identify your strengths and weaknesses. You are able to determine your positive and negative traits.

You will learn about the things that stress you out the most (and how you can handle them). You will learn about what actually motivates you. It's all about improving your life for the positive.

There are solutions that we will provide for you based on some of the negative traits you may have. For example, if you are a One, you may feel like your perfectionism may make you out to be a monster in the eyes of others. You may be angry at everything not going your own way.

So, one of the best ways to relieve your stress is to realize the negative toll it can take on your health. Especially when you are stressed out constantly over the more trivial mistakes. We will dive into how Ones and all other Enneagram types handle stress in each chapter.

The Enneagram is that one thing that will help you stay on the path so you can live a healthy life (while being able to identify some of the traits and characteristics that may be considered unhealthy and doing something about them).

Using The Enneagram to Strengthen Relationships

Not only is the Enneagram a tool for your own personal improvements, but it strengthens your relationship with others. As you read through each Enneagram type, you will understand how they want to be treated by others. You will get a good idea of their needs, their likes, dislikes, aspirations, and so on.

It is important that you know how they can handle things such as communication, feedback, encouragement from people like you, and so on. Like you, they are people with needs, wants, and emotions. Don't use the Enneagram (or your type for that matter) to belittle or make yourself look superior to them.

If the Enneagram is used as a weapon of mass destruction, you risk damaging your relationships as opposed to strengthening and maintaining them.

Final Thoughts

Now that you have a good idea of how the Enneagram is put into practice, it is time to unveil the practices for each type. You may skip to the chapter based on your Enneagram type if you so choose. But we highly suggest that you read up on the other types (especially if you want to identify them).

This will allow you to act accordingly with people who identify as Ones, Threes, or Fives. It will also give you an understanding as to why some Enneagram types work well alone instead of others. And it will also give you an idea of what your significant other, who may be a different type than you, wants in a romantic relationship.

Using the Enneagram for self-growth and building relationships both professionally and personally will be key. It will allow you to stay on the path without veering off course. Aiming for a healthy life for yourself and others is what you want and the Enneagram (and the respected practices in the next chapter) can help.

Chapter 9: Practices for Type One

First, we will be taking a look at the practices that Types Ones must follow in order to live a much healthier life based on the Enneagram. As we go over all Enneagram types, we will be looking at various types including the breathing types (as we have introduced in the breathing and centering chapter), practices for personal and professional life, and others.

As Type Ones, they thrive on making the world a better place through change. But the truth is, they may find opportunities to make things perfect. They have plenty of room to grow while carrying out what seems to be their life's mission.

There are plenty of self-care tips and practices that we will be also taking a look at for ones, as well as other Enneagram types. If you are a Type One, you can keep reading down below. Otherwise, you may skip to the chapter that corresponds to your Enneagram type.

Before you do, we highly suggest that you check out some of the sections that will allow you to communicate with Ones effectively (i.e. - Type One Practices In Professional Settings, etc.)

With that said, let's take a look now at the practices for Ones:

Personal Growth Practices

Learn to relax

For Ones, their perfectionist behavior may make them get a little irritable when something isn't going their way. You may feel like everything you thought you did was right ends up wrong. And you feel like you cannot do anything right.

It is important that you take time for yourself. Don't feel like everything has to be done all at once. And don't think it's the end of the world if you don't accomplish something.

The salvation of the world is not your responsibility. There are seven billion people on Earth. There are more than enough people that can contribute to the cause.

If the weight of the world seems to be on your shoulders, take some time to perform breathing exercises that will allow you to stay calm. Keep the pressure off of you. Instead, focus on things that you know will benefit the world.

Teach people

Circling back to our statement on responsibility, you don't have to do every little thing all at once. That's why it is a great idea to teach people how you want things done. Instead of doing everything, you can delegate responsibility in order.

You provide them with the materials that they need to learn and apply. Let them know how it should be done. Those who agree with your worldview on things are usually the best students.

While you're at it, don't demand change to be done right away. Give them a chance to marinate everything you are teaching them. Provide them with the materials and the knowledge that change occurs over time, not at the snap of a finger.

Don't work yourself up

The people you teach may or may not make mistakes. Despite being a perfectionist, you want to be at peace with that. Therefore, it is important that you resist the urge to get worked up and lash out at others for their mistakes.

They may be wrong about something and you can be irritated. What exactly does that gain? Does it make things right?

The answer is a resounding no. Your irritation with their mistakes plus the irritation based on your shortcomings can come to a head. On top of that, your inner critic can only get louder and louder over time.

Lastly, learn how to spot any attacks on your superego and figure out how they do more harm than good.

Get in touch with your feelings

This goes for your unconscious impulses as well. You might feel uncomfortable with your emotions and impulse. But we're only human.

We can be perfectionists, but we can be messy at times. If you must, we suggest keeping a journal so you can document yourself as far as developing your emotions. For better results, you should consider group therapy or work that will help you restrain yourself from condemning others just for being humans with needs and limits.

Know the risks of your anger

Ones are prone to anger because of people making mistakes or not seeing things the way they want done. Being angry all the time is risky, especially when it comes to their own health. This includes but is not limited to ulcers and high blood pressure (the latter being linked to heart attacks and strokes).

You must learn how to step back and find out that your anger will alienate people rather than whip them into shape. It will also prevent you from saying positive things about people, the project you're focusing on, and so on.

Breathing Practices

For Ones, the key here is to find breathing practices that will allow you to relax. Use your diaphragm by breathing in through your belly and exhaling through your mouth. If all else fails, consider the relaxing breath (as described in the Breathing and Centering Chapter).

While performing these breathing exercises, you'll want to be able to identify the areas where tension is present. You want to let go of that tension as much as possible. Spread as much energy and sensation throughout your body.

Do not use your chest while performing these exercises. When doing these breathing practices, you could feel anxiety creeping in. If that is the case, be sure to use the breathing practices to your advantage.

If nothing seems to be working, shift to the anti-anxiety breathing technique as a last resort. This breathing technique in particular will take away any anxiety that you may have.

Stress-busting practices for Type Ones

Type Ones may be susceptible to being stressed out a lot. And as mentioned before, that can be detrimental to your health. So, what is a One to do when they are under stress?

Let's take a look at the following practices:

Spend quality time with family and friends: To help alleviate stress, there is nothing quite like being able to spend time with people who are important to you. This can be your family, a best friend, or anyone who brings out the best in you. Do fun activities that will allow you to keep your mind off of the things that stress you out most.

Schedule a 'day off': Whether you like it or not, you're going to want to take a break to charge your batteries. This can be a day to relax and reflect. Or you can do this for chunks of hours at a time. But it's better to block off an entire day for yourself so you can rest, relax, and recharge for the next day.

Watch/read something humorous: They say laughter is the best medicine. This could be the case for a One who is stressed out. Watch a funny movie or videos of standup comedians. Anything that can make you laugh and feel good will be great for busting your stress.

Take multiple planned breaks: Depending on how long the workdays are, multiple breaks (when planned out) are essential. Especially when the last thing you want to deal with is burnout. When you're burnt out, you cannot focus. Nor will you have any interest in working on the things that need to get done.

Find out which activities made you happy as a kid: There is no shame in getting in touch with your inner child. So, take the time to investigate which activities made you happy as a kid. You may have the itch to revisit them. There may be times in your childhood when you were generally happy. Think about them, relive them, and enjoy.

Type One Practices in A Professional Setting

If you are not a Type One, you'll want to find out how you can communicate with one in a professional setting. This includes work-related activities such as meeting with them, communication, giving feedback, and more.

Let's dive right in to see how Type Ones like to work:

Communicating

While communicating with a Type One, be sure to take them seriously. Also understand what their motivations are (especially when they are doing things they believe are right).

Meeting

Ones are punctual. They abide by the scheduled times when meetings are set. They are also focused on the purpose and message of the meeting itself.

Emailing

Type Ones appreciate it when emails are short and to the point. Address specifics of a certain project and encourage them to share their input (if needed).

Feedback

Feedback should be gentle, but constructive. Since Ones want a well-detailed plan, outline specific steps that will allow them to maximize their chances of improving.

Resolving conflict

Admitting your mistakes to Ones while expressing your feelings is important. As a One, you should give them a chance to reflect by themselves if they see it as fit.

Relationships in a Professional Setting

In a professional setting, Ones can work well with others. Especially if they are outgoing and more open. They can provide stability to the team and keep them grounded.

If they work with other Ones, they need to be aligned in terms of their shared goals and values. If this doesn't happen, there may be conflicts that arise. Aside from this, Ones will work with those who appreciate their desire to improve.

They also work with high levels of efficiency and accuracy. And they are dedicated to what they see as the bigger picture. But what about when they hit obstacles?

When Ones are faced with obstacles, they may give feedback in a harsh, blunt way. They may also correct and overlook what others are doing. Lastly, they may pressure others to keep up with their high standards.

Therefore, one needs to come to the realization that these obstacles should be no big deal. And it shouldn't upset them in the slightest. They need to come to the understanding that people in their group are human and will make mistakes if and when they happen.

Relationship Practices in a Romantic Setting

If you or a partner is a One, you will notice that they place a high value on honesty and motivation. They want someone who is relaxed and open-minded. Ones who are in relationships with other Ones will typically find ways to avoid conflict.

Here are some of the practices that Ones will need to put to good use in relationships:

Communication: Communication in a relationship must be open and honest. Especially when you are a One (or if your significant other is).

Try to do what's right: Doing what's right and being consistent about it should be what you and your partner do often.

Pursue personal growth: While you and your partner can grow together, it is important that both of you should focus on your individual personal growth as well. This will allow you to both thrive at a much greater level.

Final Thoughts

Ones can perform these practices to ensure that their perfectionism (and their emotions based on them) do not cloud them in any way. They should relax and accept the fact that people can make mistakes. At the same time, they must come to the realization that not everything that doesn't get accomplished will be the end of the world.

Every task or mission that is out there isn't always there for the taking. So, they shouldn't feel the need to carry the weight of the world on their shoulders. As much as it's standard for them to get worked up and even lash out at others, it's counterintuitive when you want something and can't seem to get it.

Getting angry over the imperfections can take a toll on your health. And it may be a source of constant stress. For this reason, be extra vigilant in keeping your stress at bay by using the stress-busting practices listed above.

And lastly, don't forget the breathing exercises. These are important in helping you open up your capacity as far as your emotional intelligence goes. Other than that, Ones can live a fulfilling life with honesty, the ability to work quickly and efficiently, and knowing that sometimes, mistakes happen and they shouldn't fret about them.

Chapter 10: Practices for Type Two

Now, we will be taking a look at the practices for Type Twos. This Enneagram type in particular may be one of the most easygoing of them all. But like the rest of them, they are not the best in terms of who is good and who is evil (after all, the Enneagram principles state that no type is neither good nor evil).

Twos are like Ones to an extent. They are looking to make the world a better place. And they do that based on their actions of kindness and love.

They are the helpers who are putting their needs off to the side so they can fulfill the needs of others. So how do they do in terms of relationships both in the professional and personal sense? How do they deal with stress?

Those are the questions we will answer in this question. Twos are no doubt easy to get along with because of their caring and assuring attitudes. But how will they grow personally based on this type in particular?

Let's get right to it:

Personal Growth Practices

Focus on your own personal needs first

First off, you want to accept the fact that you come first. You may not want to hear that as it may go against your philosophy of helping others before helping yourself. But the truth is, you want to make sure that your needs are met before meeting anyone else's without any issue.

If you do not address your own issues, it may bring you a source of stress that you may not need. Especially when you are doing what you do best (i.e. - helping other people). You have to be in the best frame of mind (albeit stress-free) in order to be your happiest.

This means if you need to get a good night's rest, you better get it. Also, this means taking care of yourself properly. Meeting your own basic needs before meeting the needs of others is not selfish.

This is your health we are talking about here. Taking care of yourself is paramount if you want to live a long fulfilling life.

Become conscious of your own motives

Doing good things for others is admirable. There is no doubting that for a second. However, you want to be aware of the fact that if you are doing these things, you're expecting someone to give you appreciation or do something nice in return.

The reality is some people will reciprocate while others will not. This is something that you need to come to terms with and accept. Don't intentionally set yourself up for constant disappointment.

When you do, it sets a dangerous precedent. For one, it sets the stage for codependency. This means you will be putting pressure on other people to make you happy (when it should be your own responsibility in doing so). On top of that, you will start to develop anger and resentment for those who don't return the favor.

Ask them first before doing anything

This is absolutely key. You don't want to go out of your way and do things for people and find out that they don't need anything. That will be a waste of time and it might be a waste of energy as well.

Not to mention, you'll also be setting yourself up for disappointment. You might not know whether or not anyone may need anything or not. So, it's better to ask first before doing a good deed.

If someone says 'no thanks', that's fine. Accept it and move on. At the same time, you want to clearly communicate your intentions. Regardless if they say no or not, your act of kindness (or attempt of it) shall be noted.

Another thing to be aware of is that when they say 'no', it shouldn't be considered a sign that they dislike or reject you. They say no because they don't want something they don't need. It's as simple as that.

Resist the urge to draw attention to yourself

If you have done a good deed for someone, it is best to leave it be. Don't remind people about the good deeds you did for them. And try not to draw attention to yourself because of all the good things you do.

Doing this will put people on the spot. And that's an uncomfortable position to put them in. Doing so will not be favorable for any of the relationships that you have with other people.

Recognize the affections and good wishes of others

If you are able to recognize what others are giving you, you will know that you are loved. There are those out there who will not express their feelings in the ways you want. But don't let that discourage you in the slightest.

There are many ways to say, 'I love you' or 'I appreciate you'. And it may be in the ways that you least expect it. So, keep that in mind when you are providing those affections and good wishes to others.

Do remember that love is always available, but only to a certain extent in which we are present and able to receive it.

Breathing Exercises

With breathing exercises, Twos will need to breathe with their belly. This will allow them to open up their emotional intelligence even further.

Take breaths that are slow and deep. As you do this, make sure you are connected to the ground. Distribute the energy and sensations to your legs and feet while you feel grounded to the floor.

If there is a sense of being overwhelmed, you can turn your attention to the physical environment for a bit. This includes taking note of some of the things you notice. You are welcome to move around during this exercise but be sure not to move around as much as it may disturb your centering.

Stress-Busting Practices for Type Twos

Twos are a combination of Jekyll and Hyde. When they are stressed, they become the 'Hyde' character. It's almost akin to the negative traits that you may see in Eights when they are under stress themselves.

Twos may tend to get pushy while searching for love and affection. It can get to the point where you may be controlling or even a tyrant. The people who you see as important to you will feel like they are stepping on landmines and fear the idea of offending you in the slightest.

Lastly, you may be cornering those into making decisions about your relationship with you. Don't put them in any such position. Especially when they may despise you as a result.

With that said, let's take a look at some of the stress-busting practices that Twos can use to their advantage:

Consider art/music therapy: If there is something that will allow you to de-stress, the arts might just be what you want to dabble in. Whether it's painting, making music, or anything creative, you can unearth what may be a dormant talent and put it to good use.

Go deeper in your self-discovery: If you want to learn more about your own personal identity, go as deep as possible. You'll feel better knowing that you know more about yourself. Especially the stuff you probably didn't know.

Work on your own personal style: Another thing you want to do is make yourself feel good. Sure, caring for others is one thing. But it is a lot better when you take good care of yourself. For starters, consider building your own personal style. Go clothes shopping and see which clothes fit you in terms of your personality or personal style.

Let those important to you know about your 'self-growth': There may be people who you are in constant contact with, even on a daily basis. What you want to do is take some time off, even withdraw yourself from others for a bit with the intent of healing and self-growth. It doesn't matter how long it takes. But what you want to do is let those people know that you will be taking time to focus on yourself. You may not be visiting them as often, but you will do your best to keep in touch with them regularly. This way, they won't fear that you disappeared out of thin air because of your lack of communication.

Explore your cultural background: Ever wondered where your ancestors originated from? How far back do you know your family's history? Tying this into self-discovery, you can dive back far enough to where you can learn about your family's history. Where did they originate from? What did your great-great-grandfather do for a living? To know your family beyond yourself is quite interesting and intriguing to know.

Type Two Practices in A Professional Setting

Communicating

Twos are attentive and encouraging. They waste no time recognizing their own value.

Meetings

They listen and engage with others. Oftentimes, they are helpful in solving problems most of the time.

Emailing

They can easily create casual conversation but will stay on topic regarding the purpose of the email. They will also appreciate the hard work of others (and convey that through the message).

Giving feedback

Twos avoid being critical when it comes to feedback. They often recognize a person's contributions and can be sensitive when it comes to sharing their concerns.

Resolving conflict

They are clear when addressing conflict while sharing their own perspective on the matter. They are willing to listen to others while helping them feel valued.

Relationships in A Professional Setting

In a professional environment, Twos thrive the best when working with people who are driven and focused. They also are able to provide a solid support system for those working alongside them. Let's talk about the practices for Type Twos in this kind of setting:

They work well with those who appreciate their help: Twos will go out of their way to help others if and when asked. Or, they may have an instinct to know when someone is struggling. For this reason, they will help that person. They will work well with others who appreciate and recognize their efforts.

Easy to get to know: Twos have an easy time connecting with others around the office. So, they are easy to get to know. As a Two, you may spend time doing this when the days aren't so busy.

Have the best interest of others at heart: You may have your best interests, but you defer those in favor of the interests of others. You can do that to an extent. But when it comes time to do a project, you want to take care of that first.

Type Two Practices in A Personal Relationship

Can Twos make great friends and romantic partners? Sure they can. Especially when they provide the love and care that most people crave.

In a relationship, they should remember to take care of themselves while taking care of each other. In relationships with non-Twos, there need to be clear boundaries as to how Twos and other Enneagram types that are in a relationship with each other communicate. With that in mind, here's what Twos bring to the table in relationships:

- **Attention and care:** These needs are met with ease. Especially when it's with their partner.

- **Communicating and conveying appreciation:** Again, a key ingredient of any healthy relationship. A Two will appreciate their partners in every little thing that they do.

- **Being supportive:** Last but certainly not least, they provide their partners with a solid support system.

Final Thoughts

Twos are probably the most easygoing of the Enneagram types. They are easy to get along with because of their loving and caring nature. Especially when they are healthy.

When unhealthy, they are a complete 180 of who they are in terms of their personality. It's like they possess some kind of Jekyll/Hyde personality. It's better for you as a Two to adhere to the practices of maintaining that Jekyll personality at all times.

Meanwhile, it is important that you take care of yourself first and foremost. Even though your help and ongoing appreciation of others is commendable, you need to focus on your needs first. It may sound selfish on the surface, but the reality is that it enhances your ability to help others.

You have to be physically and mentally healthy in order to maximize your love and appreciation for others. For as long as you are of sound mind and body, you are able to give your gift for love and caring to those around you, so it spreads all over the world.

Chapter 11: Practices for Type 3

For their part, Type 3s are the kind of people who want to perform and accomplish their goals. After they accomplish them, they want recognition for their hard work. Without that, it seems that they are nobody.

However, they must be able to perform the best daily practices so they can continue pursuing the accomplishments without worrying about failure or the like. Type Threes are often driven and may not settle for the slightest failures.

While ambitious and enthusiastic, they can perform the best practices in order to be their best selves. What makes a Type Three their healthiest? And if you're a Type Three, what can you do?

Let's take a look now at the practices for Type Threes:

Personal Growth Practices

Be truthful with yourself

Type Threes have a bad habit of setting high expectations for themselves. It can get to the point where they may set the bars a little too high for themselves. As a result, they may be inadvertently lying to themselves.

The truth is, self-honesty is often the best practice. Especially when you want to be aware of your limits. You know what you can accomplish, and you can get it done with ease.

But riding on the wave of success, you'll feel like you'll want more. So, you decide to up the stakes a bit in order to reap a much greater reward. Sometimes, the 'high risk, high reward' approach will often lead to disaster.

Being honest with yourself while being genuine with your feelings is what you need to do. Furthermore, don't impress others or brag about how important you are. Your actions mixed with your authenticity will be impressive enough as it is.

As the old saying goes, actions speak louder than words. And if you just talk the talk and don't walk the walk, that's when things can go south for you. Bragging about your success or exaggerating things won't do you any favors.

Become more cooperative in relationships

While Type Threes can focus on themselves, they should not shirk anything related to relationships. Furthermore, they shouldn't eschew the idea of having to connect with other people. As a Type Three, take time out of your day to connect with someone you care about.

You don't have to be extravagant about it. Be appreciative of them, even if it's quiet. Doing this will make you more respectable in the eyes of that person.

You will be considered that friend that is authentic and faithful, something that Threes may have a hard time becoming. You will feel better about yourself knowing that you accomplished something memorable. In this context, you've accomplished the task of being an authentic human being that is appreciative of others while being able to achieve your goals and not forget those who care about you.

Take a break if needed

Type Threes are busy and on the go all the time. It seems like they are the train that just doesn't stop. Because of this, Threes are susceptible to exhaustion or overexertion.

This will not do you any favors in terms of your health. For this reason, it is important that you take breaks. Especially when you need to mentally regroup and give yourself time to think and strategize about what to do next.

Yes, your ambitions and self-image are important to an extent. And so is your intent to advance in life. But you want to rest and relax so you can be mentally and physically healthy.

Being healthy will clear a path for you to be on top of your game. Rest and relaxation will help you recharge. And you will still have that image of going 'non-stop' but with a little secret that no one may seem to know about.

Develop and maintain social awareness

Threes are focused on projects and the like. For this reason, they may seem to be lacking in the social awareness department. Which is stunningly unexpected since they are usually surrounded by people all the time.

They may be so focused on things that their personal advancement will take a backseat. And that could spell trouble. Threes will want to connect with others as it may be beneficial for future accomplishments.

The more socially aware you are, you open up the barriers that will allow you to move on up in the world. It takes that one connection in order to help you get up to the next level. Also, you can use your newfound social awareness to cooperate and help others.

Resist the pursuit of being 'accepted'

Whether you know it or not, the pursuit of being accepted is a waste of time. So, you might want to refrain from doing so. You don't want to lose touch with your true self and the situations around you.

At the same time, you may not be able to get in touch with your true core values. Do yourself a favor and get to know yourself and the values that make you...well, you. And don't worry about if some people don't accept you for who you are and what you do.

Breathing Practices

Threes will be energetic most of the time. And they may also be impatient under stress. Because of this, they may hold their breaths and even build up a serious amount of tension.

As a Three, you want to take some time and breath (as should everyone else). A few slow deep breaths using their belly and diaphragm is just what they need. Or, they should do this repeatedly for a few minutes before they move forward to what's next.

As mentioned before, an excellent personal growth practice for a Three is to sit back and relax. Especially when they need to rest, recharge, and be on top of their game when they jump back into the action. Without it, they will be a mess and their performance will be off.

An off performance will frustrate a Three immensely. So, they need to embrace the idea of rest and relaxation. And they also need to incorporate regular breathing exercises (even if they are spread out in different periods on a daily basis).

Stress-busting practices for Type Threes

If there is a Type that is exposed to stress on a regular basis, it's Threes. So, it makes a lot of sense to have stress-busting practices for them in place. What should they do if they are under stress?

If you're a Three, here's what you do:

Try out activities that are new and interesting: Threes should focus on new and interesting activities. But there is a catch. They have to be outside of their careers or what they're usually accustomed to. To do this, Threes should ask friends about what activities are available and interesting to them. Find groups of people in your area to do these activities with. Or, you can find traveling a bit interesting.

Put together a list of qualities you admire in your friends: Think about your closest friends for a moment. Name one quality you like about them. When you do, write them down. From there, you can get in contact with each friend and let them know how much you appreciate them and admire the quality that they have. To go out of your way and take time out of your busy schedule to do this will speak volumes.

Keep and maintain a gratitude journal: Journaling is a great activity to do. Especially when you are recording the happenings throughout the day. Furthermore, you can use this journal to help remind yourself how grateful you are for the things in life. When you read the pages years from now, you will look back and be proud of yourself and how far you've come.

Help others discover themselves: You may be busy creating your own identity and be recognized for it. But it would be good for you to help others discover themselves and help build their own identity. Playing the role of personal motivator or mentor might help that person help become their best selves.

Get a pet or a plant: This stress-busting technique is a little out of the ordinary. But let's explain why? The point of this is that a pet or a plant will teach you patience. And it will also provide you with the joy and happiness of watching something grow.

Type Three Practices in A Professional Setting

Communicating

In a professional setting, communicating as a Three (or with them) must be straightforward and very clear. It is important that you help them understand what is needed.

Meeting

In meetings, Threes must express their needs in a direct manner. If needed, they can designate tasks for others if they don't have the time to do them.

Emailing

Threes prefer to keep their emails concise and to the point. Address the purpose briefly.

Feedback

Threes give constructive criticism. Plus, they should have a thick enough skin to handle it themselves. At the same time, they need to feel valued while being presented with ideas on how they can improve.

Resolving conflict

With Threes, they can listen to what is bothering someone. They can also express what's bothering them as well. Either way, the emotions of themselves and others should be considered and respected.

Relationships in A Professional Setting

In a professional setting, Threes prefer to work with people who are grounded and optimistic. They also love it if the people they work with are motivated.

At the same time, they should be cautious when it comes to competition. They shouldn't push the envelope in that regard. Healthy competition is fine, but don't take it too far.

Furthermore, they need to take the time to build personal connections with others. They should also recognize and appreciate the hard work of those around them. They should also accept the fact that some goals may fail to reach on time and plan accordingly if they do happen.

Relationships in A Personal Setting

Threes can be open and driven. But as a Three, you want someone in a relationship who will tell you to slow down and not overwork yourself. That partner must be someone who appreciates a Three's accomplishments and ambitions.

They are optimistic and adaptable. They are also enthusiastic and great with people. And with their natural ability to communicate, they can do whatever it takes to make sure that the relationship lasts a long time.

At times, couples (if one or the other is a Three) may have a hard time acknowledging their roles in certain situations. Because of their habits of putting their emotions in a box, they may withhold it from their partners. Threes need to come to grips that it is okay to express those emotions with them.

Lastly, Threes need to take their time and invest in the relationship if and when possible. The more they nurture the relationship, the better.

Final Thoughts

Threes are driven, in search of constant accomplishment and recognition, and will seem like they will not stop at anything. However, it is important for them to adopt the practices as outlined above. The key practice they must take advantage of is to stop and relax.

It's never a good idea for a Three to overwork themselves. Even then, they may never enjoy the fruits of their labor or enjoy life because they may die from something like a heart attack. It is important for them to rest and relax so they can perform at top optimal levels constantly.

For Threes, it's okay to rest. It's not okay to worry about whether or not someone will 'overtake' you while you rest. If anything, those people may seem to put themselves at a disadvantage compared to you.

Regular breathing practices and focusing on your own personal growth will be key here. Furthermore, you want to be aware of what you have accomplished without being a showoff or even a 'try hard' in an effort to impress others.

Threes can accomplish great things that can be talked about for years to come without doing too much. And that is something that you can be proud of. Go forth and accomplish something but mind your boundaries and practices along the way.

Chapter 12: Practices for Type 4

Type Fours are expressive with their emotions. And they may feel like they are the 'saddest' or most depressed of the Enneagram types. That could not be farther from the truth.

Indeed, Fours are expressive, and they show it through their work. But what are the practices that they can adopt in becoming better people? Fours can grow in a personal and professional setting by taking on the practices that we will lay out below.

If there is one characteristic that Type Fours take pride in, it's their creativity. And they will use it as part of their personal growth if and when needed. They can still stay in touch with their creativity while making improvements in other areas of their lives.

If you're a Four looking to grow, you're obviously in the right place. This is a chapter that you want to pay close attention to. Especially if you are longing for special connections with people while living a happy, beautiful life.

Let's dive right in:

Personal Growth Practices

Pay less attention to your feelings

Yes, our feelings and emotions are important. But what you have to understand is that they are not the true support system. You might already know this.

Your feelings are telling you something about yourself at the moment. It's not going any further than that. You can make important mistakes and feel bad about them.

Just because you feel bad, doesn't make you bad in general. Get the idea? So, remember that the next time you make a mistake be it in your creativity or outside of that realm.

Don't procrastinate because of your mood

When we are not in the mood, we tend to put things off. Especially when it's the things that we need to do. This will allow us to pile on more work than we can handle (something that can stress us out in the long run).

Whenever you don't feel like doing anything, do it anyway. There's a reason why that is. You will find motivation in finishing what you have started.
You will gain that motivation and it becomes momentum for continuing something. Don't search for motivation or that right feeling. Just get it done and you will feel like you have accomplished a task that would otherwise seem monumental in the eyes of your emotions.

Develop your self-esteem and self-confidence

In order to develop your self-esteem and self-confidence, it is important to expose yourself to positive experiences. It doesn't matter if you are ready to take them on or not. Get yourself out there and inject some good into your life.

You will feel better about yourself. And you will feel like you can do a lot more than you originally assumed. You may feel like you're not up for the challenge, but deep down inside you, there's a dormant part that says otherwise.

Take on the challenges presented before you. Nothing is more gratifying than the sense of accomplishment that comes with it. The more you do, the better you feel.

Build self-discipline

If there is one other thing to add, it's to build self-discipline. You want to be wholesome with it. How do you go about doing this?

You can start by setting a schedule to where you are working and sleeping regular hours. This will build up over time and you will be able to have that self-discipline that may have been elusive after all this time. Regardless, they will still have their individuality and identity.

At the same time, you want to make sure that you are not partaking in a lot of things that may lead to debilitating effects. This includes refraining from the use of alcohol, drugs, or anything in which excessive use can occur. This will allow you to have self-discipline that is healthy and consistent.

Cut the lengthy conversations in your head

The conversations you have in your head should be minimal. Especially if it's negative talk. Romantic or resentful chatter in your head should be quelled as well.

Why is this? It represents the things that you want to happen, but they won't for some reason. Rehearsing a certain action in your head and not executing it is a complete waste of time.

Instead of imagining life and the relationships you desire, do your best to make them a reality.

Breathing Practices

Fours should practice breathing exercises that will allow them to focus on their breath and the physical sensations that follow it. The goal here is for them to be more grounded and connected with their instincts. It would be wise for them to do a basic breathing exercise right from the start (especially when they are beginners).

When breathing, Fours should take slow deep breaths while releasing any tension that may be located in their chest. As they exhale, they should practice holding back their diaphragm. Breathing can be switched up based on the Four's dominant wing.

Again, if you have a Three Wing, just stick with the basic breathing exercise. Just focus on following the breath every single time. If you have a strong Five wing, then you want to focus on breathing into your chest and belly (while building up an amount of energy and distributing sensations throughout your body).

If you are feeling anxious, you can always refer to the anti-anxiety breathing technique. This way, you can reduce anxiety fast and be in the present with little to no disturbance possible. You will feel a lot better knowing that you have taken the time out of your day to provide yourself with a little more calm and a little less turbulence.

Stress-busting practices for Type Fours

As expressive as they are with their emotions, Fours can get stressed out to the point where their creative process can get disrupted. But they can still find ways to beat the stress in more ways than one. Let's take a look at what you as a Four can do when under stress:

Explore different works of art through the ages: Whether it's books, films, or works of art you can explore them based on different types of periods, cultures, races, ethnicities, and more. This will allow you to expand your knowledge and perspective on all things you love the most: the arts and creativity.

Volunteer your time: If you have time throughout your day, why not volunteer? Especially when it's for a cause that you care about most. If you love animals, volunteer at an animal shelter. If you like helping other people, work at a homeless

429

shelter for a weekend during lunch. You will feel better knowing that you can give back to the community, even if you don't play an active role in it regularly.

Plan a getaway: It doesn't have to be expensive. And it doesn't have to be extravagant. You can plan a weekend getaway like a solo camping trip if that's your thing. You and the outdoors might be a match made in heaven. And it may also give you more inspiration for your next creative works. **Share your personal experiences:** Tying this into the previous practice, your getaway and experiences will give you plenty of fodder for your next creative work. You can tell this story through writing or simply talking to people. Either way, you have a story that has to be told. And it might just leave a lasting impact on others that read or hear it.

Stay up to date on personal journeys: You may be enthralled or interested in the journeys of other people. Do your best to stay up to date on them and watch their progress. Furthermore, you should also consider keeping up to date on philanthropic efforts on those who are making a difference by giving back.

Type Four Practices in A Professional Setting

Communicating

As a Four, you won't deal with things that are over logical. If you're sending the email, you will mostly focus on sharing your feelings. If someone understands them, you can appreciate the connection.

Meetings

In meetings, Fours are often encouraging and optimistic. At the same time, it would be wise for Fours to be themselves and be able to speak on their thoughts and feelings about things. Non-fours should allow Fours to do this and encourage them to use their voice.

Emailing

Fours want to keep emails to a minimum, whether they read or write them. Also, make sure that they are expressive and authentic.

Feedback

Fours want to be sensitive with their feedback. They also want to receive feedback in a sensitive tone as well. Fours should encourage (or be encouraged). Anything negative should be reframed as something where there is improvement.

Resolving conflict

In conflict resolution, Fours should not be afraid of expressing their feelings openly. Non-fours must be empathetic when dealing with Fours. You can empathize without completely agreeing with the person regardless of their Enneagram type.

The key here of course is that Fours and non-Fours should be allowed to have individuality and autonomy.

Relationships in A Professional Setting

Fours work well with people who are even-tempered. They also like working with logical people, which can help further their ability to find creative solutions. Fours should ask questions about themselves while acknowledging their own individuality.

Meanwhile, they hold a deep appreciation for those who are creative and able to express themselves (even if that person isn't a Four). They appreciate the openness of how someone feels. When it comes to creative things, Fours admire other people's creativity (even over their own sometimes).

Fours may distance themselves in stressful situations, which may be good for the long run. Expressing negative moods can hurt a professional relationship. So, the withdrawal from people can preserve the relationship rather than jeopardize it.

Practices in Personal Relationships With Fours

If there is one thing that Fours want, it's a romantic relationship. Especially when it's someone who can pull them out of their low points. At the same time, Fours should not place high expectations (or impossible ones) when looking for a romantic partner.

They should focus and pay attention to the relationship as it grows. And they must nurture and maintain it at all times. This can be done by expressing and being open with their partner regarding how they feel.

Fours and their partners must also work on being able to recognize the areas where they need to grow. They can share with their partner where they want to grow themselves (while encouraging each other to press on and go forward with the process). The more they grow, the better.

There may be times when they may have a hard time finding balance in times of stress. On top of that, when they have a disagreement, they may have a hard time detaching from their emotions. That can lead to possible arguments that can get heated.

Lastly, they may have a fear of realistic expectations of a relationship. Such expectations should not be feared. But it should set boundaries in a relationship that should last a long time between two partners.

Final Thoughts

Type Fours can still express their emotions using their creativity. At the same time, they have plenty of room for growth. Especially when they want to improve their self-esteem and self-confidence.

The whole idea of feeling melancholic should be something that can be kept in the distance rather than close by. Fours want happiness and rightfully deserve it. And it starts with implementing these practices as outlined above.

If you're a Four, the greatest takeaway from this chapter is this: do what makes you feel good. Expressing negative emotions and using them as a weapon against others is not an example of that. Do what makes you feel good both inside and out.

You want the positivity to exist in you both on the inside and the out. And when you do, you will be driven to be more creative. And if that isn't something that brings out a lot of beauty, we don't know what does.

Chapter 13: Practices for Type 5

Fives are often using their minds to search for truths and ideas. They are the most enigmatic and interesting of the Enneagram types. They have plenty of room for growth personally and professionally.

When they instill these practices, they will be able to live a healthier life while being able to do the things they love most (even if they are by themselves). They will always work on finding the 'how', the 'what', the 'why', and so on of how things work.

Let's take a look at the practices that a Type 5 can take advantage of in order to improve themselves:

Personal Growth Practices

Use your mental capacities wisely

Your mental capacities are greater than anyone else on the Enneagram. But at the same time, it can also be a curse since it may withdraw from your physicality. Use them wisely and refrain from using it as a space where you can withdraw from contact with other people.

Find ways to calm down

Fives may be intense or even high-strung at times. For this reason, they may find it hard to relax. That's why it is important for you to calm down so you can relax.

You should find a way to do this without relying on things like drugs or alcohol. Instead, you can exercise or use some biofeedback techniques that will allow you to channel the large amount of nervous energy you may have. Refer to meditation or breathing exercises as one of your go-to options.

Or you can do something that requires light physical activity. This includes jogging, walking, dancing, or even yoga. If it's light activity and keeps you in motion, give it a try.

Don't be afraid to ask questions or seek advice

There may be times when you find so many different facts, answers, and possibilities. And that can cause you to choose one out of so many. You may even shuffle them in order from more to less important.

However, this is a time-wasting activity. And it may cause stress as you are faced with so many choices. So, what can you do in order to make a decision when there are so many choices in front of you?

Ask questions? Or seek advice from someone who may be of help. Sure, you may not want to contact people under stress.

But there could be no one better than someone who can know a thing or two about your options and the current situation that you're in. They will provide you with the best possible advice that will help you make an easier decision.

You can ask others to help give you an accurate assessment of each of your options. They may also help you eliminate some of the options that may not seem like the right choice for you as well. The process of elimination is just one phone call, email, message, or door knock away (depending on who you know).

Take decisive action

You may be tied up in a project that requires a lot of your focus and energy. At the same time, it might pose a problem with your self-esteem and confidence. With that in mind, learn how to take decisive action on things.

This includes eliminating distractions or things that will drag down your self-esteem and the like. Taking decisive action will help you build confidence, and you may build some skills that you may not know about in the process.

Have a friend or two that will listen to you

Even though Fives have a hard time trusting people, they should at least have that one or two friends that they can trust. Especially when they are opening up about how they truly feel about things. They know that isolation is the easy choice, but they want to be heard by someone they know they can trust.

Find a friend or two that will help you comfortably confide in them regarding any issues you may have. They will listen to you and may have a solution to the conflict that you're facing. It's a lot better than having a solution ready to use rather than spending time and energy creating it for yourself.

Make changes for yourself

You should make changes for yourself, if needed. Especially when it's a solution to a problem you're facing. This means doing less research as well.

You have the competence and capability to create solutions based on what you know. At the same time, you can also provide a solution to those who might be facing a similar problem.

Breathing Practices

Most Fives may hold their breaths as a defensive strategy. But that can block off the vitality they need to fully function. Therefore, they need to access the energy that will allow them to enhance their instincts. To do this, they should breathe while expanding the diaphragm.

This will allow them to increase the capacity that can be filled with sensations and pleasurable feelings. Take slow deep breaths. It can get uncomfortable at the start, but it will get better once you get the hang of it.

You want to build up a lot of increased sensations so you can get plenty of vitality throughout your body. When breathing, breathe through your belly and be sure you are sitting down so you are more 'grounded'. Another option is breathing through your chest, giving you an opening to increase the capacity for empathy and emotion.

Stress-busting practices for Type 5

Stress is something that invades the personal space of Fives. This will throw off anything that makes them feel good. So rather than struggle with it, they can try out some of these stress-beating practices out:

Reconnect with people and nature: Find a friend that you don't mind spending time with and go on a hike or a nature walk. This will allow you the opportunity to reconnect with both humans and nature itself. You may even make awesome memories together with a friend who you consider close.

Find books/videos on emotional intelligence: Improving your emotional intelligence is key. Two of the best ways to do this is read books or watch videos that focus on building that emotional intelligence so you can better handle them.

Take part in certain groups: This may sound like an uncomfortable task. But this is part of the growing process so you can handle people in small doses. It's not like we are shoving you in a room where there are a thousand people present. Join small groups like Toastmasters or even a small improv group.

Eat a healthier diet and exercise: Eating healthy is key when it comes to living a long healthy life. And it goes hand-in-hand with exercise as well. A healthy diet and regular exercise routine will help you become sharper in the mind, thus making you more driven to work on things that allow you to dig deep for information.

Try activities outside of your comfort zone: If joining a small group wasn't enough, there may be other activities that you can try out as well. It can get you out of your comfort zone, but it can be tough at first. But once you try other things that you are not accustomed to, getting out of your comfort zone will be a lot easier every single time.

Type 5 Practices in A Professional Setting

Communicating

When communicating, allow Fives personal space. If you're a Five, create it for yourself. Especially when it is needed to gather your thoughts. Do not be overly emotional. Be clear when expressing and sharing your thoughts on things.

Meeting

Fives prefer to be in meetings that are productive and worthwhile. They should also be part of the discussion as well. Since they may have plenty of answers and ideas, they are often the go-to person when questions need to be asked.

Emailing

Fives hate small talk. Especially when it's email small talk. Keep it direct and clear.

Feedback

Fives want honesty when it comes to where they need to grow. They can handle constructive criticism.

Resolving conflict

When there is conflict, it should be explained to a Five in a logical manner. That's because they may have an idea that will allow both sides to work together based on a compromise. They will act like Nines in situations like this and listen to different points of view (while concocting a solution).

Relationships in A Professional Setting

Fives are often helpful to their co-workers. Especially when they have a wealth of information at their disposal. They are happy whenever they are seen as useful.

And they waste no time helping out others with the answers they have (when questions are asked). They have knowledge and input that is often valued and appreciated. When given autonomy, they work at top levels.

In a logical, balanced way they are able to express themselves. And they prefer working with people who do the same. But they may make logical decisions at times that may negatively affect their co-workers or even the group.

In times of stress, they may not have an easy time relating to the emotions of others. They may even feel overwhelmed to the point where they may need to distance themselves from others.

Relationships in A Personal Setting

Fives are calm and helpful partners. And they offer a lot of patient support and understand personal space when their partner needs it. Non-fives should be understanding of this.

When Fives are in relationships, they remain calm in tense situations. That's a huge plus for couples who want to avoid heated conflicts as much as possible. They are also great for solving relationship problems with logic.

They understand that there is a need for independence. Thus, they can allow their partner to do the things they want while they do the same. However, they may have issues with opening themselves emotionally with their partners (which may question whether or not they can trust their partner).

They may find it hard to handle difficult conversations, regardless of the topic. They also may have trouble offering appreciation for their partner.

Final Thoughts

Fives have plenty of potential to grow personally and professionally. At their healthiest, they are still knowledgeable and very helpful to others. However, a Five may find it uncomfortable to grow on a personal level at times (especially when there are steps they need to take that require them to get out of their comfort zone).

When Fives step out of their comfort zone, things can get easier from there. They can open up a bit more, but still remain guarded about their emotions. They can also open up a bit to the point where they can trust only a few people that they are close with.

Chapter 14: Practices for Type 6

Sixes are known for being hard workers and engaging. They are firm believers in loyalty. They give it but fear not getting it back in return.

They hold a high regard for security and stability. And they want to be on solid ground for the rest of their lives. They make great friends, co-workers, and lovers.

But given their constant worry of things, how will they grow into better people. As stubborn as they can be due to their loyalty, what are they willing to give up in order to grow better? As a Six, this is a question you must ask yourself as you begin your personal growth journey.

With that in mind, let's take a look now at how Sixes can improve their lives for the better:

Personal Growth Practices

Know that being anxious is nothing unusual

If you feel anxious, don't feel like you are the only one feeling that way. There are others that are feeling anxious about things. It is important that you are more present with it.

Once you are present, take the time to explore the reason why you're anxious. And then accept it as it is. Be creative when working with your tensions and refrain from such vices like alcohol or drugs.

If you must, use the breathing practices listed above to help you out. You can rely on the Energizing breath exercise that is outlined in the Breathing and Centering chapter. Meanwhile, you can make yourself productive and do more of the things you do on a regular basis.

Be aware of some of your bad traits

Being aware of some of your bad traits will allow you to recognize them and do away with them for as long as possible. For example, you may feel pessimistic about things. It may lead to dark moods and you may behave negatively.

Or if you get angry, you might get testy with other people. It can get to the point where you may lash out at them. What you want to do is eliminate any self-doubt or negativity that could turn you into your own worst enemy.
And remember, there are things that will hurt you more than the others you may have hurt yourself.

Don't overreact while under stress

When under stress, Sixes may have a tendency to overreact. If such a thing happens (or if you remember an instance when you did overreact), think back to what caused it. If things are as bad as you think, you don't want to allow such thoughts to weaken you. Especially when your mission is to change things for the better.

Accept the fact that you can't change some things

To paraphrase the famous Serenity Prayer, you want to accept the things you cannot change. Also, you will have the courage to change the things that you can. For example, there will be people who won't be as loyal and return the favor to you (even if you did something for them).

Don't blame yourself for the lack of reciprocation. It may be something on that other person's end and not so much yours. Remember that only you can manage things that are within your control (as well as your own thoughts).

Trust people more often

Your self-doubt may get the best of you. Especially when it comes to how you deal with people. It's important that you open up more and trust people as often as you normally do. That doesn't mean trust people the day you meet them.

But rather give them that trust when you know they've earned it. Don't be guarded or deny them trust (even when they return the favor in terms of security and stability). You have the ability to get along with people and make them like you, so don't blow it.

Also, don't be afraid to let people know how you feel about them (be it positive, negative, or otherwise).

Stop thinking that people are out to get you

Don't think that people are out to get you for some reason. If anything, there may be very few people or no one out there that may get you for something ridiculous. But don't let that intimidate you in the slightest.
Don't let your fears do the talking for you in terms of your attitude towards other people.

Breathing Practices

Sixes tend to be on alert at all times. Especially when they are aware of the potential threats that may affect their security and stability. They need to perform breathing exercises using slow and deep breaths.

While inhaling, they should stretch their diaphragm as much as possible. When exhaling, they should force the outbreath. Breathing through their belly will also help them reduce any anxiety they may have.

When practicing breathing, be sure to do steady breathing for 2 to 5 minutes. Allow your brain to calm down so you have the ability to think rationally when you have finished. This will allow you to think clearly and be able to focus more.

Stress-busting practices for Type 6

Sixes may get stressed out over stress itself. You may still find yourself stressed out no matter how many ways you try to manage it. But lucky for you, there are ways to deal with it (all thanks to us).

Here's how you beat stress as a Six:

Meditate regularly: You probably tried it already, haven't you? Well, try it again. But this time, use it with the breathing exercises that we have provided for you in this guide. Also, the breathing exercises specifically made for you should also help as well.

Keep a journal: Journaling is therapeutic. There is no doubting that. But you can journal what you're thinking while also making plans on how you can improve yourself.

Spend time with positive people: Positivity radiates and spreads. Especially if it is coming from other people. So, spend as much time as you can with people who will make you feel good and positive. Stress will not be found in the immediate vicinity.

Voice your concerns and be more empathetic: This should be a personal growth step more than a stress buster. But it can act as both. What are your concerns? Why are they valid? Share them with someone you can trust. Furthermore, be more empathetic when it comes to the feelings and concerns of others. A trusted friend may be someone who can give you advice and emotional validation.

Type 6 Practices in A Professional Setting

Communicating

Allow Sixes safety and security by listening and offering support when they need it. They want to be assured that they are on solid ground, so they don't worry about the future.

Meeting

Sixes will usually abide by the meeting times when they are set. They will be supporting and encouraging of others and expect the same in return.

Emailing

While avoiding small talk, explain the purpose of the email to Sixes.

Feedback

When it comes to providing feedback to Sixes, deliver it in a gentle manner. Encourage them in areas where they can improve with a mix of constructive criticism.

Resolving conflict

Sixes will usually address the situation with calm and logic. Often, they will provide their own point of view. If a Six is part of the conflict, help them feel safe while they express freely about the issue.

Relationships in A Professional Setting

In a professional setting, Sixes love working with people who are optimistic. They often provide them support. They may work with other Sixes and refrain from worrying about things based on the other Six's decision.

They are stable and predictable at best. They are someone who doesn't want to be an authority figure, but rather a subordinate. However, they are not as authoritative if they take a leadership role.

They share and express appreciation for the hard work they have created (as well as the hard work of others). So, they love to work with others that do the same. They often will have an easy time working with others that avoid being emotional when making decisions.

Relationships in A Personal Setting

Sixes make excellent partners solely on their loyalty alone. They may be happy with someone who may be idealistic and a bit of a free spirit. If they are in relationships with other sixes, they stay focused on the positive at all times.

Sixes make decisions that are balanced and thoughtful. And they work hard to solve difficult problems if and when they arise. And lastly, they have an undying loyalty for their partner.

In times of tense discussion, they may have a hard time keeping calm. And they may have trouble making key decisions that may be crucial to the relationship. Lastly, they may have a hard time with letting go of the past (especially past relationships that were unhealthy).

Final Thoughts

Sixes have room to grow in some areas. But they are loyal to the people they care about. If anything, they must improve on managing their stress better and worry less about security and stability.

It may be a hard thing to do, but at the end of the day, Sixes will think clearly and be more level-headed about things. Sixes can come to terms that there are some things that they cannot change and it isn't their fault.

Other than that, they need to be assured that while security and stability will come to them, they need not to worry about when exactly that will happen. Sixes should stay focused on the tasks that they have started and follow them through until the end.

Chapter 15: Practices for Type 7

Sevens are carefree and want to have fun. There are no limits and rules that exist in their world. But for Sevens, they must set the boundaries so they can focus on their personal growth. It shouldn't stunt or discourage them from doing fun things.

If anything, their personal growth journey should be like any other adventure they are willing to go on. They don't say no to anything that is considered an opportunity to try something out. So, it makes sense for them to be willing to try something that will be beneficial for their life.

What are the personal growth practices for Sevens? How will they deal with stressful situations? If you're a Seven (or interested in how a Seven can grow), keep reading.

Personal Growth Practices

Recognize your impulsiveness

You may act on impulse most of the time. Rather than give in on them at every opportunity, do the opposite and observe them instead. Just because you let them pass doesn't mean you're missing out.

It will also help you develop sharp judgment skills and gives you the ability to say no when you need to. At the same time, you develop self-control to the point where you won't mindlessly act on impulse if they arise. Instead, you can focus on what can be good for you.

Learn to listen to others

We suggest this in the context of searching for new ideas. These are people who could become your new friends or even travel partners. This will also give you more ideas on what you want to do for fun.

Be familiar with silence and solitude

Yes, you can have your fun. But sometimes, it's nice to break away from all the noise and distractions. This will allow you to think, reflect, and recharge before the fun resumes.
You will be happy even with less external stimulation being in your general vicinity. You will also learn to build some self-trust. Don't be surprised if you feel a bit happier being at peace for a bit.

Don't try to do everything in the moment

Sevens may worry about missed opportunities. And we can't blame them. However, there are times when you can say no to an opportunity to do something.

As long as you know that opportunity will be present tomorrow, you can say 'not now' today and say 'yes' tomorrow. Things such as food, alcohol, your friends, and other things that make you happy will also be available for tomorrow. Don't worry about the opportunities that are there every day. It's not like they are once in a lifetime thing.

Quality over quantity - always

If you're looking for new and repeated experiences, always go for quality over quantity. The quality of it all requires your full attention and makes the experience a lot more enjoyable. Also, make sure you are focused on the present rather than anticipating the future.

Know what's good for you in the long run

Some of the best things last longer than most. That is why you should consider looking for things that will last a long time. At the same time, consider what may be considered long-term consequences or even potential sources of unhappiness.

If you see something that you may think will be long-lasting, weigh the pros and cons. See if there is any good reason to jump on the opportunity so long as there is a positive return on your happiness.

Breathing Practices

Breath into your belly and pay attention to the sensations that are situated in the lower area of your body. Meanwhile, make sure that your feet act as your roots while you are planted to the floor or ground. During these breathing exercises, you may want to pay attention to whether or not you are 'staying in body'.

You may have that feeling where you slip out of your body. When that does happen, focus on the breath that is in your belly while focusing on the sensations at your feet. Be sure to follow your breaths and slow down, allowing yourself to be in the moment.

Stress-busting practices for Type 7

Sevens get stressed too. They're human like everyone else. However, when they are stressed, they act more like Ones.

Thus, they develop a more of a perfectionist attitude. And they start to nit-pick the most trivial things. Their inner child is locked away in favor of someone who is angry and irritated with what's going on.

With that in mind, Sevens can beat stress by doing the following:

Confide in a friend: Specifically, this friend should be someone who can bring you back down to reality. If necessary, find someone who will offer you practical solutions (like a friend who is a Six, since they tend to be practical). Let them know what is bothering you and they will be happy to help you destress.

Write down your goals: Map out your goals and break them down into steps that are easy and actionable. At the same time, list areas where you want to improve and share them with a friend who will cheer you on.

Explore other topics: Whether it ends in -ology or not, explore something that will allow you to read, study, or even watch videos on.

Inspire others to find their happiness: As a Seven, this is pretty easy to do. Especially with the amount of energy you have.

Type 7 Practices in A Professional Setting

Communicating

In a professional setting, Sevens bring the energy. Make sure that your communication is upbeat with Sevens. Sevens will communicate in this manner as well. Be sure that your ideas are being listened to and appreciated (especially the ideas brought by Seven themselves).

Meeting

In meetings, Sevens want clear communication. So be clear with them about what you want. They prefer meetings that are laid back and lighthearted.

Emailing

Sevens love casual conversation. Also, encourage positive dialogue in emails when dealing with them.

Feedback

Be honest and constructive. At the same time, provide Sevens with support and encouragement.

Resolving conflict

Help them express their feelings if they are difficult. At the same time, come up with a compromise that offers them multiple solutions.

Relationships in A Professional Setting

Sevens will often work with people who are practical (like Sixes). When working alongside each other, Sixes and Sevens are innovative and exciting, and their ideas will show it. As far as working with other Sevens, they must work together and hold each other accountable.

Sevens love working with people who are optimistic and energetic. They also love it when their co-workers are willing to have fun and try something new. And lastly, they look for co-workers who can appreciate their ideas (especially when they are very creative).

Sevens may have an issue with long-term commitments. At the same time, they may finish assignments on time. But they may fail to do so once in a while.

They could become bored or even limited by the work that they do.

Relationships in A Personal Setting

Sevens bring the fun in a relationship. They bring some balance to the relationship when the other is more reserved. If it's two Sevens in a relationship, they must hold themselves accountable and consider the consequences of potentially rash decisions.

They also bring enthusiasm and optimism that is not filtered in the slightest. They are also introducing and trying new things with their partner. But they may have commitment issues, which can bring the long-term idea into question in romantic relationships.

They could have negative emotions and conversations with their partners and have a hard time dealing with it. Finally, they may have an inability to listen to their partners, even in times of stress.

Final Thoughts

Sevens are the life of the party. Even if they are not fans of rules or limits, they need to set some self-boundaries so that they can honor themselves. Especially when they need to stay within them and not act on impulse.

They have the ability to grow and use their energy to their advantage. If they are willing to try new things, they have no trouble trying out a new challenge that will allow them to become better people. This won't discourage them to do fun things or the like.

But they can be better people if they practice self-restraint and self-care. A Seven can have fun, but sometimes they need to make peace with the fact that it's okay to get away from the noise at times. And there will be opportunities they are dying to try out tomorrow.

Chapter 16: Practices for Type 8

Eights are the power figures. They are the ones that don't want to be controlled because they are 'the control'. They make great leaders and authority figures. But they fear being exposed for being vulnerable.

Eights can grow despite the fact that they are more in control of their life. But still, there is always room for improvement. What areas can Eights grow in?

If you're an Eight, you can be sure that whenever there is a challenge, you are willing to take it. So why not take on the challenge of growing based on the Enneagram? With that said, let's show you some of the personal growth practices you can follow (and other practices that you can use to your advantage).

Personal Growth Practices

Practice self-restraint

This cannot be said simply enough. Even if it goes against your personal beliefs, restraining yourself and not lashing out at others is a sign of true power. If that wasn't enough, it also shows that you have control over your emotions (instead of the other way around).

Lashing out or getting angry at people will show that you're not as powerful as you think. In fact, you may be accidentally exposing a vulnerability. Wield your true power by showing restraint and your followers, subordinates, and those important will respect you immensely.

Yield to others when needed

Do this occasionally. This will not cause you to sacrifice power or your real needs. At the same time, it might also be a good idea to step back and let someone else take over for a bit.

You don't have to be the leader all the time. And you certainly don't need to be dominant over everyone every day. Plus, it will also prevent you from overinflating your ego (which could trigger issues between you and those that you want respect from).

Realize that the world isn't against you

Many people care about you. There are many that admire you and feel inspired by your words and actions. Also, allow affection when it is available.

Accepting affection does not make you weak or soft. It confirms strength and support from those that support and love you. Assuming that the world is against you may alienate those who look up to you.

Know the balance of self-reliance and dependence

Eights may seem like they are self-reliant. However, they depend on a lot of people. This is an imbalance that can come back and hurt them. Especially when they continuously dismiss or fire people they depend on most.

They don't need to question the loyalty of the people they depend on. What they need to do is balance what they can do by themselves and depend on the people who will help them out the most. They shouldn't depend on everyone to do everything for them while they themselves do nothing.

Never overvalue power

While power is nice to have, overvaluing it over love and respect is a big mistake. So be sure to have love for yourself and others. The same goes for respect. Don't let it get to a point where you care more about power over respecting and loving yourself and others.

Breathing Practices

If Eights are stressed, they should take 10 slow, deep breaths. They can repeat this process until they feel much more at ease. They should breathe using their belly as opposed to their chest.

The reason being is breathing through their chest will allow Eights the ability to 'power up', which counteracts the attempt to calm down. While you follow your breath, make sure that it is 'down and in'.

Stress-busting practices for Type 8

Obviously, Eights are prone to stress. So, it's fitting enough to provide them with stress-beating practices that they can use to their advantage. If you're an Eight, stress is one more thing you can control.

Here's how you do it:

Get in touch with your softer side: What's the one thing that helps you get in touch with a softer version of yourself? Is it your family? Someone you care about? What is it? Think about it, talk about it, and let people get to know the real you.

Do physical exercises that make you feel good: Spend time doing exercises that will allow you to keep your mind sharp while feeling good at the same time. It can be a jog, walk, run, or anything that's invigorating.

Make a list of activities: What are some things that you want to do? What are the things that excite you? Why are they exciting? Think about the activities that make you happy especially if you're sad or irritable.

Give yourself space to process your emotions: This can't be stressed enough. You need space to process your emotions. It's a lot better than taking it out on people who don't deserve it.

Type 8 Practices in A Professional Setting

Communicating

Eights are upfront and direct while open to ideas from others.

Meeting

Logical and practical. They are also willing to share ideas and suggestions.

Emailing

Not fans of casual conversation. Make sure that the emails sent to Eights are clear and concise.

Feedback

Be respectful when giving feedback. Be constructive and try to avoid Eights from getting defensive.

Resolving conflict

Eights will stand their ground when it comes to conflict. But when dealing with Eights who are a part of the conflict, stand your own ground and call them out on actions that are considered inappropriate. Also, give them a chance to consider their side of things and listen.

Relationships in A Professional Setting

Eights will help those who are relaxed or reserved make decisions and become their advocates. Meanwhile, when they work with other Eights, they maintain mutual respect and amounts of power while avoiding clashes all the time.

Eights love it when they work with people who respect their ideas and opinions. They also want people who work with them to stand up for themselves when things happen. And they are always open to thinking that is considered a new way or out of the box.

They will not be controlled and therefore not submit to an authority figure. And they may have a hard time covering their vulnerabilities if such are exposed.

Relationships in A Personal Setting

In a romantic relationship, Eights are dedicated and protective. They will often be the partner that provides balance in a relationship where they are laid-back, quiet, and gentle. Eights who are in a relationship with each other will need to de-escalate any tensions the second they arise.

Eights know that they don't want to be controlled by their partners. And they will do the same in kind with theirs. The need for independence is therefore fulfilled.

However, Eights may not be as emotionally vulnerable with their partners. And it may get to the point where they could have a hard time deferring decisions to their partner or softening up when issues need to be solved.

Final Thoughts

Eights are in control and don't want to be controlled themselves. And they fear exposing their vulnerabilities. If it's control that they want, they will need to learn how to control their stress and show self-restraint.

They should also not fear the idea of showing their softer side. It doesn't make them weak, but it shows that aside from being straightforward and driven, they are human like everyone else. They are the leaders and authoritative.

But they are protected and dedicated partners of their lovers. And they are respectful of those who work under them.

Chapter 17: Practices for Type 9

Nines want peace. And they can get it if they keep their inner peace together. And they also have their own growth practices as well. What will they need to do in order to better themselves?

In this final chapter, we cover the practices based on the Enneagram's Type 9. There may be some uncomfortable truths that a Nine will face. But in the end, they know that it will be worth it knowing that it will help them grow personally.

If you're a Nine, this is a very important chapter that you want to read. Especially when you want to make sure that you fulfill your own personal needs and growth. Let's get started and dive right into the personal growth practices.

Personal Growth Practices

Pay attention to what's going on

You may not have your attention focused on what is happening. But you should. You may avoid it as it may disturb the peace.

But you have to learn what's going on around you to keep yourself up to date. That way, you'll understand the world around you a lot better. Be an active participant.

Be mentally and emotionally engaged.

Recognize your aggressions, anxieties, and other feelings

As a Nine, you are human as well. You have feelings, anxieties, and have aggressions of your own. Keep in mind that negative feelings and impulses are nothing to have. So, stop acting like they are non-existent when in reality they are.

Get things out in the open before being more aware of how you are feeling.

Examine any issues regarding past relationships

While it may be a painful thing, you may want to examine any issues you may have had with past relationships. This also includes divorce, issues with your family members or your friends, or even breakups with a past significant other.

You want to figure out what you have contributed to the demise of such relationships. It may be difficult to face, but you will begin to understand why it was a problem to the point where the relationship disintegrated.

Exercise frequently to get in touch with body and emotions

Exercise seems to be the solution for most Enneagram types. For Nines, it's all about getting in touch with your body and enhancing your overall emotions. Exercise itself is a form of self-discipline.

Not to mention, it will increase your awareness considerably. When you are aware of your body, you can easily focus your concentration on it. Especially when you are working on breathing exercises and the like.

Breathing Practices

As you practice your breathing, your goal here is to stay focused and maintain inner peace. The breathing practices can be uncomfortable or familiar depending on past experience. But when you do these breathing exercises, make sure you are breathing in with your chest.

These breathing exercises are aimed at building your physical energy and vitality. You will feel great both inside and out. And you will feel like you have the stamina to do things that you previously thought were impossible to do with less energy.

Stress-busting practices for Type 9

Yes, Nines do get stressed. But they can beat the stress in so many ways. As easy as it is to do, Nines can't say no to restoring peace.

Let's take a look at what they can do:

Take nature walks alone: Get in touch with nature while reflecting in solitude. With the peace and quiet all over you, you will be able to get in touch with your mind.

Detox from social media: There is chaos and disturbances of peace on social media. And it can stress people out. Consider the idea of doing a social media detox for a minimum of 30 days. It may be hard, in our social media-addicted world. But you might have the willpower to pull it off.

Get a pet or a plant: Like Threes, Nines can appreciate taking care of something that has the ability to grow. On top of that, there's a certain happiness that you can acquire just by simply raising a plant or a pet.

Read motivational books: This will be perfect for whenever you make plans for yourself and need the motivation.

Type 9 Practices in A Professional Setting

Communicating

Encourage them to be open in regard to their ideas and personal needs. Create a safe environment for honest communication.

Meeting

Pressure must be avoided. Offer encouragement in terms of sharing opinions or feelings.

Emailing

Communicate with a clear purpose. But leave the door open for personal communication in case it is needed.

Feedback

Refrain from any feedback that may be overly negative or critical. Offer areas of improvement rather than mention flaws.

Resolving conflict

In conflict, make sure that they remain calm and patient. Express yourself in a gentle manner and ask if they need anything.

Relationships in A Professional Setting

Nines will help people be at more peace and acquire relaxation if they work with people who are driven. When working with other Nines, they are laid-back, and they do their best to hold each other accountable.

They avoid conflict, take the time to get to know others, and are positive all the time. They will work well with those that do the same. Meanwhile, they have a fear of being overlooked by others.

They may miss their deadlines but will always get tasks done on time.

Relationships in A Personal Setting

Nines are supportive and understanding. They will be the partner that people need when they feel misunderstood by others. However, Nines work as a team by switching off powers in terms of making decisions and leading each other.

They can adapt to unexpected circumstances and understand each other's perspectives. All the while, they are supportive of one another.

But they may struggle with issues that involve emotions. And they may not like it when such discussions about their relationship go into deeper lengths.

Final Thoughts

Nines can grow personally knowing that it is okay to have negative feelings and emotions at times. But still, they can keep the peace and help others. They are able to connect with just about anyone because of their peaceful and friendly nature.

Nines have room for growth, even if it doesn't seem like they have a lot of it. They must realize that there is a balance of positive and negative that exists.

Conclusion

This is it. You have made it to the end. At this point, you can now use the Enneagram as your guide towards improving your life in various areas. You may have already performed the growth practices and exercises based on your personality types.

If you haven't yet, that's okay. But now is a good time to start. We encourage you to keep this book as a reference guide for whenever you get stuck somewhere on your journey.

While the Enneagram is a navigational tool and a guide in its own right, so is this book. Think of it as your instruction manual that you need as part of the journey. This book might be the most important guide you've ever laid your hands on.

If you are also interested in helping others grow through the Enneagram, be sure to introduce them to this book. Explain to them in detail what the Enneagram is and how it will help them. Guide them through the process and help them identify their personality type.

From there, they can do the same practices that you're doing. Even if they are a different Enneagram type than you are, they might be dying to know what they can do with the power of this awesome tool.

What You Have Learned

In this book, you have learned that the Enneagram is a powerful tool. It is something that you use to better yourself. What it isn't is something that will be used to harm and hurt others.

It's bad enough that some of the negative traits that each personality type has may hurt others. So do not use the Enneagram to flaunt your personality type or use it as something that says, 'I am better than you are'. In short, never abuse the power of the Enneagram, or it will surely come back to haunt you.

You will come to terms with the fact that your life may need considerable changes. You may lean on different vices that you think can help with stress, but in reality they are counterintuitive. If you are religious but skeptical about the Enneagram, why not put it to the test?

You'll be surprised that you will find out more about yourself than any other religious document. What we don't realize is that we are living a life that is outlined by our conscious selves. And it's a life that may seem inauthentic at best.

The truth is, we need to peel back the layers of our conscious selves and truly get to know ourselves. We may not be surprised about some of the personality traits that we possess. But you may find out that you could be in the wrong line of work based on your type.

With the Enneagram, you could be on the verge of making life-changing decisions. And it might make you happier as a result. You may have a newfound confidence in knowing that you can thrive well in professional environments while maintaining romantic relationships with your partner.

The Enneagram test that you took was accurate. And hopefully you answered it truthfully. There are no right or wrong answers, but rather honest ones.

And we certainly hope that this book taught you to be at least honest with yourself in terms of your self-development. At the same time, it also shows you that you can come face-to-face with your shortcomings and failings since it is all part of the growing process.

After reading this book, you're about to embark on a journey that many people may never travel in their lifetime. They may find other ways to improve their lives. But there is nothing more powerful or rawer than improving your life by way of the Enneagram.

You understand the Enneagram as a tool for personal growth. As a guide to help you shed an identity that isn't the real you. And in its place is you, a true version of yourself.

You are able to let things go that were considered negative traits. And you are prepared to handle conflict in your own unique way. Now, what you do from here on out is up to you.

But we encourage you to live by the Enneagram and the practices that were given to you. Plus, it can also allow you the opportunity to pass on the knowledge and the wisdom of the Enneagram to a newer generation.

Your children and grandchildren may have the same personality type as you (or they may be different). But regardless, there is no better gift than giving them the Enneagram as a tool to help them develop the best life they can live.

What's Next?

Keep in mind that this book has actionable materials. It won't work unless you take some kind of action. This is not your standard run-of-the-mill book that was written for entertainment purposes.

This was a book that will provide you with actionable instructions on how to use the Enneagram. So be sure to read through this as many times as you can and use the practices wisely. Finally, if you loved this book, feel free to leave a positive review.

Now that you have the power of the Enneagram in your hands, it is now up to you to use it to your advantage. This kind of power requires someone to use it responsibly.

The question is: will it be you? Don't be an unhealthy Eight and overvalue its power. And do not abuse it as it will be counterintuitive.

Now, go forth and grow your life for the better. Thank you for reading.

References

3 Ways to Focus on Self-Improvement with Mindfulness. (2021, January 24). Dummies. https://www.dummies.com/religion/spirituality/3-ways-to-focus-on-self-improvement-with-mindfulness/

Berger, B. (2020, August 20). Positive Practices for Mental Health Based on Your Enneagram Type | Types 4, 5, and 6. Finding Delight. https://findingdelight.com/2020/08/20/positive-practices-for-mental-health-based-on-your-enneagram-type-types-4-5-and-6/

Bocks, S. (2020, August 11). How to Cultivate Self-Awareness and Unleash Your Creativity with the Enneagram. Shay Bocks. https://shaybocks.com/how-to-cultivate-self-awareness-and-unleash-your-creativity-with-the-enneagram/

Burgess, K. T. C. A. (2020, February 4). Why the Enneagram of Personality is becoming popular with Christians and other faith groups. Memphis Commercial Appeal. https://eu.commercialappeal.com/story/life/2020/02/04/why-enneagram-type-test-popular-with-christians/4600988002/

Cloete, D. (2021). Origins and History of the Enneagram. Integrative 9. https://www.integrative9.com/enneagram/history/

Decoding the Origins of the Enneagram. (2020, November 25). Cultish. https://thecultishshow.com/blog/decoding-the-enneagram

Energy Attacking Body and its Defense, Realities of Enneagram. (2018, January 30). Nur Muhammad Realities Biography Islam Allah Haqiqat al Muhammadia.

https://www.nurmuhammad.com/energy-attacking-body-and-its-defense-realities-of-enneagram/
The Enneagram Applied: Charting Your Path of Growth. (2020, July 30). Meritage Leadership Consulting. https://meritageleadership.com/the-enneagram-applied/
Enneagram Careers | Tips To Help All 9 Types Love Their Work. (2020, May 4). Enneagram Gifts. https://enneagramgift.com/enneagram-careers/
Enneagram Central - Idealized Self Image. (2021). Enneagram Central. http://enneagramcentral.com/Explore/SelfImage.htm
Enneagram Centres. (2021). Fitzel. http://www.fitzel.ca/enneagram/triads.html
Enneagram Growth Practices. (2020, June 5). David N. Daniels, M.D. https://drdaviddaniels.com/growth-practices/
Enneagram Personal Growth and Development System. (2021). Personal Growth Counseling. https://personal-growth-counseling.com/enneagram.html
Gottberg, K. (2020, January 30). Is The Enneagram A SMART Path To Self Awareness? SMART Living 365. https://www.smartliving365.com/a-smart-living-365-look-at-the-enneagram/
Grimes, M. (2019, September 25). Defining your life: The Enneagram. The Anchor. https://anchor.hope.edu/lifestyle/defining-your-life-the-enneagram/
How Does The Enneagram Work. (2021). Healthline. https://www.healthline.com/health/mental-health/how-does-the-enneagram-work#So-how-does-the-Enneagram-work?
How The System Works. (2021). The Enneagram Institute. https://www.enneagraminstitute.com/how-the-enneagram-system-works

How You Handle Change Based on Your Enneagram Type. (2020, August 12). Zaengle Corp. https://zaengle.com/blog/how-enneagram-types-handle-change

Keizur, H. (2019, November 8). The Enneagram: a guide to self-awareness and understanding. San Francisco Foghorn. http://sffoghorn.com/the-enneagram-a-guide-to-self-awareness-and-understanding/

Linneman, J. (2019a, August 9). Cultivating Self-Awareness. COMO Magazine. https://comomag.com/2019/05/30/cultivating-self-awareness/

Linneman, J. (2019b, August 9). Promoting Self-Awareness through the Enneagram. COMO Magazine. https://comomag.com/2019/07/29/promoting-self-awareness-through-the-enneagram/

Lubow, R. (2020, October 21). The Enneagram as Jewish Holidays. New Voices. https://newvoices.org/2020/09/24/the-enneagram-as-jewish-holidays/

McGinnis, E. (2019, October 7). How the Enneagram Can Help Find Your Life Purpose. Live Your Jam. https://liveyourjam.com/2018/01/15/enneagram-can-help-discover-jam/

Moser, D. (2020, August 18). The Enneagram's Way of Discernment. IEA Nine Points. https://ieaninepoints.com/2020/08/18/the-enneagrams-way-of-discernment/#:%7E:text=Triad%201%E2%80%94Vocation%3A%20the%20call,in%20the%20fullness%20of%20time.

Naylor, M. (2019, September 24). Introduction to Utilizing the Enneagram in Addiction Recovery & Transformation -. Enneagram Maine.

https://enneagrammaine.com/introduction-to-utilizing-the-enneagram-in-addiction-recovery-transformation/

Nine Faces Of The Soul. (2021). Nine Faces Of The Soul: A Christian Perspective Of The Enneagram. https://static1.squarespace.com/static/56d7d7fdb09f951a5 3fb8e21/t/5742a3a7e707eb8894749a06/1463985083644/ Nine+Faces+of+the+Soul%5B1%5D.pdf

Oelofsen, C. (2018). Mindfulness Practices For Your Enneagram Type. Integrative 9. https://www.integrative9.com/media/articles/11/Mindfulnes s-Practices-for-your-Enneagram-Type

Riess, J. (2019, November 22). The Enneagram as a protest against one-size-fits-all religion. Religion News Service. https://religionnews.com/2019/08/15/the-enneagram-as-a-protest-against-one-size-fits-all-religion/

Storm, S., & Yuan, L. (2020, September 9). Here's What You Need in a Friendship, Based On Your Enneagram Type. Psychology Junkie. https://www.psychologyjunkie.com/2020/09/09/heres-what-you-need-in-a-friendship-based-on-your-enneagram-type/

Thompson, J. (2020, December 10). Do You Make Decisions Through your Belly, Heart or Head? Truity. https://www.truity.com/blog/do-you-make-decisions-through-your-belly-heart-or-head

Thoughts on every Enneagram Type? (2020, September 27). Reddit. https://www.reddit.com/r/Enneagram/comments/j0qy99/tho ughts_on_every_enneagram_type/

Traditional Enneagram (History). (2021). The Enneagram Institute. https://www.enneagraminstitute.com/the-traditional-enneagram

Type Four. (2021). The Enneagram Institute. https://www.enneagraminstitute.com/type-4

Type One. (2021). The Enneagram Institute.
https://www.enneagraminstitute.com/type-1
Type Two. (2021). The Enneagram Institute.
https://www.enneagraminstitute.com/type-2
What Is Mindfulness. (2021). Mindful. https://mindful.org
What Is the Enneagram of Personality? (2021, February
23). Truity. https://www.truity.com/enneagram/what-is-
enneagram
Yuan, I. (2021, April 20). Breaking Down the Enneagram:
A Guide for Total Beginners. Truity.
https://www.truity.com/blog/breaking-down-enneagram-
guide-total-beginners

www.ingramcontent.com/pod-product-compliance
Lightning Source LLC
Chambersburg PA
CBHW031543260326
41914CB00002B/249